# MINOR PROPHETS

# Minor Prophets

Joel - Prophet of Judgment Day
Micah - Prophet of Messiah's Advent
Zephaniah - Prophet of Royal Blood

2} June 2·22

Daniel

## Fredk. A. Tatford

( 1901 - 1986 )

**JOHN RITCHIE LTD**
CHRISTIAN PUBLICATIONS

40 Beansburn, Kilmarnock, Scotland

ISBN-13: 978 1 910513 19 4


Copyright © 2015 by John Ritchie Ltd.
40 Beansburn, Kilmarnock, Scotland


**www.ritchiechristianmedia.co.uk**

Typeset by John Ritchie Ltd., Kilmarnock
Printed by Bell & Bain Ltd., Glasgow

# PROPHET OF JUDGMENT DAY

*An exposition of Joel*

by

Fredk. A. Tatford

# CONTENTS

# PREFACE

**P**OSSIBLY one of the earliest of the prophetical writings of the Old Testament, the Book of Joel has been described as one of the literary gems of the Scriptures. J. T. Carson (*The New Bible Commentary*, p. 690) says, "It is built up with care and dramatic effect; here and there throughout its chapters are beauties which shine brilliantly and even dazzle the imagination". W. G. Elmslie also declares that, "If there is a book in the Bible that is a masterpiece of literary art, it is the Book of Joel. There are other prophets who write with greater passion and greater power, who rise to loftier altitudes of divine revelation; but there is hardly a writer in the Old Testament who shows proof of so careful and detailed and exquisite pain to give his work literary polish, finish and beauty.

Joel has a peculiar relevance to this second half of the twentieth century, which has seen national and international problems, industrial disquiet, and political and economic difficulties of an unparalleled character. It is at times such as these that the burden of temporal care weighs heavily and faith too often fails. Yet, if true religion means anything at all, it is surely at such times that we should be able to prove its reality. To some extent this is the message of Joel, although the Book has, of course, a far greater significance.

J. H. Kennedy appropriately remarks, "National disasters and human sufferings have always made special demands upon thoughtful and responsible men. These experiences often become unique occasions for serious, even ultimate, questions. The Book of Joel is the record of one such calamity and the consequent human sufferings. It is also the witness to a meaningful interpretation of that crisis furnished through the spiritual resources of a man of faith. Accordingly, the book has a timeless quality of point and pertinence for every generation and for every new experience of deep distress."

Joel is of importance to the student of prophecy since he

seems to have been the first of the prophets to give a reasonably clear impression of the nature of the day of Jehovah and its relation to the judgments of every period. He looked beyond the darkness of that day, however, to the glories and blessings of the millennial age and to the complete transformation to be effected then.

Joel's book is one deserving of study and it is hoped that the following pages may be of some small help to those who seek to understand the meaning of this fascinating Old Testament book.

FREDK. A. TATFORD.

# CHAPTER 1

## Introduction

WHEN the Old Testament canon was completed, the twelve Minor Prophets were included as one prophetical book. This, according to a' rabbinical tradition, was lest any one of these smaller writings should be lost. The twelve range from the 9th century B.C. to the 5th century B.C., but they are allegedly arranged in chronological order; that this is not accurate is obvious from even a superficial examination; but it is perhaps of no great importance. G. F. Oehler takes the view that the messages of the twelve were committed to writing so that, "when fulfilled, they might prove to future generations the righteousness and faithfulness of the covenant God, and that they might serve until then as a lamp to the righteous, enabling them, even in the midst of the darkness of the coming times of judgment, to understand the ways of God in His kingdom." Keil maintains that all "the prophetical books subserve this purpose, however great may be the diversity in the prophetical word which they contain — a diversity occasioned by the individuality of the authors and the special circumstances among which they lived and laboured".

Joel's book occupies the second place in the Minor Prophets in the canon, but there is little doubt that he prophesied before Hosea, which is placed first. The book is concerned only with the southern kingdom of Judah and it seems extremely probable that Joel lived in Jerusalem. Because of

9

the accuracy of his references to the temple and its activities and to the ministry of the priests it is sometimes suggested that he was personally a priest, but there is no real support for this in the pages of his book.

The prophet's name was quite a common one and at least twelve others of the same name are mentioned in the Old Testament, viz. (1) Samuel's elder son (1 Sam. 8:2), who was the father of Heman, the Levitical singer (1 Chron. 6:33; 15: 17); (2) a Simeonite (1 Chron. 4:35); (3) a Reubenite (1 Chron. 5:4, 8); (4) chief of the Gadites at Bashan (1 Chron. 5:12); (5) a Kohathite, the son of Azariah and father of Elkanah (1 Chron. 6:36); (6) a chief of Issachar (1 Chron. 7:3); (7) the brother of Nathan and one of David's mighty men (1 Chron. 11:38); (8) a Gershonite, who helped to bring up the ark from the house of Obed-edom (1 Chron. 15:7, 11) and possibly identical with the Joel of 1 Chron. 23:8 and 26:22; (9) the son of Pedaiah of Manasseh (1 Chron. 27:20); (10) a Kohathite who assisted in Hezekiah's reformation (2 Chron. 29:12); (11) a son of Nebo who put away his foreign wife (Ezra 10:43); (12) the son of Zichri, and an overseer at Jerusalem in Nehemiah's time (Neh. 11:9).

## DATE

There has been considerable controversy regarding the date of Joel's ministry and writings, some ascribing a date to the book in the 9th century B.C. and others relegating it to the 4th century B.C. Keil (*The Twelve Minor Prophets*, p. 169) maintains that Joel "was one of the earliest of the twelve minor prophets. For even Amos (1:2) commences his prophecy with a passage from Joel (3:16), and closes it with the same promises, adopting in ch. 9:13 the beautiful imagery of Joel, of the mountains dripping with new wine, and the hills overflowing (Joel 3:18). And Isaiah again, in his description of the coming judgment in ch. 13, had Joel in his mind; and in verse 6 he actually borrows a sentence from his prophecy (Joel 1:15) which is so peculiar that the agreement cannot be an accidental one. Consequently, Joel prophesied before Amos, i.e. before the 27 years of the contemporaneous reigns of Uzziah and Jeroboam II".

Joel makes no reference to the Syrian invasion, which occurred in the latter part of the reign of Joash, 850-840 B.C. (2 Kings 12:17, 18; 2 Chron. 24:23-25). Nor does he mention Assyria, which had taken a place on the world's stage about 760 B.C., or Babylonia, which had fallen by 537 B.C. These facts suggest that he prophesied either after 537 B.C. or before 760 B.C. and possibly even before 850 B.C.

The Edomites revolted against Judah in the days of Joram, 889-883 B.C. (2 Kings 8:20-22), but they were again subdued, although the conquest was not completed until the reign of Uzziah, about 830 B.C. Since Joel predicted this (3:19), he presumably prophesied before 830 B.C.

The invasion by the Philistines, which Joel mentions, occurred during the reign of Joram, 889-883 B.C. (2 Chron. 21:10, 16, 17; 22:1). The prophet foretold their punishment, which happened in the days of Uzziah (2 Chron 26:6). His book must, therefore, have been written not later than 732 B.C. but possibly before 889 B.C.

The hostilities of the Phoenicians presumably did not occur before the fall of Athaliah (1 Kings 16:31; 2 Kings 8:18; 10:1), but Joel predicted their punishment, which occurred under Uzziah. Egypt's punishment (Joel 3:19) was doubtless because of Shishak's invasion prior to the time of Joash (1 Kings 14:25, 26).

No reference is made to the captivity, from which Driver deduced that the exile was past history, but this does not seem a justifiable conclusion. Driver again claims that the mention of Greece (Javan) establishes a late date, but this again is not really a warranted conclusion.

The reference to the valley of Jehoshaphat (3:12) is probably based on the story of the victory won by Jehoshaphat over Moab and Ammon. Forsyth remarks, "the way in which Joel refers to it shows that the event must have been a comparatively recent one and that the memory of it was still fresh" (2 Chron. 20:26).

The book makes no allusion to idolatry, which was practised in the times of Joram, Ahaziah and Athaliah, but paints a picture of correct worship of Jehovah as was practised in the earlier days of Joash, when he was under the guidance of Jehoiada (2 Kings 11:12, 17; 12:2; 2 Chron. 23:16, 17; 24:14). The priests are portrayed as carrying out their normal functions, except as prevented by the plague. No national sins are denounced and one is again thrown back to an early date.

Some commentators have made a point of the lack of any allusion to the king or to the northern kingdom of Israel, but this might be used as an argument for either view. Taking all the facts into consideration, it seems extremely probable that the book should be dated in the 9th century B.C.

### QUOTATIONS BY OTHER PROPHETS

There are some twenty literary parallels between Joel and the other Old Testament prophets, and Delitzsch pertinently remarks that "among the prophets who flourished from the time of Uzziah to that of Jeroboam, Joel unquestionably holds the position of a type or model, and after Amos, there is not one whose writings do not remind us of him."

The quotations (if such they are) from Joel are as follows:

Joel 1:15 in Isa. 13:6; Ezek. 30:2, 3; Obad. 15; Zeph. 1:7.

Joel 2:1, 2 in Zeph. 1:14, 15.

Joel 2:3 in Ezek. 36:35 (see also Isa. 51:3).

Joel 2:6 in Nah. 2:10.

Joel 2:17 in Psa. 69:10; 115:2; 43:3.

Joel 2:27 in Isa. 45:5; Ezek. 36:11; 39:28.

Joel 2:28 in Ezek. 36:27; 39:29.

Joel 2:32 in Obad. 17.

Joel 3:2 in Ezek. 38:22.

Joel 3:3 in Obad. 11; Nah. 3:10.

Joel 3:4 in Obad 15.

Joel 3:10 in Isa. 2:4; Mic. 4:3.

Joel 3:14 in Obad. 15; Zeph. 1:7.

Joel 3:16 in Am. 1:2.

Joel 3:17 in Isa. 45:5; 52:1; Ezek. 36:11; 39:28; Obad. 17; Nah. 1:15.

Joel 3:18 in Am. 9:13.

Joel 3:19 in Obad. 10.

There are other similarities of a more minor character, but there is a clear inference that most of the Old Testament prophets were aware of the contents of the Book of Joel and that it must, therefore, be regarded as of greater antiquity than their own writings.

*Covid S, 7 Nov 2022*

## BACKGROUND

The servant of God cannot ignore the circumstances in which his lot is lost. In the moving phantasmagoria of the world, there is always a significance for the spiritually enlightened. Joel, as Horton says (*The Minor Prophets*, p. 83), "had before his eyes a series of disastrous ravages, wrought by locusts, and he saw through the physical fact to spiritual realities behind and beyond." He realised that the locusts were Jehovah's army, performing the mission which He had entrusted to them, but that even the terrible havoc they wrought was merely a harbinger of the far more awful day of judgment lying in the future. He perceived, moreover, that every act of judgment was directed at securing the repentance of a sinful people in order that unbounded blessing might eventually be poured out upon them. He saw additionally that the judgment, inflicted upon God's people with a view to their penitence, was of a totally different character from that falling upon the heathen with the intention of their permanent exclusion from blessing.

The messages of other prophets may have been based, to some extent, upon current events, but Joel was perhaps the first to show plainly the ultimate significance of such happenings. In many respects, his spiritual insight was unparalleled.

The prophet's well-chosen phraseology and the perfect arrangement of his book put him in a class by himself. A. R. Fausset writes, "Joel's style is pre-eminently pure. It is characterised by smoothness and fluency in the rhythms,

13

roundness in the sentences and regularity in the parallelisms."
A certain amount of this is naturally lost in our English trans-
lations, but sufficient remains to indicate the excellence of
the style and language employed.

INTERPRETATION

There has been considerable argument regarding the basis
of interpretation appropriate to the book. J. H. Kennedy
(*Joel*, p. 64) says that "the book has been considered a
prophetic liturgy, which was used as a part of the New Year
festival. The liturgy was expanded by adding apocalyptic
fragments, including the traditional religious ideas, and was
employed on later occasions in ceremonial worship."

The majority of expositors assume that the book is a
historical record of a period of great stress in the history of
Judah. Some see little more in Joel than the factual narrative
of events with a spiritual application of some of them. The
locust plagues, in their view, were attacks by literal insects,
but the devastation they caused had a lesson for the people
to learn, a lesson which should have a practical effect upon
their lives.

There are not wanting those, however, who insist that the
book can only be interpreted allegorically. The vivid descriptions given by the prophet, in their view, are too highly
drawn to be appropriate to a literal invasion of locusts. Consequently, the picture must be of invasions by heathen
nations, whose ravaging of the land is aptly portrayed by the
symbol of locusts.

Other writers, basing their view primarily on the closing
section of the prophecy and particularly on Joel's references
to the day of Jehovah and to the blessings of the millennium,
maintain that the only tenable interpretation is an eschatological one. This, of course, ignores completely the physical and
literal experiences of Judah and treats the whole book as
fundamentally apocalyptic.

There is a measure of truth in each system of interpretation, but it seems more sensible to regard the book as partly

historical and partly predictive and also to apprehend the practical import of each section of the book.

## AUTHORSHIP AND CANONICITY

It has been generally accepted that Joel was the author of the book that bears his name, although some critics have seen differences of style and have claimed that two persons had a part in the compilation of the book. An unbiased reader will probably come to the conclusion that Joel personally committed his messages to writing and that no other hand participated.

There has never been any question as to the canonicity of the Book of Joel. It formed part of the book of the twelve and has always been included in the canon from the date of the latter's finalisation.

## ANALYSIS

It is often suggested that Joel splits into two parts at verse 18 of chapter 2, but a simple and more appropriate analysis would be as follows:

1. The locust invasion (1:1-20).
2. The day of Jehovah (2:1-32).
3. The judgment of the nations (3:1-16).
4. Millennial blessings (3:17-21).

## CHAPTER 2

## A Desolated Country

NOTHING is known of the author of the Prophecy of Joel except the book which bears his name, and the book itself contains no direct information regarding the background, character or occupation of the prophet. His prophecy was concerned solely with Judah, and he referred frequently to Zion, Jerusalem and Judah and ignored the northern kingdom of Israel. Those facts and the manner in which he spoke of the temple, the priesthood and the sacrifices, have led some to the conclusion that he was a priest who lived in Jerusalem, but this is pure speculation and there is no specific information.

### THE PROPHET'S MESSAGE
*The word of Jehovah that came to Joel, the son of Pethuel (1:1).*

Joel introduced his book with a common prophetic formula to attest his credentials (1 Sam. 15:10; Mic. 1:1; Zeph. 1:1). He declared that the message recorded was the word of Jehovah which came to him.

He described himself as Joel (i.e. "Jehovah is God"), the son of Pethuel (i.e. "enlargement of God"). The Syriac version renders his father's name as Bethuel, and the Septuagist as Bathuel. One writer suggests that Joel was the son of the prophet Samuel (1 Sam. 8:2), but there is nothing to substantiate this.

17

In Duet. 28:38, 42 Moses warned that, in the event of disobedience or apostasy, one of the instruments of Divine punishment would be devastation by locusts. Joel's prophecy arose from a visitation of locusts of unparalleled severity, accompanied by a serious drought. So badly was the land stricken that, in somewhat hyperbolic language, the prophet treated the double calamity as symbolic of the judgments of the day of Jehovah.

There can be no reasonable doubt that the plague was a literal one. "Some imagine," wrote Calvin, "that a punishment is here threatened which is to fall at some future time; but the context shows clearly enough that they are mistaken and mar the prophet's true meaning. He is rather reproving the hardness of the people, because they do not feel their plagues."

## AN UNEXAMPLED CALAMITY

*Hear this, you old men, and give ear, all you inhabitants of the land. Has such a thing happened in your days, or even in the days of your fathers? Recount it to your children, and your children to their children, and their children to another generation (1:2, 3).*

The unprecedented disaster was of such a character that the prophet turned to the oldest of his fellow-countrymen and, indeed, to all the people of Judah, to ask whether their experience held any recollection of an occurrence so dreadful. Had an affliction on such a scale ever been known before? To an agricultural and pastoral people, there could, in fact, be nothing more serious than the complete loss of crops and herds and the infliction at the same time of a drought. It was not an isolated happening to which Joel referred. The locust plague had descended upon the land in successive years (2:25) and everything had been stripped.

It was the responsibility of elders to transmit knowledge to succeeding generations (Ex. 10:2; Deut. 4:9; 6:7; 11:19), and the nature of the calamity justified the prophet's injunction that the details were to be recounted to future generations, presumably as a warning of the judgments which fall upon a sinful people.

The awful devastation caused by a locust swarm can scarcely be realised by a western mind. *The Encyclopedia Britannica* says, "The size and destructiveness of a large locust swarm are tremendous. Many cover 100 square miles while in flight; some have been estimated to cover as much as 2,000 square miles. It has been reliably reported that the total coverage of the desert locust swarms that invaded Kenya in January 1954 was 500 square miles. An outbreak of desert locusts weighing approximately 50,000 tons and eating their own weight in green vegetation daily while growing or migrating occurred in Somalia in 1957. Migrations usually are with the wind and aided by it. . . . Some flights are near the ground, others more than a mile above it. Flying with the wind is advantageous to the locust because air currents that aid in transportation often drop rain, creating a congenial breeding ground where the swarm settles."

No details are given of the extent of the plague in Joel's day, but it was obviously extremely extensive and its effects accentuated by repetition of the invasion.

### Repeated Attacks

*What the shearer has left, the swarmer has eaten; what the swarmer has left, the lapper has eaten; what the lapper has left, the stripper has eaten (1:4).*

The prophet described the locust swarms by four names and declared that what one had left, the next had devoured—the implication being that there had been at least four successive swarms and this may possibly have recurred in succeeding years. But there are not wanting those who consider that there was only one invasion and that the names used by Joel related to different stages of growth of the insects.

According to J. D. Davis (*The Westminster Dictionary of the Bible*), "The insect referred to is evidently the migratory locust (*oedipoda migratoria,* or in some cases possibly an allied insect, *oedipoda cinerescens, aeridium peregrinum,* or other species). The locust is two inches or more in length. It is a winged, creeping thing. Like other insects of the order *orthoptera*, it has four wings. Those of the anterior pair are narrow, while those of the posterior pair are broader, folded up when not in use, and transparent. It has six legs, on four of which it walks, while the hindmost pair, which are much longer than the others and equal to the body in length, it uses for springing. The mouth is furnished with cutting jaws, by means of which it nips off leaves and blades of grass. Locusts were clean insects (Lev. 11:21, 22), and John the Baptist ate them, as many Orientals did before him and still do (Matt. 3: 4). They are prepared by being slightly roasted, dried in the sun, and salted. When used, the head, wings, legs and intestines are commonly removed, and only the fleshy portion is eaten."

"The locust is exceedingly destructive to vegetation, and locusts blown into the valley of the Nile by the east wind constituted the eighth Egyptian plague (Ex. 10:4, 5, 12, 15, 19). In some passages, as Jud. 7:12 and Jer. 46:23, the A.V. renders *'arbeh* 'grasshopper'; the R.V. uniformly translates it 'locust'. The locust is distinguished from the grasshopper by the shortness of its antennae. . . . Many other words refer to different species of locusts difficult to identify, or some of them may mean the migratory locust in different stages of development (Lev. 11:22; Joel 1:4). The eggs of the various species of locust are deposited in April or May, in a cylindrical hole excavated in the ground by the female. They are hatched in June. The young insect emerges from the egg a wingless larva. It enters the pupa state, when it has rudimentary wings enclosed in cases. It is more voracious in this stage of its development than at any other period. In another month, it casts the pupa or nymph skin, and has become the imago or perfect insect".

The terms used by the prophet to describe the insects were the shearer *(gazam)*, swarmer *('arbeh)*, lapper *(yelek)* and stripper *(hasil)*. Pusey says that there were over eighty kinds of locust, all possessed of an insatiable voracity. The Old

20

Testament mentions at least ten, viz.:

(1) *'Arbeh.* This is the most common (Ex. 10:4, 12, 13, 14, 19; Joel 1:4; 2:25). The name is derived from a root meaning to be numerous and it has been translated "swarmer" above. Olivier describes clouds of them coming from the interior of Arabia and says that the air was "filled on all sides and to a great height by an innumerable quantity of these insects, whose flight was slow and uniform, and whose noise resembled that of rain: the sky was darkened, and the light of the sun considerably weakened. In a moment the terraces of the houses, the streets, and all the fields were covered by these insects, and in two days they had nearly devoured all the leaves of the plants. Happily they lived but a short time, and seemed to have migrated only to reproduce themselves and die."

(2) *Chageb* or "concealer" (Lev. 11:22; Num. 13:33). This apparently referred to the locust at its fourth stage of growth, although it has sometimes been said to apply to a smaller size of insect.

(3) *Chargol* or "galloper" (Lev. 11:22) is sometimes incorrectly translated in the A.V. as "beetle" and in the R.V. as "cricket".

(4) *Salam*, the "bald locust" (Lev. 11:22). The Talmud says that this insect has a smooth head and that the female is without the sword-shaped tail.

(5) *Gazam* or "shearer" (Joel 1:4; 2:25; Am. 4:9), is translated "palmerworm" by the A.V. in Joel.

(6) *Gob* or "gatherer" (Isa. 33:4; Nah. 3:17; 7:1). This may represent the normal larva stage of the locust.

(7) *Chanamal* (Psa. 78:47). There is some dubiety about this form and it has been said by some to refer to hail or frost.

(8) *Yelek* or "lapper" (Jer. 51:14, 27; Psa. 105:34; Nah. 3:15, 16; Joel 1:4; 2:25) has also been incorrectly translated "cankerworm" or "caterpillar". It refers to the pupa stage of the locust, in which the wings are found in a horn-like sheath.

21

(9) *Hasil* or "stripper" (1 Kings 8:37; Joel 1:4) is sometimes translated as "finisher".

(10) *Tselatsel* or "creaker" (Deut. 28:42) is so named because of the noise produced by the insect rubbing its leg against its wing.

There have been various interpretations of the four types mentioned by Joel. The majority of commentators conclude that the four designations referred to four different stages of development. Ewald, for example, suggests that the first was the newly hatched, the second those with growing wings, the third those able to fly, and the fourth those who are changing colour. Others have argued, however, that the prophet was describing four successive invasions of locusts: this is unlikely since locusts seldom follow the same path. Those who regard the prophecy as allegorical see the four names as symbolic of the "four sore judgments" of Ezek. 14:21 or the four forms of punishment of Jer. 15:3. There are not wanting expositors who insist that the reference was to four invasions of the land, viz, by the Assyrians, Chaldeans, Macedonians and Romans. It seems more logical, nevertheless, to regard the insect invasions as actual and historical, whatever symbolic significance may be attached to them.

### THE DRUNKARDS SUMMONED

*Awake, you drunkards, and weep; and wail all you drinkers of wine, because of the sweet wine, for it is cut off from your mouth (1:5).*

The devastation had been complete: every green thing had been devoured and the vines had suffered with all other plants. The intoxicated, sunk into inebriated slumber, were called upon to awake and to realise that the vintage had been ruined. The wine which stupefied them — a concoction of honey, raisins, dates and grapes—would no longer be available, since its ingredients had been destroyed. The sweet wine, or must, made from the fresh juice of grapes, pomegranates or other fruits (S.Sol. 8:2), could no longer be made: the fruit had perished. Pictorially, the prophet declared that the drink, which delighted these wine-bibbers, was cut off from their mouths. The cup was dashed to the ground just as they prepared to drink it, There was, of course, no condonation of drunkenness here, but wine is frequently used figuratively of joy (Psa. 104:15; Eccles. 10:19).

Joel called upon them to weep and to wail. In place of their raucous laughter and besotted merriment, the air should now ring with their lamentations. Gratification was to be replaced by unrestrained grief. He described the reason for their deprivation in the next two verses. To quote Driver (*The Books of Joel and Amos*, p. 37), "an army of depredators had invaded Judah, countless in numbers and equipped for their work."

### THE INVASION

*For a nation has come up upon my land, strong and numberless; its teeth are lion's teeth and it has the fangs of the lioness. It has laid waste my vines and splintered my fig-trees; it has peeled off their bark and thrown it down; their branches are made white (1:6, 7).*

The countless numbers of the locust swarms seemed to the prophet like a mighty army, and he declared that a nation had invaded Jehovah's land. The strength of limb which enabled the insects to engage in long flights and then ruthlessly to indulge in this work of destruction also impressed him. This was an irresistible force.

Their teeth were edged like a saw and were extremely powerful and he likened them to the teeth of a lion and to the fangs or sharp prominent eye-teeth of a lioness. They had laid waste the vines and splintered the fig-trees, even stripping off the bark and leaving the trees white and bare. They first attacked plants, vegetables and grass and, when these had been devoured, they consumed the foliage of the trees and then the bark, leaving the uneatable fragments strewn on the ground.

The vine and fig were two of the most common fruit trees in Palestine. Both were also used as symbols of Israel, the vine in Psa. 80:8, 14; S. Sol. 2:13, 15; Isa. 5:1-7, and the fig in Hos. 9:10; Matt. 21:19, etc.

Kelly (*Lectures Introductory to the Study of the Minor Prophets*, pp. 70, 71) sees a reference in the scourge to the Assyrian invasion which still lay in the future. He says, "Joel uses the present visitation as a fact, but withal employs language which forms an easy passage to the prediction of a nation that would deal with the Jews in an unparalleled way. There need be no doubt that the nation in question is the Assyrian. The first chapter starts with the repeated and frightful depredations of the locusts in the prophet's day, but looks on to the trouble of a terrible day. The second chapter directly notices no such havoc from insects, but mingles figures taken from them with the Assyrian who should surely come up."

### OVERWHELMING GRIEF

*Lament like a virgin girded with sackcloth for the bride-groom of her youth (1:8).*

Picturing the land as a young widow, who has just been bereaved of her bridegroom, the prophet enjoined the country to indulge in the deep, bitter lamentation which might be anticipated in such circumstances. No sorrow could be greater than that of the bride bereft of her all. Coarse sackcloth would be girded about her to afflict her body in common with her mind and emotions (Am. 8:10). The LXX puts it even more aptly, "Let thy song of woe before me be more plaintive than that of a bride clothed with sackcloth for the husband of her youth."

A. B. Davidson comments, "The interruption of the fellowship between the land and Jehovah through the failure of the sacrifices the prophet throws into the figure of a young wife bereaved and in mourning. The land is the virgin; the dreary bleak aspect of it is the mourning which she wears. The bereavement lies in this: that through the cutting off of the meal offering and the drink offering, the tokens of Jehovah's presence and favour, manifested in His acceptance of the offerings, have been removed; communications between the

24

land and its God have been removed, and the land is bereaved." It was the severance of this relationship that plunged the nation into grief.

*The meal offering and the drink offering are cut off from the house of Jehovah; the priests, Jehovah's ministers, mourn (1:9).*

The scene of devastation was heart-breaking, but there was a far greater calamity than the loss of the means of subsistence. The greatest national misfortune lay in the loss of the sacrifices in the temple of Jehovah. The temple was the visible sign of God's presence among His people. But upon the continuance of the requisite sacrificial system depended the people's communion with God. There could be no greater misfortune than the inability to supply the materials for the offerings, but the denuding of the land had robbed the people of the means to provide them.

Here was cause for no ordinary grief. Material loss sank into oblivion by comparison with the religious loss—a lesson which it seems difficult to learn nowadays, but which was more obvious in that day because it was linked with the tangible by the material offerings which had now become impossible.

The cessation of the offerings was a serious matter for the priests also, because it meant the loss of their normal means of subsistence. Consequently, they mourned, not only as the ministers of Jehovah, but on their own account as well.

Two offerings were specified as representative of the whole sacrificial system. The loss of pasture would naturally react upon cattle and sheep and affect animal offerings as well, but Joel referred only to the meal and drink offerings. Meal offerings, composed of fine flour, oil and frankincense (Lev. 2) were presented, not only with all burnt offerings in general, but in particular with the morning and evening sacrifices (Exod. 29:38-42). Drink offerings of strong wine (Num. 15:1-10) were poured out as a libation at the same time. Because of the plague, it was impossible to provide these daily offerings for the temple, and the priests, who were consequently unable to carry out their normal sacerdotal functions, were filled with grief.

## A BLASTED COUNTRY

*The fields are laid waste, the ground mourns; because the grain is destroyed, the sweet wine is dried up, the oil pines away. Be abashed, O you husbandmen, wail, O you vine-dressers, for the wheat and barley; because the harvest of the field has perished. The vine withers and the fig-tree langui-shes. The pomegranate, palm, apple and all the trees of the field are withered; because joy fails from the sons of men (1:10-12).*

The scene was one of desolation. The fields were blasted, and the prophet pictured the ground as mourning over what had happened. The three principal products—corn (i.e. the threshed grain), must (or new wine, the fresh juice of the grape) and oil (the fresh juice of the olive)—had failed, and shame and frustration took the place of joy and gladness.

The prevalent sense of shame and frustration was to be overtly demonstrated by the husbandmen (or tillers of the soil), and the vinedressers (or vineyard-keepers) were bidden to wail. Well might they in view of the devastation on every side. The staple crops had perished. The wheat and barley had been destroyed and the harvest was irretrievably lost.

The vine had been laid waste and the fig-tree had also suffered desolation. The pomegranate (greatly prized for its fruit), the palm (admired for its beauty and the shade it afforded), the apple (possibly the apricot) and, in fact, all the trees of the field had withered, not only because of the locust invasion, but also because of the protracted drought from which the land was also suffering. The labour of the past months had been for naught, and the possibility of famine now confronted the despondent people. The joy which should have come from the harvest and the vintage had vanished from the sons of men as though it was personally ashamed.

26

Indeed, the keynote of this section of the prophecy seems to be the word "shame", used not in the sense of humiliation or dishonour for wrongdoing, but rather with the idea of frustration or loss of face.

## PRIESTLY LAMENTATION

*Gird on sackcloth and lament, you priests. Wail, you ministers of the altar. Come, lie all night in sackcloth, you ministers of my God (Elohim). For the meal offering and the drink offering are withheld from the house of your God (Elohim) (1:13).*

The prophet turned to the priests and bade them not merely to lament over the disheartening conditions but, in their deep grief, to follow the usual eastern practice in times of deepest mourning and to clothe themselves in sackcloth (Nah. 9:1). Moreover, he exhorted them to spend the whole night in vigil in the temple, presumably pouring out their souls in penitential prayer because of the cessation of the regular bloodless offerings to God.

They might justifiably lament and wail, but grief was not sufficient: there must be contrition and supplication. "Such a calamity", says one writer, "is a judgment, not merely betokening God's present anger with His people, but awakening the apprehension of sorer judgments in the future, which it behoves the nation, by timely penitence, if possible, to avert." The loud cries of grief were appropriate, but more was needed.

## A NATIONAL FAST

*Sanctify a fast. Call a solemn assembly. Gather the elders and all the inhabitants of the land to the house of Jehovah your Elohim and cry to Jehovah. Alas for the day! For the day of Jehovah is near and as a destruction from the Almighty (Shaddai) it comes (1:14, 15).*

So serious was the position that a summons to national prayer was obviously demanded, and Joel bade the priests to set apart a time for fasting and to call together all the people —the elders and all the inhabitants of the land—in solemn assembly to the temple to abase themselves before God and to pour out their supplications to Him. The prophet implied that abstention from food, humiliation of soul and penitential petition might propitrate God and avert the threatened destruction.

The Septuagint renders the injunction to the people as "cry incessantly". Possibly the people's very importunity might gain them a hearing with Jehovah. Schmoller (*Joel*, p. 14) says that "all public calamities are divine dispensations designed to awaken men to a sense of their sins and to bring them to repentance". Certainly this was true in the case of Judah, but it is equally relevant to conditions of the present day.

The calamitous experiences through which the land was passing aroused even deeper concern in Joel's mind. There seemed a possibility that a far more alarming experience was imminent: the plague of locusts and the drought were only harbingers of the day of Jehovah. He, therefore, urged the people to seek Jehovah's face and entreat Him to stay the threatened judgments.

"Alas for the day! The day of Jehovah is near", cried the prophet. "The day of Jehovah, or of the Lord," writes Ellison, "is a fundamental concept in the Old Testament, never really introduced or formally explained. The Hebrew saw that the world does not know the perfection of God's rule, and that the righteous man does not fully reap the reward of his righteousness. The Old Testament does not look for a redress of this world's wrongs and sufferings in heaven, but expects God's intervention by which His sovereignty will be perfectly and for ever established on earth. This intervention with its accompanying upheavals and judgments is called the Day of the Lord (see also Am. 5:18ff; Isa. 2:12; 13:6, 9f; Zeph. 1:14f; Jer. 46:10; Ezek. 30:2f; Obad. 15; Zech. 14:1; Mal. 4:5)."

"It is that day," writes Driver, "when Jehovah is conceived as manifesting Himself in His fulness, striking down wrong-doing and illusion, and giving the final victory to righteous-

28

ness and truth". References to that day are found in most of the prophetic books of the Old Testament. Obadiah and Joel, who were possibly among the earliest of the prophets, both mention it, and Joel refers to it so fully that he has been called the prophet of the day of Jehovah. It is clear from the description given by the different prophets that the day of Jehovah is to be one of unparalleled judgment. The visible and glorious manifestation of Jehovah will be accompanied by the outpouring of His wrath upon the nations. The earth itself will reel to and fro like a drunken man and will be utterly broken down. At the same time. Israel will be restored to blessing in their own land. But so dreadful will be the judgments of that day that fear will grip the hearts of all nations.

The trials through which Judah was passing seemed so utterly crushing that Joel conceived that they might quite possibly be the precursors of the day of Jehovah, which was to come with devastating effect from the Almighty. Indeed, every judgment is a reflection, in some measure, of that day. Well might the people voice their fear of the horrors which seemed so imminent.

The assonance between devastation *(shod)* and Almighty *(Shaddai)* is lost in the English versions. "Shaddai", says Driver (*ibid*, p. 81), "is a Divine title, occurring (a) as an adjective attached to God (El) in the name El Shaddai (God Almighty) (Gen. 17:1; 28:3; 35:11; 48:3; Ex. 6:3)....(b) as a poetical name of God (Num. 24:4, 16; Ezek. 1:24; Isa. 13:6; Joel 1:15)". It was from that all-powerful One that destruction would come on the day of Jehovah. His governmental actions would then be seen clearly and unmistakably.

### HOPELESS CONDITIONS
*Is not the food cut off before our eyes, joy and gladness from the house of our God (Elohim)? The seed shrivels under the clods; the storehouses are desolate, the granaries are broken down, because the grain has failed. How the beasts groan! The herds of cattle are bewildered, because there is*

29

*no pasture for them. Even the flocks of sheep are made desolate (1:16-18).*

The situation was extremely grave, for all means of subsistence had disappeared. What little had been spared by the locusts had apparently suffered from a drought. In consequence, hunger and thirst confronted man and beast, since food had been destroyed and streams had dried up. Conscious of their inability to arrest the course of events, the people watched helplessly while the crops perished before their eyes.

Their mortification was deepened by the fact that, in addition to the threat of famine, their service for God was involved. Not only were the meal offerings and drink offerings affected, but it was impossible for firstfruits and thankofferings to be brought to the temple to be eaten there in joy and gladness (Deut. 12:6,7; 16:10, 11; 26:1, 2, 10, 11). The harvest and vintage festivals (the Feasts of Weeks and of Ingathering) could not be celebrated with the customary rejoicing (Deut. 16:10-15).

A drought frequently attended a plague of locusts, and now the scorching sun beat down upon the parched fields, and the burning heavens withheld their moisture. As the streams and brooks dried up, the grains shrivelled up—even the very seeds under the clods of earth—and the corn withered. There was no harvest to gather in and no wine or oil to store, and the unused storehouses and barns fell into a pitiable state of dilapidation and disrepair. What use were granaries without grain?

In their distress the irrational creation was pictured as groaning. As Kennedy (*Joel*, p. 71) says, "the hot quick breath and longing eyes (cf. Jer. 14:5, 6) of the beasts offered imploring prayer . . . to the God of provident mercy." But their prayer was ineffectual. The cattle seemed bewildered as they hopelessly sought food in different directions, wandering hither and thither in perplexity, but finding no pasture. The sheep, which did not demand such rich grazing land as the cattle, also suffered through the lack of pasture.

## The Forest Fire

*Unto Thee, O Jehovah, I cry. For fire has devoured the pastures of the wilderness, and flame has burned all the trees of the field. Even the wild beasts cry to Thee, because the water brooks are dried up and fire has devoured the pastures of the wilderness (1:19, 20).*

Frustrated and helpless, Joel cried to Jehovah, Who alone could help. "The gnawing of the locusts", writes Pusey (*The Minor Prophets*, pp. 168-9), "leaves things as though scorched by fire; the sun and the east wind scorch up all green things, as though it had been the actual contact of fire. Spontaneous combustion frequently follows". It does seem that, an top of all that the land had endured, the terrifying swarms of locusts and the devastation they caused, and the distressing effects of the drought, a forest fire now swept through the land, destroying all that remained of the parched herbage and trees in the ensuing conflagration.

The water-courses had dried up and the brute beasts sought in vain for water. The prophet had previously voiced his own petition to God, but he now declared that the desire of the very beasts mounted to God in longing. Only He could satisfy the needs of man and beast, and even the insensate animals were pictured as seeking the satisfaction of their need in Him. It is possible that the prophet intended to imply that the calamities through which they were passing had been deliberately permitted by God in order to drive the people back to Him, and that, in consequence, even the animals were turning to Him. The providential dealings of God are seen in the days of trouble as well as in the days of prosperity, and it may frequently be the case that He uses trials and difficulties in order to bring His people back to Himself.

The "wilderness" *(midbar)* referred to by Joel meant a large uncultivated prairie or steppe, which normally yielded pasturage in the rainy season. The water brooks were the farmers' irrigation ditches. There was no pasturage in the wilderness and the ditches had dried up.

# CHAPTER 3

## The Unparalleled Catastrophe

JOEL had called the people of Judah to mourning and lamentation in view of the calamities which had befallen them. He now plunged into a more detailed description of the day of Jehovah—to which he had already referred—still employing the imagery of the locusts. He warned that other swarms were about to attack, which he regarded as the immediate precursors of the day of Jehovah. Warning of impending danger was normally given by the sounding of the trumpet and Joel commanded that it should now be blown to warn the people of what was about to happen.

### THE WARNING

*Blow the trumpet in Zion. Sound an alarm on my holy mountain. Let all the inhabitants of the land tremble, for the day of Jehovah is coming: it is near; the day of darkness and gloom, a day of clouds and thick darkness. Like the dawn spreading over the mountains there is a great and powerful people. Their like has never been from of old, nor will there be again after them through the years of all generations (2:1, 2).*

The *shophar,* or curved cow's horn, was used principally to give directions in war or to announce some public event or give warning of approaching danger, and was a secular rather than a religious instrument. So convinced did Joel seem of the imminence of the day of judgment (whether actually or

33                                                    c

prophetically) that a sense of desperate urgency ran through his words. The day of Jehovah was approaching: nay, it was practically upon them! Soon God would burst upon them in His judicial power and might.

"Blow the shophar in Zion. Sound an alarm on my holy mountain", cried the prophet. The alarm was sounded by a continuous blast, but the "blowing" took the form of short, sharp blasts (Num. 10:1-10). The warning was to go forth that all might be aroused from the slumber into which they had been lulled by a feeling of false security. Let them tremble in view of the coming dread event.

Multiplying metaphors, Joel declared that it was a day of darkness and gloom, of clouds and fog. The words were, of course, more fully applicable to the future day of judgment and to the dread calamities which will accompany it, but the immediate reference was obviously to the dark cloud of locusts, so dense that it would presently obscure the sun and sky and convert a summer day into one of gloom and shadow. As Taylor says (*The Minor Prophets*, p. 22), "the language oscillates between the immediate threat of the locusts and the eschatological prospect of God's judgment".

Those who have witnessed an attack of locusts, say that the cloud of insects may be often several hundred feet in depth and sometimes as much as four miles in length. Yet the reflection of the sun upon the wings of the locusts conjured up for Joel the vision of the early dawn touching the mountain-tops with an irridescent brightness. The whole imagery was singularly appropriate to the day of Jehovah, to which the prophet had likened it. That too will be a day of darkness and of light, of judgment and of blessing, a day to be feared and one to be eagerly anticipated. George Adam Smith sees the picture as one of the struggle between dawn and the thick clouds of the night (or of the locusts). He says, "The figure is of dawn crushed by and struggling with a mass of cloud and mist, and expresses the gleams of white which so often break through a locust cloud".

Suddenly changing the figure, the prophet then likened the

34

locust invaders to "a great and powerful people" and hyperbolically declared that nothing comparable had ever been seen previously nor would be again. Like a well-disciplined and perfectly organised army, they moved on in irresistible and overwhelming force: nothing could withstand them. The description was a completely accurate one. Horton (*The Minor Prophets*, p. 84) says that "locusts fly in serried and orderly ranks like soldiers; when in an erect position, their appearance at a little distance is like that of a well-armed horseman. They advance in a cloud, which rises 12 or 18 feet from the ground. They blot out the sun and produce darkness. Their noise in flight is described as like the crackling of fire or the hissing of thunder-rain. Their numbers are so prodigious that no attempts at destruction avail; over millions of dead, and ditches filled with corpses, the unfailing host pours on." They were well termed a great and powerful people. They advance in tremendous numbers with the order, precision and unyieldingness of a thoroughly organised host, and all measures against them are completely unavailing.

## THE ARMY'S ADVANCE

*Fire devours before them, and a flame burns after them. The land is like the garden of Eden before them but like a desolate wilderness after them. And nothing escapes them. Their appearance is like the appearance of horses; and like war horses, so they run. Like the rattling of chariots on the tops of the mountains, they leap, like the crackling of a flame of fire devouring stubble, like a powerful people set in battle array. Before them peoples are in anguish; all faces grow pale (2:3-6).*

Opinion is divided among commentators as to whether Joel referred in verse 3 to the forest fire he had mentioned earlier or whether he was (as is more probable) likening the devastating effects of the locusts to those of a fire. The insects swept the land as clear as though a raging fire had swept over it, a fire devouring before them and a flame consuming after them. Although, prior to the plague, the land had been as beautiful and well-preserved as the garden of Eden, it had now become a desolate waste. Nothing had escaped the destructive hosts.

Moving compactly and swiftly they looked and ran like horses. The prophet's simile was apt. An Arab proverb says, "The locust has the form of ten of the giants of the animal world, weak as he is—face of a man, eyes of an elephant, neck of a bull, horns of a hart, chest of a lion, stomach of a scorpion, wings of an eagle, thighs of a camel, legs of an ostrich, and tail of a serpent." The head of the locust is so similar to that of a horse that the Italians call it *cavalette* (little horse), and the insect has the speed and tirelessness of a war-horse.

The noise of their wings sounded like the rattling of chariots travelling over the hill-tops. (It has been said that the noise can be heard six miles away). The sound of their feeding was like the crackling of a prairie fire sweeping over the dried stubble. With their solid phalanxes they had all the appearance of a great army prepared for the fray (Prov. 30: 2⁷). It was a fearful prospect to gaze upon.

At the sight of the frightening hosts, the nations were struck with fear, and faces blanched at the realisation of their terrible potentialities. Fear and anguish usually cause a draining of blood from the face, and this occurred in the experience of the people in Joel's day. The descriptions given were not overdrawn but coincide remarkably with experience. Feinberg (*Joel, Amos and Obadiah*, p. 21) considers that the happening discloses one of the great principles of God's dealings with mankind. He writes, "God only inflicts punishment after great provocation, and when He does so, it is meant to draw man back from further and more severe visitations of the wrath of God. The plague of locusts was severe, but it could not approximate to the devastation to be wrought in that time known as the Day of Jehovah".

Having stripped the countryside, the locusts advanced upon the city, no defence being able to impede their progress. It was primarily in anticipation of this attack that the people

36

had been filled with fear. Now their fear was realised as the ordered ranks climbed the walls and penetrated the houses.

## JERUSALEM INVADED

*They run like warriors; they scale the wall like men of war. Everyone marches on his way; they do not break their ranks. They do not jostle one another; each marches in his path. When they fall by the sword, their ranks are not halted. They run to and fro in the city; they run upon the wall; they climb up into the houses; they enter through the windows like a thief (2:7-9).*

With amazing steadiness and regularity, the insect army moved upon the city. "They seemed to march in regular battalions," says Morier, "crawling over everything that lay in their passage, in one straight front". Pusey (*ibid.*, p. 177) sees this as typical of the spiritual. He writes, "So the judgments of God hold on their course, each going straight to that person for whom God, in the awful wisdom of His justice, ordains it."

The locusts climbed the walls of the city in marshalled order and as if by a common impulse. Nothing broke their ranks. Attempts have sometimes been made to check the advance of a host of locusts by filling trenches with water or making fires in their path, but the trenches simply became filled with the bodies of the first ranks, while the others crossed over the bodies, and the fires were extinguished by the thousands who were cremated thereon while hordes of others made their way directly over the ashes of those who had been consumed. Nothing makes any impression upon the mighty army.

The host moved on, each following his own path straight forward, none jostling another or being diverted to a different course. They entered the city, making their way through the lattice-work windows into the houses. Weapons were completely ineffective against them: they moved on with unbroken ranks. Nothing could arrest their progress. They coursed through the city and took possession of the walls and

37

then of the houses. Well might the people be fearful.

## JEHOVAH'S ARMY

*The earth quakes before them; the heavens tremble. The sun and the moon are darkened, and the stars withdraw their light. Jehovah utters his voice before his army, for his host is very great, for he is strong who executes his word. The day of Jehovah is great and very terrible: who can endure it? (2:10, 11).*

The locust invasion was apparently accompanied by a great storm and by an earthquake, and the prophet depicted the earth and the heavens as trembling, and the sun, moon and stars as withdrawing their light before the approach of the locust bands. Again Joel linked the circumstances with the day of Jehovah. Envisaging Jehovah as captain of the great army (itself symbolic of the hosts of heaven), he heard His thunderous shout and realised the vastness of His forces and the greatness of His power.

The locusts were envisaged as the army of Jehovah, executing His word, indicating quite clearly that every judgment was by His command and that it was figurative of that greater judgment yet to come. "Behind and beyond the locust ravages and the earthquake and the storm, looms up the day of Jehovah", writes Horton (*ibid.*, p. 98). "a camp more impregnable, a host more irresistible, a punishment great and terrible".

Throughout Joel emphasised that the tribulations inflicted upon the people were warnings of the future and the means divinely used to bring the people back to God in repentance. "The march of the locusts", writes Ewald, "appears like an innumerable well-organised army of irresistible rapidity, before which the whole earth trembles and the heavens grow dark, ... an irresistible terrible army at the head of which Jehovah Himself appears as commander, with His thunder, issuing His commands to destroy the land and chastise its inhabitants . . . In this darkness, this onward march of an army of a far more destructive character than an army of

38

human enemies, amidst this thunder and storm, the great day of vengeance and judgment, Jehovah Himself seems in reality to be coming." If these were only typical of that day, how terrible must the reality be, and the prophet pertinently asked, "Who can endure it?"

Although the day of judgment seemed so imminent that nothing could now avert it, God pleaded with His people to turn to Him in true penitence and contrition. To the repentant heart He would prove Himself gracious and compassionate, and even yet blessing might take the place of judgment.

## PLEA TO RETURN

*Yet even now, says Jehovah, return to me with all your heart, with fasting, weeping and mourning: and rend your hearts and not your garments. Return to Jehovah your God (Elohim), for he is gracious and merciful, slow to anger and great in kindness, and repents of evil. Who knows but that he will turn and repent, and leave a blessing behind him, even a meal offering and a drink offering to Jehovah your God (Elohim) (2:12-14).*

The prophet had looked beyond the passing scourge of locusts and had envisaged the whole aggregate of Divine judgments culminating in the final judgment of the day of Jehovah. Nevertheless, the impending doom might even yet be averted. If the people returned to Jehovah sincerely and with purpose of heart, demonstrating the reality of their repentance by evident tokens of their regret for their sins (tokens which must be inwardly felt and not merely outwardly indicated), God implied that He would hear their cry and avert the judgment for their sake.

"Return to Me with all your hearts", said Jehovah. In Hebrew psychology, the heart was the organ of intellect and moral intention, rather than of the affections. There must be deliberate resolution to turn the back upon sin and definitely to show allegiance to God. Joel did not specify the particular transgressions for which punishment was threatened and which must, therefore, be eschewed if contrition was to be regarded as sincere.

Old Jeremy Taylor has well said, "Although all sorrow for sin has not the same expression, nor the same degree of pungency and sensitive trouble, yet it is not a godly sorrow unless it produces these effects: (1) that it makes us really to hate and (2) actually to decline sin; and (3) produces in us a fear of God's anger, a sense of the guilt of His displeasure; (4) and then such consequent trouble as can consist with such apprehension of the Divine displeasure; which, if it express not in tears and hearty complaints, must be expressed in watchings and stirrings against sin; in patiently bearing the rod of God; in confession of our sins; in perpetual begging of pardon; and in all the natural productions of these according to our temper and constitution; it must be a sorrow of the reasonable faculty, the greatest of its kind."

The penitence was to be characterised by fasting, weeping and wailing. The humbling of the flesh by fasting was directed to producing a humbling of heart. The tears and mourning were evidence of the regret and remorse consciously realised as the character of the iniquities committed became apparent.

"Rend your hearts and not your garments", enjoined the prophet. The rending of the clothes was an expression of grief and exceptional sorrow or sometimes of anger or other strong emotions (1 Sam. 4:12; I Kings 21:27). The sorrow experienced now, however, was to have a far deeper effect: the rebellious heart was to be torn; the former motives and intentions were to be sent, and the grief was to strike the very root of the feelings and emotions. There was to be an inward reality.

Is not this what is required today? True repentance does not consist in sloppy sentimentality or in empty and meaningless phraseology, but in a heartfelt remorse and a sincere and deliberate change of attitude. The tears of regret, which were once in evidence when the Holy Spirit wrought conviction of sin, seem to be a feature of the past. It might be of greater spiritual value if the supercilious superficiality of the present was exposed for its unreality and artificiality, and the torment of transgression again realised in all its heart-rending grief.

If the people unreservedly abandoned their sinful habits and practices, Jehovah's grace and compassion would be manifested, for He was "slow to anger and great in kindness". If His hand fell in chastisement upon His people, it was only in order that they might be convicted of their wrongdoing and be restored to Him. His reluctance to inflict punishment was evidenced by the period allowed for repentance. His wrath was never unrestrained and His mercy and loving-kindness were always awaiting the prodigals who returned.

The prophet declared that He "repents of evil". But God "is not a man that He should repent". When the conditions which demand punishment are changed by repentance, a just God cannot continue to impose punishment. The change of conduct by the sinner is reflected in a change of attitude on the part of Jehovah. He must remain consistent with His own character. The justice which must punish the guilty must equally pardon the penitent.

Yet there was no presumption demonstrated by the prophet. "Who knows but that He will turn and repent", he said. Because of Judah's sin, Jehovah was estranged from them and His attitude towards them could only be one of judgment, but if they turned to Him in sincere contrition, showing the fruits of repentance, He could turn to them in forgiveness. Schmoller (*ibid.*, p. 23) says, "God's glory and our salvation are so intimately conjoined that the pardon of the guilty is facilitated thereby, since the salvation of the sinner redounds to the glory of God".

It was possible, therefore, that He would amend His original intention and bestow upon His people blessing instead of castigation. The earth might again yield her increase, and the meal offering and the drink offering for the temple again become available. The deprivation of Jehovah of the offerings due to Him was one of the most serious aspects of the people's trials, since it implied a severance of communion with Him. But now the possibility of providing the offerings was once more envisaged.

God ever delights in mercy and, even to this day, He waits
to welcome the prodigal home and to shower His love and
affection upon him. For Judah the curse had become a
blessing—one which Jehovah had left behind Him.

## A Solemn Assembly

*Blow the trumpet in Zion; hallow a fast; call a solemn
assembly. Gather the people; hallow the congregation.
Assemble the elders, gather the children and the sucking
infants. Let the bridegroom leave his room and the bride her
bridal chamber. Let the priests, the ministers of Jehovah,
weep between the porch and the altar, and let them say,
Spare Thy people, O Jehovah, and make not thy heritage a
reproach, that the nations should rule over them. Why should
they say among the peoples, Where is their God? (2:15-17).*

Joel had earlier called for the *shophar* to be blown as a
warning of impending danger (v. 1), He now bade the priests
to blow it, but on this occasion to summon the people to a
solemn assembly and a period of fasting. Conditions were
serious and their gravity demanded that all normal occupations should be laid aside and the people gathered together
before God. None was exempted from this occasion of
national humiliation: every member of the nation, from the
oldest to the youngest, was summoned. Elders, children and
even babes were called upon to attend, and the vast congregation was to be hallowed as set apart to Jehovah.

Even the newly wedded couples were summoned. A bride-
groom was legally exempted from military duties and certain
other responsibilities for a year after marriage (Deut. 24:5),
but the circumstances of this fast were such that the legal
privilege was suspended. Despite the fact that it may have
been the actual wedding day, the couple were to leave the
nuptial tent erected for the consummation of the marriage
(2 Sam. 16:22) and to participate in the common austerity of
repentance.

As mediators and intercessors, the priests were to stand
in the court of the priests at the temple and to supplicate

God for mercy on His people, while they wept bitter tears of contrition. As true ministers of God, they interceded with Him on behalf of His people, taking the burden of the nation's case upon their own shoulders. Their plea was subtly based upon the fact that Jehovah had avouched Judah as His people and His inheritance and that, in consequence, He had a particular responsibility towards them.

Not only was the onus on God to defend His property, but there was an obligation upon Him, in Joel's view, to save His people from reproach, since both they and He would otherwise suffer the taunts of the heathen for His non-intervention. If He allowed the heathen to ravage His own country and to take possession of it, they would be able to turn round contemptuously and enquire where Judah's God was. It was a logical argument, which God did not seek to refute.

## CHAPTER 4

## Deliverance from Trouble

THE people presumably responded to the summons to national prayer and fasting, although the book records no information regarding the solemn assembly. Jehovah was clearly not oblivious to His people's circumstances, however, and the second half of Joel's book opens with a series of Divine promises, given in response to the nation's repentance and supplications for mercy.

### DIVINE JEALOUSY

*Then Jehovah was jealous for his land and had compassion on his people. Jehovah answered and said to his people, Behold, I am sending you grain, wine and oil, and you will be satisfied therewith: and I will no longer make you a reproach among the nations (2:18, 19).*

Joel had urged the priests to plead with God that His people should not be the subject of mockery to those around them. The reply was immediate. Jehovah recognised His liability: the land was His and He was jealous for it. The people were His and His compassion went out to them. The fast had been effective. The penitence was sincere and He accepted their expressions of remorse and contrition.

The prophet declared that Jehovah was jealous for His land. Driver says (*ibid.*, p. 58), "Jehovah is 'jealous' when His power is doubted, or the honour which is His due is given to another . . . this happens, however, when His people or His

45

land suffer, and the heathen argue in consequence that He is unable to relieve them; accordingly the feeling of 'jealousy' prompts Him then to interpose on their behalf". The Divine 'jealousy' is, of course, in no way comparable with the "green-eyed monster" so well known in human experience.

In view of the change of attitude on the part of Judah, Jehovah's heart went out to them. No longer should they be the subject of ridicule or reproach. They had mourned the loss of the corn, the must (new wine) and the fresh oil, but God now declared that there would be a full restoration. He was supplying the very things they had lost and they would receive sufficient to be completely satisfied.

The plain implication of the promise was, of course, that they would be delivered from the plague of locusts and this assurance at once followed. God is ever faithful and He never turns the needy away or refuses to listen and respond to the cry of His people. Never again would they be a reproach among the nations. The complete fulfilment of the Divine promise is, of course, postponed until the future restoration of Israel, when God will indeed be jealous for His land and have pity on His people.

"It is clear," writes Pusey (*ibid.*, p. 187), "that the chastisements actually came, so that the repentance described was the consequence, not of the exhortations to repentance, but of the chastisement. What was removed was the chastisement which had burst upon them."

### THE NORTHERNER

*I will remove the northerner far from you and will drive him into a barren and desolate land, with his front towards the east sea and his rear towards the western sea. His stench and his ill savour will rise, for he has done great things (2:20).*

A predictive element was now imported into Jehovah's words. The locusts normally invaded Palestine from the south or the south-east, but God here referred to them as the northern foe. Since it is extremely unlikely (although not impossible) that they came from the northern quarter, it

46

seems clear that the words go beyond any irruption of locusts and refer prophetically to the great northern power which has been Israel's enemy in the past and will yet be again in the future. As one writer says, the prophet "takes a name employed in Israel since Jeremiah's time to express the instruments of Jehovah's wrath in the day of His judgment of Israel. The name is typical of doom, and therefore Joel applies it to his fateful locusts".

The prophecy can scarcely refer to the destruction of Antiochus Epiphanes of Syria, a notorious oppressor of God's people, since the description given of the end of the northern foe was not applicable in his case. Other prophets reveal that, in the day of Jehovah, of which Joel spoke, God will use the Assyrians (a term used in a general sense rather than a particular one and referring to an invader from the north—the same direction from which the Assyrians came) as a means of inflicting punishment upon His ancient people (Isa. 10:5, 6). Details of the activities of the future "king of the north" are given in Dan. 11:36-45; Nah. 1:11-14; Ezek. 38 and 39 etc., and these prophets reveal that this great power will perish between the Mediterranean and Mount Zion (cf. Joel's description of the end of the locusts of his day). A fuller discussion of this subject will be found in the author's exposition of Daniel, *The Climax of the Ages*, pp. 212-225.

So far as the immediate problem was concerned, Joel declared that the invading host of insects would be removed far away from Judah and that Jehovah would drive it into a barren and desolate land and ultimately into the sea. This seems to have been precisely what occurred. The locusts disappeared as quickly as they came. A sudden wind carried them into the desert and, then veering, deposited them not only in the desert but on the Dead Sea in the east and then (at a further change) on the Mediterranean on the west (cf. Ex. 10:19), so that the shores of both seas were strewn with putrefying insects, the effluvia from which polluted the air over a wide area.

Jerome says, "we have seen the land of Judea covered by

47

swarms of locusts, which, as soon as the wind arose, were precipitated into the . . . Dead Sea and the Mediterranean. And when the shores of both seas were filled with heaps of dead locusts, which the waters had thrown up, their corruption and stench became so noxious that even the atmosphere was corrupted, and both men and beasts suffered from the consequent pestilence." In our own time, Chapelle, writing in *National Geographic Magazine* of April 1953, said, "Some swarms inexplicably commit suicide, flying out to sea after veering away from good feeding areas. Others blunder into cold or are shrivelled by intense heat."

The prophecy may have had in view the future invasion of the land by the great northern armies of Gog referred to in Ezek. 38 and 39 and the complete destruction of these hostile forces by the Almighty. It is recorded that the annihilation of that tremendous host will provide work for seven months to those appointed to bury the dead.

In view of the miraculous salvation which Jehovah had promised, the prophet declared that He had done greatly, or had done great things. Keil (*ibid.*, p. 203) takes the view that the reference was not to God but to the locust army and he says, "to do great things is affirmed of men or other creatures, with the subordinate idea of haughtiness," or boasting. This would be a legitimate interpretation of verse 20.

### FEAR TURNED TO JOY

*Fear not, O land, be glad and rejoice, for Jehovah has done great things. Fear not, you beasts of the field, for the pastures of the wilderness are springing with new grass, for the tree bears its fruit; the fig-tree and the vine give their full yield (2:21, 22).*

As he realised what the power of Jehovah would accomplish, the prophet jubilantly bade his fellow-countrymen to exult. Unable to restrain his joy, Joel called upon the land, the beasts and the people to rejoice in the great goodness of God. Truly He had done great things for them.

The ground, which had been stripped by the locusts, dried

up by the drought and burned by the forest fire, could rejoice that the visitation was past and its period of mourning ended. The sufferings of the brute beasts had been indicated by their groaning and bewilderment (1:18); their food was gone and the brooks had dried up. But now their needs had been miraculously supplied and they could rejoice in the mercies of God. A carpet of fresh verdure was already beginning to cover the ravaged ground, the trees which had been stripped even of their bark had again revived to put forth their strength and to show the signs of life in blossom and fruit. Well might the people rejoice in Jehovah.

## ABUNDANT RAIN

*Be glad, you sons of Zion, and rejoice in Jehovah your God (Elohim): for he has given you the early rain according to righteousness, and he has poured down for you the winter rain, the early and the latter rain as aforetime. The threshing floors shall be full of grain, and the vats shall overflow with wine and oil (2:23, 24).*

There was further cause for rejoicing, however. The tormenting drought had ended and the seasonal rains had begun to fall. As Jehovah's righteousness prompted Him, He had bestowed the early rain, and the people could now rely upon the early rain in October and the latter rain in March as previously. The early rain was essential to prepare the soil for sowing: the latter rain was vital to the growth of the young plants. Both were promised unconditionally.

In consequence, the grain would fill the threshing floors, and the new wine and fresh oil (i.e. the grapes and olives to be crushed) would fill the vats to overflowing. The whole scene was completely transformed by the touch of the divine hand.

The Septuagint and the Syriac version render the second sentence of verse 23, "for he has given you this (LXX only) food for righteousness". Laetsch and some earlier translators render it, "He will give to you the Teacher unto Righteousness" (in some cases, "Teacher *of* Righteousness"). The word *moreh,* translated "the early rain" above, does, in fact, mean "teacher" and the question arises whether it was intended to mean an actual teacher in this case, or merely spiritual blessings. Some expositors maintain that the correct interpretation is a teacher and that the reference was to Joel personally, but others see in it a promise of the Messiah.

Keil (*ibid.,* p. 205) says, "Most of the Rabbins and earlier commentators have followed the Chaldee and Vulgate, and taken *moreh* in the sense of 'teacher'; but others, in no small number, have taken it in the sense of 'early rain' . . . But although *moreh* is unquestionably used in the clause of this verse in the sense of early rain, in every other instance this is called *yoreh* (Deut. 11:14; Jer. 5:24)." Nevertheless, we prefer the rendering already suggested. The introduction of the Messiah, or the Teacher of Righteousness, into the verse is awkward and out of harmony with the context.

### Restoration

*And I will restore to you the years which the swarmer has eaten, the lapper, the stripper and the shearer, my great army which I sent among you. And you shall eat in plenty and be satisfied, and praise the name of Jehovah your God (Elohim), who has dealt wonderfully with you: and my people shall never again be put to shame. You shall know that I am in the midst of Israel, and that I am Jehovah your God (Elohim) and that there is none besides; and my people shall never again be put to shame (2:25-27).*

It is a plain inference from the prophet's words that the visitation of locusts had lasted for a long period, since he referred to lost *years,* and the opening words of the prophecy take on an added significance in the light of this fact. There had evidently been repeated swarms year after year and the people must have been deprived of practically all means of subsistence.

Whilst no reason was given for the infliction, Jehovah now revealed that it had been at His behest: the swarms were His army and had been sent among them by Him. No indication was given as to whether the reason was punitive or disciplinary, or whether it was exemplary or part of the tribulations of life which are providentially imposed upon men for the training of their character, although it can presumably be deduced from the injunction to penitence contained in the early part of the chapter that the cause was the sin of the nation.

But now Jehovah promised a full restoration of all that had been lost and declared that prosperity would again be experienced and the physical needs of the people would be completely satisfied. The Almighty's dealings are always equitable and there is ever a compensation for the trials He imposes.

"I will retore the years which the locust has eaten". What glad assurance the words have brought to many a humbled heart. The failures of the past may bring regret and remorse; the contrite soul pours out its confession of sin and transgression. But the Eternal Lover not only pardons the guilty and restores the penitent to communion again: He also restores the lost years! The possibility of service for Him has not ended: a new door opens wide: the past is forgiven and forgotten.

At the realisation of the goodness of God and the wonderful way in which He had dealt with His people, praise ascended to Him. How marvellously had life been transformed: it was only fitting that worship should flow out to Him. Never again would they be abashed or put to shame. The words doubtless anticipated the still future day of deliverance when the hordes of the northern enemy will be Divinely routed and Israel will be conscious that salvation came only from God. Their fears and sufferings will have been dismissed solely in consequence of His intervention.

With the restoration of prosperity, the people were also given the assurance that Jehovah was permanently in their midst as their sufficiency and defence, that He was their God and that there was no place for any other. He alone was capable of transforming the picture and His people would never again be put to shame. The prophet patiently anticipated the glorious millennial day, when God will again dwell in the midst of His people and the shame which still envelops them in their present humiliation will then for ever be removed.

# CHAPTER 5

## Spiritual Blessing

THE remainder of Joel's prophecy is very largely predictive in character and is concerned principally with the day of Jehovah and the signs attending it. The term "the day of Jehovah", or "the day of the Lord", has a primary reference, as Wm. Kelly points out, to "the public and governmental side of His coming", and it is, therefore, to be anticipated that it will be associated with signs, portents and indications of His power and glory. He first referred, however, to the spiritual blessings to be bestowed.

In the Hebrew text, verses 28-32 of Joel 2 form Chapter 3.

### OUTPOURING OF THE SPIRIT

*It shall be that afterwards I will pour out my Spirit on all flesh; your sons and your daughters shall prophesy, your old men shall dream dreams, your young men shall see visions. Also upon your menservants and maidservants in those days will I pour out my Spirit (2:28, 29).*

When fertility had returned to the barren field and the physical needs of the people had been met, Jehovah declared that He would add spiritual blessing to material prosperity. Like the outpouring of a shower of blessing, the Holy Spirit would be poured out upon all flesh.

That the promise was not strictly applicable to Joel's own day was evident from its non-fulfilment at that date, and there is, of course, no doubt that it was prophetic in character.

The introductory expression, "It shall be that *afterwards*," linked the promise, not with the circumstances of Joel's time, but with the latter days (Hos. 3:5).

It is frequently stated that the apostle Peter expressly claimed that the descent of the Holy Spirit at Pentecost was the fulfilment of Joel's prophecy (Acts 2:16-21), but the accompanying details, which the apostle quoted, were not, of course, fulfilled at Pentecost. Peter merely implied that what had transpired at Pentecost was of the same nature as the events foretold by Joel, and it is obvious that the complete fulfilment awaits the outpouring of the Holy Spirit in the millennium (Ezek. 39:29).

The prophecy refers to the outpouring of the Holy Spirit *on all flesh*. It seems clear that this relates primarily to the nation of Israel, since the following chapter describes the destruction of the Gentile nations. During Messiah's earthly reign, blessing will be centred in Israel, and throughout Israel the enduement of the Holy Spirit will evidently be received. In earlier days, the Holy Spirit had been bestowed upon an individual for a specific purpose or a particular work (see Appendix), but the experience was now to be universal.

"It had been Moses' wish," writes Taylor (*ibid.*, p. 24), "that all the Lord's people might be prophets and that they all might have His Spirit upon them (Num. 11:29), but it is left to Joel to predict this as a feature of the last days." The young and virile, Joel declared, would then burst into declarations of God's will and purpose. The Pharisees declared that "prophecy does not reside except on one wise and mighty and rich". But Joel implied that it would be found in all the young—"your sons and your daughters". God is no respecter of persons.

While the old men will dream dreams in those days, the young men will see visions, but both will be freshly inspired and enlightened. It has always been the case that it is the older who meditate (and perhaps ruminate) and ponder, dreaming of what might have been and of what might still be. But it is the younger who seem to catch the glimpse of life's potentialities and, with the vigour and inspiration of youth go forth, conquering and to conquer.

In earlier days, no slave apparently received the gift of the Holy Spirit, although this was completely reversed in New Testament days. But Joel disclosed that, in the age to which he looked, even the menials would share in the spiritual blessing and power. Pusey (*ibid*, p.195) says, "Under the law, God had provided for slaves that, even if aliens, they should, by circumcision, be enrolled in His family and people; that they should have the rest and the devotion of the sabbath; and share the joy of their great festivals, going up with their masters and mistresses to the place which God appointed. They were included in one common ordinance of joy". But this went much farther and must have seemed almost incredible to the Jew of the prophet's time. Yet such was the grace of God.

### THE DAY OF JEHOVAH

*And I will give portents in the heavens and on the earth, blood and fire and columns of smoke. The sun shall be turned to darkness, and the moon to blood, before the great and terrible day of Jehovah comes (2:30, 31).*

If the outpouring of the Holy Spirit was to occur in the millennial age, it was to be preceded by other events, and the remainder of chapter 2 assumed an apocalyptic character and was concerned with the physical forewarnings of the imminence of the day of Jehovah. "This", said R. B. Girdlestone (*The Grammar of Prophecy*, p.55), "is the time of the manifestation of some special attribute or purpose of God. In Isa. 2.12 it marks a judicial crisis; in Ezek. 13:5 a day of battle; in Amos 2:18 it is pointed out that the day will prove very different from what some people expected".

In many instances, it was stated that the day of Jehovah was near. "This expression", said Girdlestone, "had to do with the fall of Babylon (Isa. 13:6), with the punishment of Egypt (Ezek. 30:3), and with the destruction of Israel and

Jerusalem (Joel 1:15; Zeph. 1:7, 14, 18). Similar expressions, which refer to temporal judgments may be noted in Isa. 13:9; Joel 2:1; and Zech. 14:1. These passages throw light on kindred utterances in the New Testament, and justify us in looking upon the fall of Jerusalem (A.D. 70) as a special manifestation of the day of the Lord; though the full force of the expression is yet in the future", (See also the author's book, *God's Programme of the Ages*, pp. 109-115).

Joel declared that before the coming of the day of Jehovah, celestial and terrestrial phenomena would be seen—blood, fire and columns of smoke, while the sun would be darkened and the moon crimsoned as with blood. Blood and fire are considered by many commentators to be symbols of bloodshed and war (Ex. 7:17; 9:24), and the columns of smoke to be symbols of the destruction of cities in times of military conflict, the clouds of smoke from the burning towns telling of the enemy's victory (Isa. 9:17). The figures employed all suggest forms of judgment.

Signs in the heavens have often allegedly been seen at critical periods of history. For instance, Josephus relates that, prior to the destruction of Jerusalem by the Romans in 70 A.D., a bright star was seen standing over the city, and that chariots and armed troops were seen coursing through the clouds. Even if the stories told are dismissed as figments of the imagination, the fact remains that accounts of similar happenings were widespread.

The sun and moon were originally set in the heavens as a symbol of authority in this scene (Gen. 1:18), the sun being representative of the supreme authority of the Eternal God, and the moon—which takes its light from the sun—signifying all derived authority. Driver (*ibid*, p.66), writing of the signs given in these two heavenly bodies, considers that the "imagery may be suggested partly by eclipses, partly by universal obscurations of sun or moon through atmospheric disturbances—by sandstorms, cyclones, flights of locusts, etc."

Blood is frequently indicative of death (Gen. 9:5, 6; Hab. 2:12; Matt. 27:23) and, when transferred metaphorically to the spiritual realm, it probably implies the cessation of spiritual life, or apostasy from God. When the moon was pictured as being turned to blood (cf. the similar manifestation under the sixth seal of Rev. 6:12), there was the implication of the destruction of all derived rule and authority.

The sun is the natural light of the earth (it is also used in Mal. 4:2 as a type of the Messiah, the spiritual light of the world), and its darkening was a sign of impending judgment (Ezek. 32:7; Rev. 6:12; 8:12; 16:10). Keil remarks (*ibid.* p.213), "The darkening and extinction of the lights of heaven are frequently mentioned, either as harbingers of approaching judgment, or as signs of the breaking of the day of judgment." They were regarded as accompaniments to major catastrophes in human history. One of the plagues of Egypt was the enshrouding of the land in thick darkness (Ex. 10:21-23; cf. Isa. 50:3). If, immediately prior to the day of Jehovah, the sun is to be darkened and the earth is to be clouded by columns of smoke, it would seem that, in consequence of man's apostasy and his refusal to recognise the authority of God, spirtual enlightenment and understanding will be withdrawn, and men left to their own darkened ways. This, in itself, would be a judicial punishment.

The portents also included fire, which again was a feature in the plagues inflicted upon Egypt (Ex. 9:22-25). Fire is an apt symbol, not only of war, as suggested above, but also of the wrath of God, who is Himself a consuming fire (Heb. 12:29; Isa. 33:14). It is used in relation to Divine judgment in Deut. 33:24; Mal. 4:1; Luke 16:24; etc. After the final assize, the last judgment will consign the wicked and impenitent to the lake of fire (Rev. 20:10-15).

Symbols of death and judgment will give the world—and particularly Israel—terrifying warnings of the horror of the impending judgment day. It seems from Matt. 24:29 that the particular period described is that which immediately follows the great tribulation and which introduces the coming of the Son of Man in power and great glory. The day of Jehovah is one of judgment for this world and may well, therefore, be feared. In relegating it to that future period, it should not, of course, be overlooked that the term is sometimes used additionally in a more restricted sense and in reference to an immediate judgment. Every act of Divine judgment is apparently related to the final judgment of the day of Jehovah.

In His Olivet discourse, our Lord predicted the events which are to happen in the latter days and warned those who would then be living in Judea to "flee into the mountains", when they saw "the abomination of desolation, spoken of by Daniel the prophet, stand in the holy place", since this would herald the commencement of the great tribulation (Matt. 24:15-21). Those who trust in God will obey our Lord's injunction in that day and will escape the unparalleled horrors of that period.

## SALVATION IN GOD

*And it shall be that all who call on the name of Jehovah shall be delivered: for in Mount Zion and in Jerusalem there shall be an escape, according as Jehovah has said, and among the escaped shall be those whom Jehovah calls (2:32).*

The period of judgment will not be completely devoid of hope. All who, in that day, call on the name of Jehovah (i.e. who put their trust in Him, for the invocation of God is not merely oral, but is the expression of the heart's deep feelings) will be delivered. As Obadiah also foretold (Obad. 17), many in Zion and Jerusalem will escape from the judgment which falls upon the guilty nation. There will also be some of Jehovah's own (His called ones) among the fugitives who have fled from the persecutions in other countries. The prophet probably envisioned the Jews who are dispersed among the nations: those who demonstrated their loyalty to God would also participate in the deliverance now offered.

Laetsch (*ibid.*, p. 130) sees in the picture only those who are members of the church. "In this church", he writes, "the heavenly Jerusalem (Gal. 4:26; Heb. 12:22), alone is found deliverance, for the church is the whole number of escaped ones, all those whom the Lord shall call." This ignores the peculiar character of the church and the clear teaching of the apostle Paul that this mystery had not been revealed until his day.                           30 June 2022

The prophetic Scriptures reveal that, in the latter days, Israel will be found once more in her own land, that she will suffer dreadfully at the hands of the Gentile nations and under the disciplinary dealings of God during the great tribulation period. The Bible also discloses that the Lord will come forth to judge the nations, to deliver His people and to reign over them in peace and equity for a thousand years. Joel 2:32 foretold Israel's deliverance, and the third chapter of the book predicted the restoration of the people and the judgment of their oppressors.

# CHAPTER 6

## The Second Advent

*Shabbat, 29 Oct 2022*

THE return of nearly three million Jews to their own land in the twentieth century and the re-establishment of the State of Israel once again have been one of the most amazing facts of history. But this return has in no way fulfilled the purposes of God and His intention to restore all His people to their land once more. This is not only inevitable but today it seems imminent.

### THE DAY OF RECKONING

*For, behold, in those days and at that time, when I bring again the captivity of Judah and Jerusalem, I will gather all the nations and bring them down to the valley of Jehoshaphat, and I will enter into judgment with them there on account of my people and my inheritance Israel, whom they have scattered among the nations, and have divided my land. And they have cast lots for my people; and have given a boy for a harlot, and sold a girl for wine and have drunk it (3:1-3).*

The great tribulation, alluded to in the previous chapter, will end with the coming of Christ in glory for the deliverance of His people (Zech. 12:8, 9; 14:3; Rev. 19:11-21). The power of God was now to be demonstrated in the salvation of Israel. He would "turn again their fortunes" (possibly a more accurate translation than "bring again the captivity"). They were to be gathered back to their own country and their own capital (Jer. 23:8). Distress was to be transmuted into happiness once more.

At the same time God intended to deal appropriately with those nations which had maltreated the people of Israel. In Matt. 25:31-46, our Lord disclosed that, when the Son of Man comes in His glory, all nations will be assembled before Him for judgment, and that the basis on which they will be dealt with will be the treatment they have accorded to His brethren, the Jews. Those who showed kindness to the Jews will enter into blessing; those who persecuted them will be banished into everlasting punishment.

Joel's prophecy indicates that the nations will be gathered together for the purpose of the judgment in the valley of Jehoshaphat (meaning "Jah judges", so that there is a play upon words—God's judgment is to take place in the valley of "God judges"). There is no valley known by that name in the vicinity of Jerusalem, but Joel probably had in mind the great victory over the Moabites and Ammonites, won by Jehoshaphat in the valley of Berachah (2 Chron. 20). Since the same valley is described in verse 14 as the valley of Decision, the name may perhaps be regarded as allegorical. The location is usually identified with the valley of the Kidron, but it is impossible to be dogmatic regarding the appointed site of the judgment.

Joel daringly portrayed Jehovah as contending as a litigant in respect of His people against the nations. A parallel passage in Jer. 25:31, which probably relates to the same time, declares that "Jehovah has a controversy with the nations, He will plead with all flesh." God's people are the apple of His eye and any attack upon them is tantamount to an attack upon Himself.

The subject of His dispute or litigation with the Gentiles will be His people and inheritance of Israel. (It is significant that He does not restrict it to Judah but refers to the united kingdom). The Gentiles had followed the practice of Nebuchadnezzar (to whom the passage may prophetically refer) and other pagan rulers, and had dispersed the Israelites far and wide among the nations. Josephus says that the Romans, for example, chose out of the Jews "the tallest and most beautiful, and reserved them for the triumph; and as for the rest of the multitude that were above 17 years old, he put them in bonds; and sent them to the Egyptian mines . . . and those that were under 17 years of age were sold for slaves."

The land had then been divided up among the new inhabitants imported to replace the deported Israelites. Following the common practice, moreover, the Jewish captives had been shared by lot among the soldiers who had captured them, and were so lightly esteemed that a boy was given up as the equivalent of a prostitute's hire for a night's debauch, while a girl was casually exchanged for a bowl of wine. It was a complete violation of rudimentary morality. God could not ignore the affront to Himself contained in the indignities suffered by His people and He accordingly announced that He would enter into legal dispute with the Gentile nations.

### PHOENICIA AND PHILISTIA

*What are you to me, O Tyre and Zidon and all the regions of Philistia? Are you rendering me a recompense? If you are recompensing me, I will swiftly and speedily return your recompense upon your own head. For you have taken my silver and gold and have carried my precious treasures into your temples (3:4, 5).*

Although other nations were equally culpable, God marked out the Phoenicians and Philistines as particularly deserving of condemnation. They had stolen the treasures of the land and presumably also of the temple at Jerusalem. The gold and silver and precious things which had been carried away were deposited in their own temples. This was a double insult to Jehovah. Not only had they carried away His possessions, but they had dedicated them to the lifeless idols which they worshipped.

"What are you to Me?" asked Jehovah. Their actions implied that He had done them some injustice, for which they were revenging themselves. But their attack and their theft had been without provocation. Was there some wrong which had been done to them which had inspired them to repay Him in such a way? What had happened was irrational and without the slightest justification, but God declared that their wrongdoing would recoil upon their own heads. He would "swiftly and speedily" bring retribution upon them.

They had ruthlessly denuded the temple of its silver and gold and had robbed God's people of their possessions, and the most precious treasures had been carried away to adorn the palaces of the wealthy and the temples of their false gods. Divine requital was inevitable.

### THE SLAVE TRAFFIC

*You have sold the sons of Judah and Jerusalem to the sons of the Greeks, so that you might remove them far from their own border. Behold, I will stir them up from the place to which you have sold them, and I will return your recompence upon your own head. I will sell your sons and daughters into the hand of the sons of Judah, and they will sell them to the Sabeans, to a nation far off: for Jehovah has spoken (3:6-8).*

Not content with their ill-gotten material gains the mercenary spirit of the Phoenicians and Philistines led them to adopt the infamous slave traffic. They had made captives of the people of Judah and Jerusalem and had sold them into slavery to the Greeks, who had transported them far from their homes, thereby minimising the prospects of their return. This was, of course, fortuitous rather than deliberate.

Jehovah warned them that He was stirring up His people to desert the land of their servitude and He threatened these guilty nations that He would fittingly repay those who had so ill-treated His people and dishonoured Him. "The punishment", moreover, as Driver remarks, would be "awarded according to the *lex talionis*". The Phoenicians and Philistines had sold the Jews into slavery to the Greeks. God declared that He would sell their people to the Judahites, so that they in turn might sell them to the Sabeans, or men of Sheba—a distant nation dwelling in south-west Arabia (Job 6:19; Jer.

6:20; Ezek. 27:22; 38:13). God's dealings are always just and equitable, and as the enemy had dealt with Israel, so would He deal with them. The retribution was meet.

Further information was now given of the judgment of the nations mentioned in verse 2.

## A Military Proclamation

*Proclaim this among the nations. Hallow a war. Arouse the mighty men. Let all the fighting men draw near; let them come up. Beat your ploughshares into swords, and your pruning hooks into spears. Let the weak say, I am a warrior (3:9, 10).*

Again Jehovah indicated that the nations were to be brought together for judgment in the valley of Jehoshaphat. A proclamation of war was to be heralded among the nations, and the war was to be sanctified or hallowed—possibly an allusion to the customary sacrifices slain prior to embarking upon a military campaign. (In some cases the animals were used by the pagans to ascertain the omens for the commencement of the war or of the battle).

The Gentile warriors were aroused from their inactivity to prepare themselves for the coming conflict with Israel in the valley of Jehoshaphat. In the millennial age, swords will be beaten into ploughshares and spears into pruning hooks (Isa. 2:4). Here the process was reversed, and the agricultural implements were to be converted into military weapons. Stirred by the martial preparations around him, even the weakling will declare himself a warrior. All will be prepared to participate in the great battle.

Joel does not disclose the specific cause of the conflict and it is left to other prophets to provide fragmentary details, from which it is possible to gain a more comprehensive picture. Zech. 14:2, for example, declares that Jehovah will gather all nations to battle against Jerusalem immediately prior to the Second Advent. Rev. 19:19, also referring to the same period, portrays the rulers of the earth and their armies gathered together to make war upon the Lamb. Dan.

65                                          E

11:44, 45 implies that the forces of the north will be involved,
Rev. 16:12 those of the far east, and Dan. 2:35, 44 and 7:26
suggest that the western powers will also be associated in the
great armies to be destroyed. The prophet's picture presumably relates to the final military outburst at the great tribulation and prior to the return of our Lord in judgment.

### JEHOVAH'S JUDGMENT

*Hasten and come, all you nations round about, and
assemble yourselves. Thither cause thy warriors to come
down, O Jehovah. Let the nations be stirred up and come up
to the valley of Jehoshaphat. For there will I sit to judge all
the nations round about (3:11, 12).*

The final dénouement was now at hand, and Jehovah
urged the nations to hasten and assemble together in the
valley. They would gather under the impression that it was
for a contest with Israel and would be totally unaware of the
real purpose. Joel pictured the mighty armies gathering together from every direction for the tremendous battle.

He accordingly turned to Jehovah and prayed Him to
intervene by causing His warriors, the mighty angelic hosts
(Psa. 68:17), to descend to do battle in the valley. In reply,
Jehovah declared that the nations would be stirred up and
gathered to the valley of Jehoshaphat. Nothing could frustrate
His purposes. There He would meet them, for there it was
His intention to sit to judge the nations. Wünsche points out
that "The decision of a judge made by him standing was
generally deemed to have no legal force", and this judgment
of the living nations was, therefore, to be delivered sitting.

No longer was Jehovah the litigant standing to plead as in
verse 2. He was now the Judge sitting to pass sentence upon
the guilty (Psa. 9:4, 5). The picture is, of course, of the final
battle prior to the setting up of His earthly kingdom. The
Gentile forces will be gathered together by the Beast, the
great western dictator, and "the kings of the earth". The
Apocalypse reveals that then the Lord will ride forth to judge
and to make war, all the armies of heaven following Him in

His judicial descent (Rev. 19:11-14).

The Apocalypse views Him as treading "the winepress of the fierceness and wrath of Almighty God" (Rev. 19:15), and somewhat similar language was used by Joel.

UNMITIGATED JUDGMENT

*Put in the sickle, for the harvest is ripe. Come, tread down, for the press is full, the vats overflow; for their wickedness is great. Multitudes, multitudes in the valley of decision: for the day of Jehovah is near in the valley of decision (3:13, 14).*

When judgment was about to break in the Patmos visions, the Son of Man was bidden, "Thrust in Thy sickle and reap: for the time has come for Thee to reap; for the harvest of the earth is ripe" (Rev. 14:15). Sin had come to fruition and it was time that the ripened harvest was cut down. The sentence to be executed following the decision of the Judge in the valley of Jehoshaphat was in almost precisely identical terms. "Put in the sickle, for the harvest is ripe", was the command.

The figure was an apt one. The development of iniquity is gradual but, in due course, it grows to completion, and it is evident today that the harvest is ripening fast. The full growth is, of course, arrested at present by the restraining influence referred to in 2 Thess. 2, but when the Holy Spirit and the Church have been removed at Christ's coming, there will be nothing to prevent a speedy ripening. But evil cannot continue for ever unchecked. At the appointed moment, the grain will be cut down. Ultimate judgment is inevitable.

In the apocalyptic vision, the reaping of the harvest was followed by the gathering in of the vintage and the crushing of the grapes in the winepress (Rev. 14:18-20). Although the harvest is not often used as a symbol of judgment, the treading of the winepress is consistently used in this sense. The prophet Isaiah pictures Jehovah as coming from Edom with blood-stained garments, having "trodden the winepress alone" (Isa. 63:1-3). Joel portrays the guilty nations as crowded together like grapes in the winepress, the vats already overflowing, their wickedness demanding unrelieved punishment and awaiting the crushing judgment of God.

As the New Testament subsequently reveals, the relentless crushing of His foes is undertaken by the Lord Jesus Christ. The day of mercy will then be over and, iniquity having come to full fruition, the unalleviated weight of Divine judgment must then be borne. Our Lord will tread down His adversaries and crush the rebels beneath His feet.

Joel's prophecy pictures multitudes assembled in the valley of decision, i.e. the valley of judgment, when the Divine decision is announced and the sentence executed. The distant hum of the tremendous masses, thronging tumultuously into the valley, seemed to fill the prophet's ears. The noisy, vociferous crowd would probably be boasting loudly of what their arms would accomplish in battle and the marvellous victory they were about to win. But the day of reckoning had come. The day of Jehovah, the dread day of judgment, was at hand, and the penalty was to be exacted in the valley of decision.

### THE VOICE OF GOD

*The sun and the moon are darkened, and the stars withdraw their shining. And Jehovah roars from Zion and utters His voice from Jerusalem: and the heavens and the earth shake. But Jehovah is a refuge to his people and a stronghold to the sons of Israel (3:15, 16).*

Joel had already described the preternatural signs of the impending day of Jehovah and he again referred to the celestial and terrestial phenomena (to which others of the prophets also make reference, of course).

If his language is taken literally, a mighty storm breaks out: the sky darkens, the sun and the moon cloud over, the stars are lost to view, the roar of the thunder breaks upon the ears of the terrified earth-dwellers, and the heavens and the earth seem to be convulsed by a terrible earthquake. The same preternatural signs of the coming day of judgment are mentioned in Isa. 13:10; Matt. 24:29; Mark 13:24; Rev. 6:12, and other passages. In the height of the storm, the roar of God's voice is heard (cf. Amos 1:2; Jer. 25:30) above the roll of the thunder (itself often employed as a metaphor of the voice of God), and the nations are struck down and destroyed as if in a cataclysm.

Whilst the Second Advent may quite literally be attended by physical signs of this nature, the language may very well have been intended figuratively and simply as indicative of the awful retribution which will overtake the Gentiles at the end of the great tribulation period. The celestial luminaries were set in the sky as rulers and signs (Gen. 1:14-18), and the obscuring of their light implies the complete overthrow of authority in that dread day, and the withdrawal from earth of divine grace and compassion. It is a day of judgment and no place will then exist for mercy. In the dreadful convulsion of nature, the prophet depicts the complete dissolution of social and governmental order and its supersession by utter chaos. Truly the day of Jehovah is one to be feared.

In the midst of the awful scenes of judgment upon the Gentiles, however, Israel will be divinely protected. Despite the storm around them, they will find a shelter in God. He will be their refuge. Danger and destruction may threaten the guilty world, but Jehovah sees no defilement in His people and He assured them that He would be their refuge from the storm and their stronghold in which they could shelter from the foe—terms frequently used of God in the Old Testament (e.g. Psa. 46:1). The Syriac version admirably (even if not accurately) renders the second half of verse 16, "the Lord will have pity on his people and will strengthen the children of Israel".

Jehovah's presence was known among His people in their earlier history and this was now to be repeated.

## GOD IN THE MIDST

*So you shall know that I am Jehovah your God (Elohim), who dwell in Zion, my holy mountain. And Jerusalem shall be holy and strangers shall never again pass through it (3:17).*

God's covenant name to Israel was Jehovah and He now declared that they should "know that I am Jehovah your

69

God". Their Deliverer in the coming day of judgment will be no other than the One who has been their Protector throughout their history. God will dwell in the midst of His people, the guarantee of their security, and the holy city will be sanctified and protected by His presence (cf. Joel 2:27). The same pledge is reiterated by other prophets (e.g. Ezek. 43:9; Zech. 14:16, etc.).

Strangers have trodden the streets of Jerusalem down the centuries. The invader has plundered and devastated the city. In that millennial age, which Joel anticipated, no stranger would ever defile the city again (Isa. 52:1; Rev. 21:3, 27). Nothing defiling is tolerable where His presence is known. The glory of God, filling the city, will sanctify it to Him. Zion will be His holy mountain and Jerusalem will be His holy city.

Judgment past, the prophet continued to depict the millennial scene, where blessings abound on every side.

## A LAND OF BLESSING

*And it shall be in that day that the mountains shall drip sweet wine, and the hills shall flow with milk, and all the stream beds of Judah shall flow with water. And a spring shall go forth from the house of Jehovah and water the valley of Shittim (3:18).*

The land originally promised to Israel was to be "a good land and a large . . . flowing with milk and honey" (Ex. 3:8). Every promise to the nation in the past will be fulfilled in detail when the people are eventually established in their own land in the millennium. The once desolate waste will be superseded by a land of extraordinary fertility. The country, which had been torn by strife and devastated by invaders, will then enjoy undisturbed peace for ever. The presence of Jehovah will transform even the natural and material.

While the language used by Joel of the conditions of that age may be hyperbolical, it does give some impression of the prosperity and blessing of "the golden age". The prophet pictures the mountains as giving rise to streams of sweet wine (cf. Amos 9:13)—the symbol of joy and gladness—and the hills of rivers of milk (figurative of nourishment and satisfaction). In the summer practically all Israel's rivers and streams dry up. No dry river bed would ever be seen again, declared the prophet. The rivers would constantly flow with water (one of the greatest material blessings of the East). Drought would never again strike the land.

Ezek. 47:1-12 portrays a river issuing out of the temple at Jerusalem, and Zech. 14:8 describes waters for ever flowing out of the city to the Mediterranean and the Dead Seas. Joel also declared that a spring would issue from the temple to water the gorge of Shittim—the desert acacia valley near the Jordan, which was the last encampment of Israel before they entered the promised land (Num. 25:1; Josh. 2:1; 3:1).

The mountains will be covered with terraces of vines, herds of cattle will be pastured on the hills, rivulets will trickle down the slopes and an inexhaustible river flow through the valley. Life, refreshment and fertility will be the characteristics of the country, and the exaggerated description given by the prophet suggests the abnormal fertility which will exist.

By contrast, the lands of Egypt and Edom, the age-long enemies of Israel, will be barren wastes. Even in natural things, there will be divine retribution for the past.

## STRICKEN COUNTRIES

*Egypt shall become a desolation, and Edom a desolate wilderness for the violence done to the sons of Judah, because they have shed innocent blood in their land (3:19).*

Egypt was so prolific that it was maintained by ancient writers that the waters of the Nile had some power of fecundity. The country enjoyed great prosperity because of the river and, at the time of Joel's prophecy, there was not the slightest symptom of potential decay.

Edom, as Pusey (*ibid.*, p. 219) remarks, "was the centre of the intercourse of nations. Occupying, as it did in its narrowest dimensions, the mountain between the south end of the Dead Sea and the Atlantic gulf, it lay on the direct line between Egypt and Babylonia . . . Petra was the natural halting-place of the caravans . . . In Joel's time, not the slightest shadow was cast on her future".

Yet the prophet Ezekiel had predicted that "the land of Egypt shall be desolate and waste" (Ezek. 29:9)—despite the abundant irrigation normally possible through the waters of the Nile—and that Edom shall be desolate (Ezek. 25:13). Joel repeated the prediction and in almost identical language.

The two countries had wreaked their cruelty upon Judah and had inflicted unprovoked bloodshed upon God's people. Hence they should be desolate and barren. The reference is probably to the consistent behaviour of these two nations and their constant vindictiveness and cruelty rather than to an isolated incident, although Driver (ibid., p. 78) argues that the prophet had in mind "the sudden and unprovoked massacre of Jews, who were settled and living peaceably in the two countries named, possibly at the time of a revolt". The land mentioned by Joel, however, was probably that of Israel and not that of her enemies. One fact was quite clear, viz. that the Eternal, who takes account of nation's actions metes out His punishment in precise relation to the deeds committed.

### JUDAH'S FUTURE

*Judah shall abide for ever, and Jerusalem to all generations. I will avenge their blood which I have not avenged. For Jehovah dwells in Zion (3:20,21).*

While their enemies suffered, Judah and Jerusalem would permanently flourish, declared the prophet. The land would remain inhabited for ever and the city of Jerusalem would be a populated city to all generations.

The penultimate sentence of the prophecy has been rendered in various ways. The A.V. translates, "For I will cleanse their blood that I have not cleansed", whereas the R.S.V. renders it, "I will avenge their blood, and I will not clear the guilty". Laetsch adopts the rendering suggested above, but the LXX says, "I will make inquisition for their blood, and will not pass it over unavenged". The Syriac version puts it, "I will avenge their blood, and I will not absolve the offenders".

Driver translates, "I will hold as innocent their blood, which I have not held as innocent", and comments, "By the desolation of Egypt and Edom, Jehovah will show openly that the murdered Israelites (v. 19 b) had suffered innocently".

It seems reasonably clear that the purport of the prophet's words was that God would now vindicate His people, who had been massacred by their inveterate foes. Since He had not previously intervened, it might possibly have been assumed that the people of Israel were guilty and deserving of the death inflicted upon them. But He now demonstrated their innocence by His judgment upon their foes. In further confirmation, He, who could not tolerate sin, abode in Zion —the conclusive evidence of His satisfaction of His people's innocence.

# APPENDIX

## The Holy Spirit

IN his book, *The Doctrine of the Holy Spirit*, Prof. H. Berkhof claims that pneumatology is a neglected field of systematic theology and that one of the primary reasons lies in the character of the Holy Spirit. "The Spirit constantly leads our attention away from Himself to Jesus Christ," he says. "So He hides Himself on the one hand in Christ; and on the other hand He hides Himself in His operations in the life of the church and the lives of individuals." Whilst this is true it would be equally correct to say that, in many circles, there is a strong disinclination to listen to ministry on the subject of the Person and work of the Third Person of the Holy Trinity.

The Hebrew word *ruach* and the Greek word *pneuma* which are often translated "spirit" in the Old Testament and the New Testament respectively, might equally well be translated as "wind" or "breath", or occasionally, in a more metaphorical sense as "vitality" or "principle of life". The Scriptural teaching is nevertheless clear that the Holy Spirit is not some abstract influence or power but a vital Personality. In *The Holy Spirit in the New Testament*, H. B. Swete says that, although "in His workings and gifts He is regarded as a power and a gift rather than a person, and described under figures borrowed from external and inanimate nature, yet in His own Divine life it is impossible to doubt that He possesses that which answers in some higher, and to us, incomprehensible way to personality in man."

The personal pronoun is repeatedly used in reference to Him, e.g. "He shall testify," "He will guide you," "He will show you," "the Holy Ghost said" (John 15:26; 16:13, 15; Acts 13:2). As T. Houghton points out in *The Holy Spirit*, it could only be said of a Person that He "teaches, brings to remembrance, testifies, comes, is sent, reproves, guides, speaks, shows things to come, glorifies and receives."

The Bible attributes to Him a mind, will and emotions, which are exclusively characteristics of a person and cannot possibly apply to an influence or some abstract conception. That He has a mind and is capable of knowing is evident from 1 Cor. 2:10, 11, where the apostle Paul declares that the Spirit searches the deep things of God and that such things are known by none but the Spirit of God. In Him is the Divine self-consciousness and self-knowledge.

His possession of a will is equally plain. He instructed the church at Antioch, for example, to set apart to Him Barnabas and Saul for the work to which He had called them (Acts 13:2). He guided Philip to join the chariot of the Ethiopian eunuch (Acts 8:29). When Paul, Silas and Timothy purposed to go to Bithynia, He suffered them not (Acts 16:7). It is said that He distributes gifts to men as He wills (1 Cor. 12:11).

Again, it is clear that He has emotions and feelings. "Grieve not the Holy Spirit of God," the apostle bade the Ephesians (Eph. 4:30), while, in assuring the Roman believers of the intercessory prayers of the Holy Spirit, he implied an intensity of sympathetic feeling in "groanings which cannot be uttered" (Rom. 8:26).

It is said of Him that He can be resisted, obeyed, lied to, sinned against and vexed. His activities are always described as personal. Before the flood, for instance, God declared that His Spirit would not always strive with man (Gen. 6:3) while in New Testament days, James plainly referred to a Person when he said, "It seemed good to the Holy Spirit and to us, to lay upon you no greater burden" (Acts 15:28).

But the Holy Spirit is not merely a Person: He is a Divine Person, possessed of all the attributes of Deity. As Wm. Hoste says in *Studies in Bible Doctrine*, He "is co-equal, co-eternal and co-substantial with the Father and the Son . . . That He is called the Spirit is not because the other Divine Persons are not Spirit, for 'God is Spirit,' but only because His mode of existence is 'spiration'."

One of the primary characteristics of the Godhead is eternity of being. No one is eternal but God, yet the Holy Spirit is described in Heb. 9:14 as "the eternal Spirit." He is uncreated. Again, God alone is inherently and indefectibly holy, but the Spirit is repeatedly referred to as the Holy Spirit. God is obviously the origin of life, but the apostle Paul refers to the Holy Spirit as "the Spirit of life" (Rom. 8:2, 10) and Peter plainly describes Him as God (Acts 5:3, 4).

By the very nature of things, omnipotence belongs to the Deity, but it is plain from the part He played in creation and continues to play in providence that this attribute is possessed by the Holy Spirit. The Psalmist declares that all animal life was brought into existence by Him and that, by Him, the face of the earth is renewed (Psa. 104:30). Job disclosed that the heavens were decorated with stars by Him (Job 26:13). Our Lord indicated that the same One had authority over Satan and his kingdom of darkness (Matt. 12:25).

Only the Almighty can be omniscient, but this attribute is patently attributed to the Spirit. "Who hath directed the Spirit of Jehovah," asks the prophet, "or being His counsellor has taught Him? With whom took He counsel, and who instructed Him and taught Him in the path of justice, or taught Him knowledge, and showed Him the way of understanding?" (Isa. 40:14). He needed no guide or teacher: all knowledge is His.

The Divine attribute of omnipresence is also His. "Whither shall I go from Thy Spirit?" cried the Psalmist. "If I ascend up into heaven, Thou art there; if I make my bed in hell, behold Thou art there" (Psa. 139:7, 8).

The Spirit is given equal rank with the Father and the Son

in the commission and baptismal formula of Matt. 28:19, as well as in the apostolic benediction of 2 Cor. 13:14. Of His Divinity there can be no doubt. "As spirit is nothing less than the inmost principle of life, and the spirit of man is man himself," says A. H. Strong in his *Systematic Theology*, "so the Spirit of God must be God" (1 Cor. 2:11).

At the same time, it is evident that, although the Holy Spirit is one with the Father and the Son, He is also distinct from both. At our Lord's baptism, for example, the Son stood in the water, the Spirit descended as a dove, and the Father spoke from the opened heavens (Matt. 3:16, 17). Again, to His disciples, our Lord said, "I (the Son) will pray the Father, and He shall give you another Comforter" (John 14:16). In his sermon at Pentecost, Peter told the vast congregation, "Being by the right hand of God exalted and having received of the Father the promise of the Holy Spirit, He (the Son) hath poured forth this" (Acts 2:33). Bishop Pearson, in his book, *On the Creed*, says that He "is truly and properly a Person, of a true real and personal subsistence, not a created but uncreated Person, and so the true and eternal God; . . . yet is He not the Father, nor the Son, but the Spirit of the Father and the Son, the third Person in the blessed Trinity, proceeding from the Father and the Son."

There are not only different relationships in the Godhead, but differences in operation as well. The Son is begotten of the Father; the Holy Spirit is not, but our Lord's conception is said to have been His work (Matt. 1:18, 20; Luke 1:35). The Holy Spirit proceeds from the Father and the Son, but the reverse is never true. Although, as C. Hodge says in his *Systematic Theology*, "He is the same in substance and equal in power and glory," yet "He is subordinate to the Father and the Son as to His mode of subsistence and operation, as He is said to be of the Father and of the Son; He is sent by them and they operate through Him . . . His eternal relation to the other Persons of the Trinity is indicated by the word 'Spirit', and by its being said that He is out of God, i.e. God is the source whence the Spirit is said to proceed."

In the Old Testament, the Father was in prominence. Then for 33 years the light shone upon the Son. But from Pentecost unto today, it has been the age of the Spirit. This is true, for example, of regeneration (John 3:5), sanctification (1 Pet. 1:2), teaching (John 16:13), indwelling (1 Cor. 3:16; 6:19), and the inhabiting of the temple of the church (Eph. 2:21, 22). This distinction cannot be pressed too far, however. In the case of redemption, for instance, the Father loved, the Son paid the price, and the Spirit applies it to the individual.

The Holy Spirit is the author of the Scriptures. He moved and inspired men to write, using their own personality and style, but guiding them in their thoughts and choice of words (2 Pet. 1:21); yet if it was the voice of the Spirit, it was also the word of Jehovah (1 Tim. 4:1; Jer. 7:1, etc).

It seems clear that the fuller revelation of the Holy Spirit's activities was reserved for New Testament days. "The Holy Spirit had not been unknown in human history prior to the coming of Christ," writes G. Campbell Morgan in *The Teaching of Christ*. "Men had been taught that the Spirit had been specially associated with the cosmos from that hour of restoration which the first page of Genesis records. The restoration of a lost order was accomplished by the brooding of the Spirit over the abyss. In the Old Testament men spoke of the Spirit, and a ministry of the Spirit was constantly referred to . . . . We read of the Spirit, clothing Himself with a man, clothing a man with Himself; coming to inspire men for special work, the singing of a song, the weaving of a fabric, the working in gold for the perfecting of the tabernacle. The suggestion throughout is of special wisdom and illumination and power for special occasions."

The New Testament paints a different picture. A Man came into this world, who was conceived of the Holy Spirit. That One "grew and waxed strong in spirit, filled with wisdom" (Luke 2:40), and as another has written, "We must ascribe to the Holy Spirit all the progress in Christ's mental and spiritual development, and all His advancement in knowledge and holiness." When our Lord was baptised, the Spirit descended upon Him to *abide* upon Him. This had never happened to man before. Isaiah (11:2) had foretold centuries earlier that the Spirit of the Lord would rest upon Him, and at His baptism this actually happened, and our Lord declared in the synagogue at Nazareth, "The Spirit of the Lord is upon Me" (Luke 4:18). The Holy Spirit was given to Him without measure. The full plenitude of the Spirit was His unction. He was anointed of the Spirit and all His teaching was by the power of the Spirit. It was through the eternal Spirit that He offered Himself to God (Heb. 9:14), and it was the Holy Spirit who raised Him from the dead (Rom. 8:11; 1 Pet. 3:18).

When our Lord ascended to heaven, He sent the *paraclete* He had promised (the Comforter of John 16:7). The word used is indicative of one called to another's side as a helper and was particularly relevant to an advocate to plead the cause of another in a court of justice. The same word is used in 1 John 2:1 and is there translated *advocate*. We have a representative with the Father, but Christ has also His representative in us.

When the Holy Spirit came upon the disciples at Pentecost, it was with tongues of fire and miraculous signs. What had never occurred in Old Testament days came to pass then. The Holy Spirit came to indwell individuals permanently and not temporarily, and to make them living temples for God's glory. By this men and women are regenerated or born again; by Him they are kept; by Him spiritual fruit is produced in their lives; by Him they are fashioned like Christ. He is the guide and teacher of God's people, and His mission is to reveal the glories of Christ to them. His power and wisdom are available to them and He equips for all the circumstances of life.

He came, as Christ foretold, to convince the world of sin, righteousness and judgment (John 16:8). His presence acts as a restraint upon the full manifestation of sin, and preserves the world from complete corruption. When He is withdrawn (2 Thess. 2:7), iniquity will break out on an unparalleled scale.

As Joel 2:28, 29 indicates, however, the Messianic age will see an unprecedented effusion of the Spirit, with effects unequalled by anything in past history. Even during the church era, in which we live, the results of His coming at Pentecost were beyond anything realised in previous ages.

Not long before His ascension, our Lord told His disciples that "John truly baptised with water, but you shall be baptised with the Holy Spirit not many days hence" (Acts 1:5). Subsequently, reporting the outpouring of the Holy Spirit on the Gentile Cornelius and his household, Peter declared that "the Holy Spirit fell on them as on us at the beginning" (Acts 11:15), implying that Pentecost was the fulfilment of the Master's statement. That baptism with the Spirit was a historical and initiatory fact. W. E. Vine pertinently remarks that, at Pentecost, "the whole church was by the Holy Spirit's action incorporated into one integral company, a spiritual entity; those who were already believers on that day, and those who would afterwards believe, were thus actually and prospectively formed into the body of Christ, all the members having been in the mind of God according to His eternal counsel."

In Eph. 4:8 the apostle Paul declared that, when the Lord Jesus Christ ascended, "He led captivity captive and gave gifts unto men," and the Holy Spirit's distribution of these gifts occurred at Pentecost. The gifts were bestowed for the furtherance of the work of God and the edification of the body of Christ (Eph. 4:12). They were (and still are) bestowed in Divine sovereignty, and are no reflection of the merit or spirituality of the recipient, and consequently provide no basis for self-glorification. It is clear from I Cor. 12:7 that every believer has been the recipient of one or more gifts and is responsible for their exercise for the good of the whole. If they are not used, the whole body suffers.

The gifts are not natural talents, but spiritual endowments (or "manifestations") and must, therefore, be exercised in the power of the Holy Spirit. Whilst the Corinthians were exhorted to "covet earnestly the best gifts" and, in particular, that of prophecy (I Cor. 12:31; 14:39), we cannot choose our own gifts or the sphere in which we shall exercise them. "God has set the members every one in the body as it has pleased Him" (I Cor. 12:18). He has determined our place and He has given the gift to be used in that particular place in the body.

In the exercise of the gifts, it is clear that, whilst acting under the direction of the Holy Spirit, the individual still remains responsible for his actions and cannot plead that some extravagance or excess is attributable to the leading of the Holy Spirit. "The spirits of the prophets are subject to the prophets" (I Cor. 14:32). "God is not the author of confusion" and everything must "be done decently and in order" (I Cor. 14:33, 40). There is a control of the exercise of gift in church gatherings: "let the prophets speak two or three," said the apostle Paul, and those who listen are to judge whether what is said is in accord with the Word of God (I Cor. 14:29). The gift is to be used for the profit of the hearers: otherwise it is not to be used (I Cor. 12:7). Above all, every gift is to be exercised in the spirit of love (I Cor. 13).

It is sometimes argued that I Cor. 13:8, 10 indicates that certain of the charismatic gifts—prophecy, tongues, and knowledge—no longer exist, since they were to disappear "when that which is perfect is come," and it is maintained that this refers to the completion of the canon of Scripture. This is a somewhat doubtful interpretation, however, and it seems more probable that the reference is to the Second Advent of our Lord. It is often urged that these gifts were simply bestowed for signs at the ushering in of a new dispensation and that they disappeared when the need for them had gone. Some gifts have certainly not been in evidence to any great extent over the centuries, although a revival of their use has been alleged in recent days. It is, of course, possible that the end of the age may be characterised by similar phenomena to those at the beginning, and that special spiritual manifestations may be anticipated in view of the imminence of our Lord's return. The dogmatism, which dismisses these features as carnal, or even diabolical, may not be so completely justified as is sometimes assumed.

The gifts bestowed in this age are detailed in four lists, given in Rom. 12:6-8; I Cor. 12:8-10; I Cor. 12:28-30; and Eph. 4:11, 12. These lists do not agree, and it is significant that prophecy is the only gift to appear in all four lists. In some instances, the gift itself is referred to, and in others the person who possesses the gift. The differences may also be explained in part by the context in which they are found. It may be useful to consider briefly the individual gifts.

1. An' *apostle* (I Cor. 12:28; Eph. 4:11) was an envoy or ambassador entrusted with a special mission, an emissary who spoke with the authority of the power by whom he had been sent. It is used of the twelve who, in a special sense, formed the foundation of the church (Eph. 2:20), and whose names appear in the foundations of the heavenly Jerusalem of the future (Rev. 21:14). But the same word is used of our Lord (Heb. 3:1), of Barnabas (Acts 14:4, 14), as well as of Titus and others (2 Cor. 8:23), and it would not be unreasonable to describe some of God's servants today as apostles with a special mission to a particular country or to a certain race. Although often described loosely as a "foundation gift," in its broadest sense the gift of apostleship (as distinct from the technical office in the early days of the church) may still be in evidence in our own time.

2. The gift of *prophecy* (Rom. 12:6; I Cor. 12:10, 28; Eph. 4:11) has again been referred to as merely an initiatory and temporary gift, employed in the founding of the church (Eph. 2:20), but prophets were to be found in Jerusalem and Antioch (Acts 11:27; 13:1), as well as at Rome, Corinth and Ephesus, and the use of the gift seems to have been widespread. Although Agabus, one of the prophets of Jerusalem, was, on at least two occasions, used to predict future events (Acts 11:27; 21:10), it is evident that the gift was not re-

stricted to prediction: indeed the New Testament prophet seems to have been more of a *forthteller* than a *foreteller*. The apostle Paul explained that the prophet spoke to men "to edification and exhortation and comfort" (I Cor. 14:3), and enjoined the Corinthians to covet this gift, which he clearly esteemed as of greater importance to the church than some others (1 Cor. 14:39). With a complete revelation, it is not to be expected that predictive powers will normally—if ever—be in evidence now, but the need for prophetic edification, exhortation and comfort is as great as ever.

3. The *teacher* (1 Cor. 12:28; Eph. 4:11) is envisaged as a minister of divine things, who takes the Word of God and explains its meaning to others. As with all the gifts, it is essential for that of teaching to be exercised in the power of the Holy Spirit in order that understanding may not be merely academic or intellectual, but spiritual.

4. The *evangelist* (Eph. 4:11) is one who carries the glad news of the gospel to those in need. Philip was so described (Acts 21:8) and Timothy was exhorted to "do the work of an evangelist" (2 Tim. 4:5). The gift is not synonymous with the ability to preach: rather does it conjure up the picture of one with a heart for souls, who seeks to present the love of Christ to the unsaved.

5. The *pastor* (Eph. 4:11) is, in some respects, the most necessary gift to the church. As a shepherd of the flock, he cares for their spiritual needs and condition, binding up the broken knees, visiting the sick, seeking the restoration of the backslider, and generally comforting God's people. In Old Testament days, God promised to give His people pastors according to His heart, who would feed them "with knowledge and understanding" (Jer. 3:15). God's people are regarded as sheep and the pastor as a shepherd who is constantly watching over their souls.

6. *Ministry* is detailed as a gift only in Rom. 12:7. Sandwiched as it is between prophecy and teaching, this gift might appear to relate primarily to the ministry of the Word. Prof. John Murray, however, prefers to apply it to the other use

made of the word as "the ministry of mercy with reference to physical need" (cf. Acts 6:1; 11:29; 12:25; 2 Cor. 8:4; 9:1, 12, 13). The term is, in fact, used in Rom. 15:31 in regard to Paul's mission to Jerusalem. If this view is adopted, the ministry of mercy to the poor and infirm is the spiritual work of a deacon. Archippus and Timothy were both enjoined to fulfil their ministry (Col. 4:17; 2 Tim. 4:5), but its precise character is not stated.

7. *Exhortation* (Rom. 12:8) is derived from the same root as the word *paraclete* and may perhaps be better rendered "consolation" and ability to come alongside and help. The implication is a spiritual ability to provide consolation to the afflicted. Murray says, "As teaching is directed to understanding, so is exhortation to the heart, conscience and will. Exhortation needs to be directed to the cultivation of patience and perseverance".

8. *Giving* (Rom. 12:8) is naturally expected of all believers, but this spiritual gift seems to be a special grace divinely bestowed. As in the case of the Macedonians, it involves more than the giving of material resources—"they first gave their own selves" (2 Cor. 8:5). The apostle states that this giving is to be with simplicity or with single-minded purpose.

9. *Rule* or *government* (Rom. 12:8; 1 Cor. 12:28). In every sphere there must be those with the ability to control and direct operations. In the church, there is also the need for the spiritual rulers who, under the guidance of God, will channel activities into the right course and who will guide in the conduct of the work.

10. *Mercy* (Rom. 12:8) as a spiritual gift is vitally essential in the church. Among the saints generally there is always a need for sympathy and understanding in the circumstances and difficulties of life; for many there is a call for compassion, and for the faltering and wayward there is a cry for succour. Mercy reaches out and covers all with its cloak of kindness.

11. *Wisdom* (1 Cor. 12:8). This gift is mentioned only in 1 Cor. 12 and is there described as "the word of wisdom". The reference seems to be to one who is possessed of spiritual

discernment and sound judgment in the interpretation of the deeper spiritual truths contained in the Scriptures and revealed by the Holy Spirit.

12. *Knowledge* (1 Cor. 12:8). The "word of knowledge" is also mentioned only in the Corinthian epistle. Wisdom has rather a theoretical connotation, whereas knowledge is eminently practical. The one with this gift has the ability to make a practical application of spiritual truth to the life and daily experience and to impart some spiritual counsel in practical circumstances.

13. *Faith* (1 Cor. 12:9). All Christians must obviously have faith, but there is a special gift of the Holy Spirit, which enables the possessor, as one writer says, "to stand upon revealed truth and trust in a power that is beyond the sphere of human possibilities." Such special faith is not given to all. George Müller's story is an outstanding example of the exercise of this gift.

14. *Healing* (1 Cor. 12:9, 30). It is sometimes said that all sickness is due to personal sin, and that repentance and faith bring healing because Christ bore our sicknesses at Calvary, but this is not true. Heb. 12, for example, makes it plain that physical suffering is sometimes due to the loving chastisement of God. Paul had the gift of healing (Acts 19:12; 20:10) and he certainly had faith, but healing from his "thorn in the flesh" was not granted to him (2 Cor. 12:7-9). This gift is exercisable only at the direction of the Holy Spirit and not at the will of the possessor himself.

15. *Miracles* (1 Cor. 12:10, 29) or, as the apostle expresses it, "workers of miracles". This gift was of particular significance in the authentication of the message in the early days of the church (Heb. 2:4) and is still, on rare occasions, found in exercise in the mission field for similar reasons.

16. *Discerning of spirits* (1 Cor. 12:10), God's work has often suffered from counterfeits and it is not always easy to recognise Satan's deceptions. Hence upon some has been bestowed the gift of spiritual discernment, so that they can say what is true and what is false.

17. *Help* (1 Cor. 12:28). This gift seems to be related more to the practical aspect of the work and it has been associated by some with the deaconal work of the church and the spiritual care of practical matters. But there is undoubtedly an application also to those who are always ready with spiritual guidance and practical help.

18. *Tongues* (1 Cor. 12:10, 28). This has been described as "a supernatural manifestation of the Holy Spirit" enabling the individual to speak "in a language he has never learned". The apostle Paul clearly intimates that this gift is not to be exercised in public unless an interpreter is present and that, even then, there is a restriction on the number taking part of those so gifted (1 Cor. 14:27, 28).

19. *Interpretation of tongues* (1 Cor. 12:10, 30). Since this is a spiritual manifestation, the gift is obviously more than an ability to translate, acquired by learning. It is an imparted power to interpret without a previous knowledge of the tongue being used.

Upon every believer in this church age, God has bestowed some gift, and the well-being of the whole body is dependent upon the exercise of those gifts. We are, therefore, responsible to ascertain our own spiritual endowment and to use it in the power of the Holy Spirit for the blessing and upbuilding of the church.

The manifestations of the Spirit in the millennial age are apparently to be of a different character, but to be extremely widespread (Joel 2:28, 29).

87

# BIBLIOGRAPHY

J. A. Bewer: *A Critical and Exegetical Commentary on Obadiah and Joel*, T. & T. Clark, Edinburgh, 1959.

L. H. Brockington: *Joel* (in *Peake's Commentary on the Bible*), Thos. Nelson & Sons Ltd., London, 1967.

S. R. Driver: *The Books of Joel and Amos*, Cambridge University Press, Cambridge, 1915.

C. L. Feinberg: *Joel, Amos and Obadiah*, American Board of Missions to the Jews, New York, 1948.

R. F. Horton: *The Minor Prophets*, T. C. & E. C. Jack, Edinburgh, 1906.

W. S. Hottel: *Hosea — Malachi*, Union Gospel Press, Cleveland.

H. A. Ironside: *The Minor Prophets*, Loizeaux Bros. Inc., Neptune, n.d.

C. F. Keil: *The Twelve Minor Prophets*, Wm. B. Eerdmans Publishing Co., Grand Rapids, 1961.

W. Kelly: *Lectures Introductory to the Study of the Minor Prophets*, W. H. Broom & Rouse, London, 1897.

J. H. Kennedy: *Joel* (in *The Broadman Bible Commentary*, *Vol. 7*), Marshall, Morgan & Scott Ltd., London, 1973.

T. Laetsch: *The Minor Prophets*, Concordia Publishing Co., St. Louis, 1956.

J. P. Lange: *The Minor Prophets*, Zondervan Publishing House, Grand Rapids, n.d.

E. B. Pusey: *The Minor Prophets*, Baker Book House, Grand Rapids, 1970.

O. Schmoller: *Joel* (in *Lange's Commentary*), Zondervan Publishing House, Grand Rapids, n.d.

G. A. Smith: *The Book of the Twelve Prophets*, Hodder & Stoughton Ltd., London, 1905.

J. B. Taylor: *The Minor Prophets*, Scripture Union, London, 1970.

# PROPHET OF MESSIAH'S ADVENT

# PROPHET OF
# MESSIAH'S ADVENT

*An exposition of Micah*

by

Fredk. A. Tatford

# CONTENTS

# PREFACE

**W**HEN king Herod was confronted with the Magi's disturbing question, "Where is he that is born king of the Jews?" it was to Micah's prophecy that the chief priests and scribes referred him for an answer (Matt. 2:2-6). The prophecy was a surprising one. If Isaiah had predicted the virgin birth of Immanuel (Isa. 7:14), his contemporary revealed that it would take place, not at Jerusalem, but at the relatively unimportant village of Bethlehem (Mic. 5:2). It was centuries before either prophecy was fulfilled, but both came to fruition in Herod's day. It is doubtful whether Micah could possibly have realised how long the fulfilment of his words would be delayed: he may well have conceived that the dawning of fame for Bethlehem was very much nearer than it was and that the advent of Israel's ruler was imminent. But although the centuries had to elapse, the predicted One was eventually born at the ancient village of Ephrath.

The First Advent took place over nineteen centuries ago, but the closing verses of Micah's book evidently anticipated the Second Advent of that same Ruler, and it seems today 2/Oct 23 that that event cannot long be postponed. Events, which are to be fulfilled before His Second Coming, seem already to be casting their shadows before. The restoration of Israel and her re-establishment as a State once more appears to many to be an outstanding sign of the imminence of the end times. The attitude to Israel of Egypt and Russia, the rise of power in the Orient, the linking of western powers in the European Community, the movement towards a one-world church, and many another political detail, all seem confirmatory indications. The current prevalence of the conditions described in Matt. 24:6, 7, 12, 37-39 and 2 Tim 3:1-7, etc. provide additional evidence of the nearness of Christ's return to earth.

The Christian, however, looks for another event—one which will precede all others foretold by the prophets—the coming of the Lord Jesus Christ to the air to remove all who belong

9

to Him (1 Thess. 4:15-17). If events, which are to happen at a later stage, appear to be extremely close, how very near must be the fulfilment of the church's hope—its rapture to meet its Lord. This is the event for which we wait.

Micah described conditions leading up to the First Advent. Similar conditions may be seen today, possibly the precursors of the Second Advent. The prophet quite clearly has his message for the present day.

FREDK. A. TATFORD.

# CHAPTER 1

## Introduction

THE eighth century B.C. was a period of great material prosperity for both Israel and Judah. In the north Jeroboam II had forced back the frontiers of Israel and had seized control of the major trade routes. Uzziah had acted similarly in the south and had developed the commercial activities of Judah to such a degree that the country was more prosperous than it had been for centuries. Peace and security had been won by the sword, and there seemed no fear of invader.

Uzziah was succeeded by his son, Jotham, a good king, who followed the principles and practices of his father; but Jotham was succeeded by Ahaz, an evil character who led his people astray spiritually during his reign of twenty years. He was succeeded in turn by Hezekiah, an able ruler, who initiated considerable religious reforms, which unfortunately had little effect upon the majority of the people. Religion had become a formality and the reformation was not accompanied by true penitence or any desire to render sincere worship to Jehovah. To quote one writer, "Morals were low, government was decadent, courts were corrupt, religion was formalistic, the nation had lost its integrity".

The internal corruption of the nation was particularly evidenced in the days of Ahaz. This flagitious monarch was instrumental in introducing the worship of Baal and in making arbitrary changes in the temple, but he was also detested for his sacrifice of his children to Moloch. Even in the times of the good king Hezekiah, the people of Judah had become thoroughly unscrupulous and barren of charity and sympathy. To quote S. Goldman (*Micah*, p. 153), "Extremes of wealth and poverty, which had been impossible in an agricultural society based on the Biblical system of land tenure, were dividing the nation into the classes of possessors and dispossessed. The rich built up large estates, and with the help of corrupt judges, added house to house and field to field, while the oppressed and dispossessed peasantry sought in vain for legal redress. The pursuit of commerce encouraged the development of cities and city-life; and it was to the cities that the landless farmers migrated in search of a livelihood, where wealth, luxury and vice dwelt side by side with poverty, misery and squalor."

### THE MORASTHITE
It was at this period of history that Micah of Moresheth commenced his prophetic ministry. A contemporary of Hosea, Isaiah and Amos, he seems to have prophesied for over sixty years. Tekoah was only twenty miles to the east of Moresheth and it is extremely likely that he was not only acquainted personally with Amos of Tekoah but that he was strongly influenced by his words. There are possibly reflections of Amos in the Morasthite's book. It has been suggested that he may have been a descendant of Eliezer of Moreshah (not necessarily identical with Moresheth), who prophesied against Jehoshaphat (2 Chron. 20:37), but this is pure speculation.

A small town dweller, Micah may have been no more than a peasant or a humble tradesman, but no clue is given as to his occupation. He was certainly a fearless critic of the social injustices of his day and intrepidly flayed the wealthy and the influential. His words were evidently held in memory, for a century later his sayings were quoted in defence of Jeremiah (Jer. 26:18, 19). "His denunciations of injustice and oppression," says one writer, "were as fierce and categorical as any in Hebrew poetry."

Duff (*Old Testament Theology*, i. p. 307) declares that he was a brave man "and that in moments of real danger. No fancied sketch of an attack is that in ch. 2. When he protected the fugitives, the thieving Gittites turned on him with gnashing wolves' teeth. It is far too realistic and too probable to be a fiction; such blows as he brings down in ch. 3 on princes, prophets, traders, must have been resented. We feel this before we turn to Jeremiah's book (Jer. 26:17-19), and read how they seized this Micah to destroy him in their rage."

### AUTHORSHIP

The consistent forcefulness apparent throughout the Book of Micah is a strong presumptive evidence for the unity of its authorship, but modern critics have urged that the difference in style of the last two chapters and of certain other parts of the book indicate more than one author. George Adam Smith (*The Book of the Twelve Prophets*, Vol. 1, pp. 359, 360) declares that "all critics are practically agreed as to the presence of interpolations in the text, as well as to the occurrence of certain verses of the prophet out of their proper order." This, however, is by no means as certain as is suggested.

It is reasonably clear that the prophet gathered together the messages he had uttered and committed them to writing at a later date. It is usually claimed that his and the writings of other prophets were subsequently edited by another hand, but there is no direct proof of this and there is really no logical reason for assuming that the whole of the book did not spring from the hand of Micah.

### DATE

The prophet specifically stated that his ministry was during the reigns of Jotham, Ahaz and Hezekiah, so that he presumably commenced his public work about the middle of the 8th century B.C. and continued into the 7th century. He was clearly contemporaneous with Isaiah, although E. B. Pusey considers that he was called to the prophetic office later than Isaiah. As C. F. Keil (*The Twelve Minor Prophets, Vol.* 1, pp. 419-20) remarks, "he agrees so thoroughly with Isaiah in his description of the prevailing moral corruption, as well as in his Messianic prophecies, that we are warranted in inferring the contemporaneous labours of the two prophets". In more than one instance, it seems evident that Isaiah quoted from his younger contemporary: in others, it may be that the reverse applied. The points of similarity are numerous, e.g.

| Micah 1:9-16 | Isaiah 11:28-32 |
|:---:|:---:|
| 2:1, 2 | 5:8 |
| 2:6, 11 | 30:10, 11 |
| 2:11 | 28:7 |
| 2:12 | 10:20-23 |
| 3:5-7 | 29:9-12 |
| 3:12 | 32:14 |
| 4:1 | 2:2 |
| 4:4 | 1:20 |
| 4:7 | 9:7 |
| 4:10 | 39:6 |
| 5:2-4 | 7:14 |
| 5:6 | 14:25 |
| 6:6-8 | 58:6, 7 |
| 7:7 | 8:17 |
| 7:12 | 11:11 |

There is no doubt that the two prophets must be dated in the same period.

That Micah's first words were uttered before the destruction of Samaria in 721 B.C. is evident from ch. 1:5. The contents of his book, in J. D. Davis's view, "show that it was written after the reigns of Omri and Ahab (ch. 6:16), at the time when Assyria was the power which the Israelites dreaded (ch. 5:5 seq.), and in part at least while Samaria and the northern kingdom were still in existence (ch. 1:6, 14); but how long before the fall of Samaria the words of ch. 1:5-7 were uttered cannot be determined, for from the time of Uzziah and Jotham the prophets were foretelling the approaching doom of Samaria . . . and the desolation of Judah . . . The prophecy of ch. 3 : 12 was spoken during the reign of Hezekiah (Jer. 26 : 18), though Micah may have discoursed on this theme before."

Since Hezekiah extirpated idolatry in Judah, it is clear that Micah must have prophesied not later than the earliest years of Hezekiah's reign, for his book refers to idolatry as still being practised. The corruption of the upper classes and of the judiciary, which Micah so vividly describes, was prevalent in the days of Ahaz, but had been brought under control in Hezekiah's time, so that, once again, the book must be dated primarily before Hezekiah's accession. Pusey suggests that the conversion of Hezekiah and many of Judah was probably the final harvest of Micah's life and that he probably lived to see only the first dawning of the reformation resulting from his preaching.

Despite the critics, there seems every justification for accepting the prophet's own statement in verse 1 regarding the date of his utterances.

The Book of Micah was patently composed of discourses uttered at various times and brought together by the prophet at a later date. This is evident from the abrupt transitions and changes of theme which occur and which would obviously not appear in an argued and coherent treatise the whole of which was written at one time. The book is unparalleled for the consistent and unflinching severity of its tone but, at the same time, for its vividness and forcefulness. T. K. Cheyne also draws attention to the pungent irony employed by the prophet.

"His words," says Keil (ibid, p. 421), "are never deficient in cleanness and evenness; whilst in abundance of figures, similes (ch. 1 : 9, 16; 2 : 12, 13; 4 : 9, etc.), and rhetorical tropes, as well as in speciality, paronomasia, in play upon words (ch. 1:10-15), and dialogue (ch. 2:7-11; 6:1-8; 7:7-20), his style resembles that of his highly cultivated contemporary, Isaiah."

No question ever seems to have arisen regarding the canonicity of the book. Its position in the twelve Minor Prophets is not, of course, an indication of the date of its origin, but probably of its size.

The book is apparently a condensation of the various oral messages delivered by Micah and it consists of three discourses (probably representing a far larger number in actual fact) contained in chapters 1 and 2, 3 to 5, and 6 and 7. Each message commenced with a call to hear and concluded with a promise.

The whole may be analysed as follows:—

1. Judgment on Samaria and Judah (chapters 1 and 2).
   (a) The Superscription (1:1).
   (b) Judgment threatened (1:2-7).
   (c) The prophet's lamentation (1:8-16).
   (d) The causes of judgment (2:1-11).
   (e) Restoration promised (2:12, 13).
2. The Messianic salvation (chapters 3 to 5).
   (a) Sins of the nation's leaders (3:1-12).
   (b) Vision of restoration (4:1-5:1).
   (c) The Messianic deliverance (5:2-15).
3. Jehovah's controversy (chapters 6 and 7).
   (a) The Divine case (6:1-16).
   (b) Confession and penitence (7:11-14).
   (c) The Divine promise (7:15-17).
   (d) Final doxology (7:18-20).

It is interesting to note that there is a twofold strand in Micah's messages—denunciation on the one side and comfort on the other. Sin is first exposed and then the promise of salvation and deliverance is presented.

# CHAPTER 2

## The Threatened Judgment

NOTHING is known of the prophet Micah outside the book which bears his name. His was a common name and was an abbreviated form of Micaiah, which means "Who is like Jehovah?" At least seven others of the same name are mentioned in the Old Testament, viz.:

1. An Ephraimite who set up images in his house (Jud. 17 and 18).
2. A son of Mephibosheth (2 Sam. 9:12; 1 Chron. 8:34, 35; 9:40, 41).
3. A descendant of Reuben (1 Chron. 5:5).
4. A descendant of Asaph (1 Chron. 9:15; Neh. 11:17, 22; 12:35).
5. A descendant of Kohath (1 Chron. 23:20; 24:24, 25).
6. The father of Abdon (2 Chron. 34:20; 2 Kings 22:12).
7. A Levite who sealed the covenant (Neh. 10:11).

The prophet gave no details of his genealogy or his circumstances, but merely stated that he came from a small town in the maritime plain near Gath.

### THE SUPERSCRIPTION

*The word of Jehovah that came to Micah the Morasthite in the days of Jotham, Ahaz and Hezekiah, kings of Judah, which he saw concerning Samaria and Jerusalem (Mic. 1:1).*

Micah described himself as the Morasthite. Moresheth was less than twenty miles from Tekoah, the home of Amos, and the two prophets were presumably acquainted with one another. The little town was located on one of the terraces of the Shephelah, the range of low hills between the hill country of Judah and the Philistine plain, and was nearly a thousand feet above sea level. The valley mouth near the town was virtually the south-western gate of Judea. It has sometimes been identified with Moreshah and also with Tell-el-Judeideh, six miles north-east of Gath.

Moresheth was sufficiently far from Jerusalem for its inhabitants to cultivate a spirit of sturdy independence, but the capital was near enough for its problems and attitudes to be well known. As G. A. Smith (*ibid*, p. 379) says, "Micah must have seen pass by his door the frequent embassies which Isaiah tells us went down to Egypt from Hezekiah's court, and seen return those Egyptian subsidies in which a foolish people put their trust instead of in their God."

The prophet dated his ministry by kings of Judah and his messages were concerned with the country of Judah. He declared, however, that "the word of Jehovah", which came to him, "he saw", that is, of course, by an inner spiritual perception, and that it concerned both Samaria and Jerusalem. The fate of Samaria was described primarily as a warning to Jerusalem and not merely for its own sake.

Micah was faced by a corrupt society, an oppressed peasantry, a venal judiciary and an unjust administration. Judgment was inevitable and he fearlessly denounced the guilty people. He declared that Jehovah Himself would descend into the arena in judgment.

### JEHOVAH IN THE STORM

*Hear, all you peoples; hearken, O earth and all that is in it; and let Adonai Jehovah be witness against you, Adonai from his holy temple. For, behold, Jehovah is coming forth out of his place, and will come down and tread on the high places of the earth. And the mountains will melt under him and the*

18

*valleys will be cleft, like wax before the fire and like waters poured down a steep place (Mic. 1:2-4).*

Micah took up the expression employed by his earlier namesake, Micah ben Imlah (1 Kings 22:28) and called upon all nations to hear his message, as though he was continuing the testimony of his predecessor. The son of Imlah had inveighed against the false prophets who had deceived the king and the people, and had announced the judgment which was to fall upon the nations of Israel and Judah. The Morasthite similarly denounced the false prophets of his day and foretold the judgment to fall upon both kingdoms.

All nations were called upon to listen, because the impending judgment would have repercussions upon the whole world. The prophet declared that the Sovereign Lord God, Adonai Jehovah, would Himself bear testimony against the people from His holy temple. Like a mighty, victorious conqueror, He was issuing forth from the heavens, to descend to tread on the high places of the earth. A glorious and dreadful theophany was to take place.

His coming was to be accompanied by earthquake and storm and volcanic eruption (cf. Psa. 18:6-15). In picturesque language the prophet described the mountains as melting before Him and the valleys split into deep channels. The hills dissolved like wax before the fire, and the valleys were cleft as by torrential waters pouring down the steep, precipitous slopes. The whole contour and configuration of the land would be altered. He saw the mountains disappearing as the eruption took place and the burning lava flowing down like sheets of water. His description was consistent with that of other prophets. M. L. Margolis says, "Jer. 4:23 ff. shows how, to the mind of the prophets, the Divine judgment caused by Israel's sin meant nothing short of a cataclysm reducing the earth to chaos."

The language may have been hyperbolical, but it was indicative of the seriousness of the terrible outpouring of wrath invoked by the people's sin. Jehovah was holy and, in the inner recesses of His temple, there was no place for sin and injustice. When He emerged in His inherent holiness and intrinsic purity, the whole earth suffered.

Wrongdoing can never escape His eye and He cannot tolerate sin and uncleanness on the part of His people. He is infinitely holy and His people should be holy too. Failure to maintain the standard can only invoke His chastisement. The terrifying theophany which shook the earth was a judicial interposition by Jehovah because of the apostasy of Israel and Judah.

## THE CAUSE

*All this is for the transgression of Jacob and for the sins of the house of Israel. What is the transgression of Jacob? Is it not Samaria? And what are the high places of Judah? Are they not Jerusalem? (Mic. 1:5).*

The judicial action of God was because of the transgression of Jacob and the sins of Israel, the prophet declared. He obviously used the term Jacob as a synonym for the whole of Israel (including Judah), and the name Israel for the southern nation of Judah alone. The whole nation—Israel and Judah—had virtually revolted against God. Both kingdoms had accepted Baalism and the people's impiety impressed itself upon Micah's mind.

This was the reason for the Divine intervention. The apostasy of Israel centred in the capital of Samaria; through it the whole country was infected. Similarly, the source of Judah's corruption and of the *bamoth*—the idolatrous worship of the high places—must inevitably be regarded as the metropolis of Jerusalem. "Ahaz brought thither," says Pusey (*ibid*, p. 18), "that most hateful idolatry, the burning children to Moloch in the valley of the son of Hinnom."

By implication, Samaria must suffer for her wrongdoing but, if she did, Jerusalem could not be regarded as any less culpable and, by inference, must suffer too.

## THE JUDGMENT

*Therefore I will make Samaria a heap in the field and a .*

*place for planting vineyards; and I will pour down her stones into the valley and uncover her foundations. All her carved images shall be beaten to pieces, and all her hires shall be burned with fire, and all her idols I will lay waste. For from the hire of a prostitute she gathered them, and to the hire of a prostitute they shall return (Mic. 1:6, 7).*

God now disclosed the fate of Samaria—intended, at least, in part, as a warning to the kingdom of Judah. Since the city was not destroyed until 721 B.C., this prophecy must have been uttered before that date. Israel's capital was to be completely destroyed. The proud, impregnable fortress would be captured and demolished, the materials from its ruins being heaped up in the valley below. An old report said, "There is every appearance of the ancient buildings having been destroyed, and their materials cast down from the brow of the hill, in order to clear the ground for cultivation; masses of stone are thus seen hanging on the steep sides of the hill, accidentally stopped in the progress of their descent by the rude dykes and terraces separating the fields." The stones of the city were, in fact, toppled down the 300 feet into the valley, as Micah predicted, and the foundations of the city laid bare.

The hill of Samaria and the surrounding area was an extremely fruitful region, and the prophet predicted that when the site of the city had been cleared, vineyards would be planted there, as they had been before Shemer sold the land to Omri. It would return to its original condition. This was what actually occurred at the time of Sargon's invasion.

It was because of the nation's idolatry that the punitive hand of the Almighty was to be laid upon the capital. Accordingly the prophet declared that the idolatry would be dealt with and all Samaria's carved images would be beaten to pieces. The Assyrians did, in fact, destroy all the idols they found in Israel and carried away the gold and silver of which they were constructed.

Idolatry was consistently regarded in the Old Testament as spiritual adultery and Micah declared that the wages of prostitution would be consumed by fire. Also all the nation's

21

idols would be destroyed. They had been produced by the wages of prostitution, i.e. by the votive offerings presented by the people as part of their worship of the false gods. They would likewise be carried off by the conqueror as an offering to the false deities in his own land as his votive offerings or wages of prostitution (or idolatry). The reference is presumably to the gifts presented by the people in their idolatrous worship, but some commentators refer it to the actual gifts received by temple prostitutes from the worshippers to whom they offered themselves (Deut. 23:17, 18).

### THE LAMENTATION

*For this I will lament and wail. I will go barefoot and naked. I will make lamentation like the jackals, and mourning like the ostriches. For her wound is incurable, and it has come to Judah; it has come to the gate of my people, even to Jerusalem (Mic. 1:8, 9).*

When he envisioned the terrible judgment impending for Samaria and the northern kingdom, Micah realised the inevitability of it reaching to Judah and Jerusalem as well. For this reason, he lifted up his voice in lamentation and loud wailing, after the manner of his people in times of unusual grief and distress. He declared that he would accompany his dirge-like utterances with the outward signs of mourning common in his day: he would walk barefoot and naked (2 Sam. 15:30; Isa. 20:2)—not completely devoid of clothing, of course, but wearing only the undergarment (cf. Job 22:6; 1 Sam. 19:24). T. K. Cheyne (*Micah*, p. 20) suggests that "the appearance of the prophet is significant of the enforced nakedness of his people on their way to captivity (Isa. 20:3, 4)." His mourning was certainly not solely because of the prospective condition of Israel; he foresaw also the approaching calamity for his own people of Judah, and his actions were obviously intended to awaken them to a sense of their sinful condition.

Mourning was frequently likened to the cries of animals and birds, and Micah declared that his lamentation would be like the haunting piteous cry of the jackal and that his mourning would be like the fearful screech of the ostrich (Job 30:29). His groans would resound through the countryside as he bewailed the lot of his people.

The prophet described the conditions as though they had already occurred but, as Goldman points out (*ibid*, p. 158) regarding Micah's language, "The tenses in the Hebrew are prophetic perfects, vividly presenting future events as if already realised. It need not be assumed that the calamities were actually in progress." The stripes of chastisement to fall upon Samaria and Israel were, however, so heavy that Micah declared that her wound was incurable.

The punishment had been detailed centuries earlier in Deut. 28:15 et seq. What concerned him now was that Judah also was evidently destined to suffer in similar fashion. Anticipating the future, he declared that the punitive calamity had reached Judah also and that destruction was at the very gate of Jerusalem (cf. 2 Kings 19:1-5; Isa. 37:1-4).

In the mercy of God the judgment, which then seemed impending and which the guilty city so richly deserved, was Divinely averted (2 Kings 18:13-37). But the day of reckoning was only postponed and Micah's words ultimately came to fruition.

## PUNS ON THE CITIES

Mic. 1: 10-16 consists of a series of puns on the names of the towns and villages of the country around the prophet. In a unique dirge, he described the desolation awaiting Judah. His grief used the vehicle of a series of paronomasias unparalleled in literature.

F. W. Farrar (*The Minor Prophets*, pp. 130-1) provides a translation (perhaps a little exaggerated) which makes clear the way in which the figure of speech was employed in this section. "In Gath (Tell-town) tell it not; in Akko (Weep-town) weep not! In Beth-le-Aphrah (Dust-town) roll thyself in the dust. Pass by, thou inhabitress of Shaphir (Fair-town) in nakedness and shame! The citizen of Zaanan (March-town) marched not forth. The mourning of Beth-ezel (Neighbour-town) taketh from you its standing-place. The inhabitress of Maroth (Bitter-town) is in travail about good, because evil hath come down from Jehovah to the gate of Jerusalem. Bind the chariot to the swift horse, thou inhabitress of Lachish (Horse-town); she was the beginning of sin for the daughter of Zion, for the transgressions of Zion were found in thee. Therefore wilt thou, Oh Zion, give dismissal (farewell presents) to Moresheth-Gath (The Possession of Gath). The houses of Achzib (False-spring) became Achzab (a disappointing brook) to Israel's kings. Yet will I bring the heir (namely, Sargon, king of Assyria) to thee, thou citizen of Mareshah (Heir-town). Unto Adullam (the wild beasts' cave) shall the glory of Israel come! Make thyself bald (Oh, Zion) for the children of thy delight. Enlarge thy baldness as the vulture, for they are gone into captivity from thee."

### EXPERIENCES OF THE SHEPHELAH

*Tell it not in Gath. Weep not in Accho. In Beth-le-Aphrah roll yourselves in the dust. Pass on your way, inhabitants of Saphir, in nakedness and shame. The inhabitants of Zaanan do not come forth. The mourning of Beth-ezel has taken away from you its refuge place. For the inhabitants of Maroth wait anxiously for good; because evil has come down from Jehovah to the gate of Jerusalem (Mic. 1:10-12).*

G. A. Smith (*ibid*, p. 382) sees Micah "on his housetop, pouring forth his words before the hills and the far-stretching heathen land. In the name of every village within sight he reads a symbol of the curse that is coming upon his country, and of the sins that have earned the curse." It is one of the most vivid and imaginative sections of the prophecy.

Gath was located near the prophet's home of Moresheth, but it is probable that it had been destroyed by the time of his words. In the course of his lamentation over the death of Saul and Jonathan, David cried, "Tell it not in Gath" (2 Sam. 1:20), and the words became a common saying, which is still

24

employed today. Micah picked up the words and repeated them in this section. Although a pun was employed, it was not perhaps quite as plain as most commentators would have us believe, for the primary meaning of Gath is really "winepress" rather than "tell-town". The plea that the threat to Judah should not be narrated in Gath may have been, as one writer suggests, that they might be spared the sight of the malicious joy of their envious neighbours, but this is not consistent with the remainder of the paragraph. The simplest explanation is that the prospective troubles were so great that there was no desire to discuss them.

The threatened punishment might justifiably give rise to bitter lamentation, but Micah exhorted the people not to weep in Accho. Later known as Ptolemais, Accho was one of the towns out of which Israel were unable to drive the Canaanites at the time of the invasion of Canaan (Jud. 1:31). Not only was no public proclamation to be made, but none of the usual signs of grief and penitence were to be displayed.

On the other hand, he enjoined those in Beth-le-Aphrah (which means "the house of dust") to roll themselves in the dust in token of their sorrow and sense of shame and humiliation (cf. Job 16:15; 42:6). The location of this town is not known. Since most of the eight towns mentioned lay in the Shephelah—the low country between Gaza and Jaffa—it is unlikely that it was identical (as has been proposed by some expositors) with Ophrah cf. Bethlehem (Josh. 18:23).

Turning to Saphir or Shaphir (which means "beautiful") the modern Suafri, a few miles south-east of Ashdod, the prophet bade the inhabitants pass on their way in nakedness and shame. He presumably saw the people in the future on their way to captivity and suffering. "She will be stripped of every vestige of her beauty", writes Laetsch (*The Minor Prophets*, p. 251), and stand before the world in shameful nakedness (cf. Hos. 2:3)". He also sees a possible "allusion to the shameful treatment accorded by Assyrian and Babylonian armies to their captives, men and women (Jer. 13:22,

25

26; Neh. 3:5)". The beautiful city would be denuded of her charm.

Once an awareness of danger had dawned, the cities might have been expected to empty themselves. The population would surely forsake the walls to find shelter elsewhere. Yet Micah said that the inhabitants of Zaanan (i.e. "going forth") do not come forth. This city has been identified with Zenan (Josh. 15:37) by some commentators, but Keil and others reject the identification. If the people did not leave the city when the invader eventually came, they could only perish of starvation: they had no means of supporting themselves.

The reason for Zaanan's dilemma was made clear in the next clause. Beth-ezel (i.e. a "neighbour" or a "place near"), the modern Deir-el-Asal, would no longer provide a shelter to refugees. The mourning in that city would only fill others with despair. Who would want to shelter in a town where the death wails could already be heard? Keil, however, considers that the correct interpretation was that the calamity would not stop at Beth-ezel: it would provide no protection from the oncoming enemy. The lamentations from the overrun city would only cause consternation to those who had hoped that it would have halted the invader's progress.

The inhabitants of Maroth (i.e. "bitterness"), which stood on the route of any invading army coming through Lachish, waited anxiously for deliverance or help, declared the prophet. But they would appropriately taste bitterness for no salvation would come. On the contrary, the feared calamity had descended from Jehovah to the gate of Jerusalem. If Jerusalem, the city of peace, was not to be spared, there was little hope for Maroth. The evil had been sent by God.

### THE TIDE FLOWS ON

*Harness the swift steeds to the chariots, O inhabitant of Lachish. You were the beginning of sin to the daughter of Zion; for in you were found the transgressions of Israel. Therefore you shall give parting gifts to Moresheth-Gath. The houses of Achzib shall be a deceitful thing to the kings of Israel* (Mic. 1 : 13, 14).

The next paronomasia was not so apparent as those already used and it lay in the assonance of *rechesh* (steed) and Lachish. This royal city of the Amorites was one of the chief fortresses of Judah (2 Chron. 11 : 9) and was situated south-west of Jerusalem. It was almost on the border of Egypt. Its strategic position gave it both a military and a commercial importance. It is said to have been one of the cities where Solomon conducted a trade in horses (1 Kings 10 : 28, 29).

Lachish lay on the route of the invader and it was, in fact, captured later by Sennacherib. Because of its vulnerability in this respect, Micah instructed the inhabitants of the city to harness the swift steeds to the chariots, in order to prepare for flight at the advent of the foe.

The prophet accused Lachish of being "the beginning of sin to the daughter of Zion" and added that, in Lachish, "were found the transgressions of Israel" (i.e. patently "Judah"). The city's sin is not specified. It may be that its location led to the people's reliance upon Egypt and her subsidies of horses and chariots, or it may have been that the idolatry of the northern kingdom spread into Judah through Lachish. Trade with the heathen nations naturally led to idolatry, marriages with heathen and undesirable alliances. Some Jewish commentators have argued that Lachish was the centre of an idolatrous system of worship, which spread throughout Judah, but there is no evidence for this.

Because of Judah's sins, Micah disclosed that she would be compelled to renounce the town of Moresheth-Gath. He declared that the nation would have to give parting gifts to the city. The term used referred to bridal presents and particularly the dowry bestowed upon a daughter by her father and with which he sent her away to belong to another. Anticipating the conquest of the land, the prophet virtually declared that Judah would relinquish Moresheth to the conqueror—the town would be surrendered to the enemy and delivered up with the farewell presents of a dowry.

Achzib (Josh. 15:44) was probably identical with Chezib (Gen. 38:5). Its name meant "falsehood" or "deceit". The houses of Achzib, said Micah, would become a deceit to the kings of Israel (by which presumably Judah was intended). The winter brook of Achzib would fail in the drought of summer and prove a deceitful hope. Horton (*ibid*, p. 232) says that "the pun is 'Achzib shall be Achzab', a winter brook that fails in the heat (Jer. 15:18) to the kings of Israel, affording no real defence or check to the invader".

*I will yet bring a conqueror to you, inhabitants of Mareshah. The glory of Israel shall come to Adullam. Make yourselves bald and cut off your hair, for the children of your delight; make yourselves as bald as the eagle; for they shall go from you into captivity (Mic. 1:15, 16).*

Mareshah (not Moresheth) was the next town to which the prophet turned. To it, he declared, a conqueror would be brought—one who would possess himself of the city and dispossess its inhabitants. Mareshah was located near Gath and Achzib (Josh 15:44; 2 Chron. 11:8). Micah again introduced his pun, connecting the name with *yarash* "possess" or *yoresh* "conqueror". Mareshah, which means "chief place", is said also to have a secondary meaning of "possession". She was to become the property of the conqueror.

Adullam, a very ancient city of the Shephelah, once provided shelter in one of its caves for David and his followers (1 Sam. 22:1, 2). Now, declared Micah, the glory of Israel was to come to it. Laetsch interprets this of the aristocracy of Judah (Isa. 5:13) finding a shelter in Adullam from the enemy, and Cheyne says that the worthy part of Israel will take refuge in the fort. It can hardly refer, as some commentators suggest, to the Second Advent of Messiah and, in particular, to His coming to His people.

Addressing Judah as a mother sorrowing for her children, the prophet bade the people to make themselves bald and to cut off their hair because of the children of their love. This form of mourning was specifically forbidden by the law (Lev. 19:27, 28; Deut. 14:1), but it was a practice which was nevertheless adopted (Isa. 22:12; Jer. 16:6). Although it is sometimes suggested that the children were the cities of Judah, there seems no reason to interpret the expression otherwise than literally. Both the Assyrians and the Babylonians deported whole populations as a common practice.

The people were to make themselves as bald as the gier eagle (or possibly the griffon-vulture), because their children were to be carried away into captivity. Keil (*ibid*, p. 438) remarks that "we must not exclude the Assyrian oppression altogether; for Sennacherib had not only already conquered the greater part of Judah, and penetrated to the very gates of Jerusalem (2 Kings 18:13, 14; 19; Isa. 36-38), but could have destroyed the kingdom of Judah . . . if the Lord had not heard the prayer of His servant Hezekiah, and miraculously destroyed Sennacherib's army before Jerusalem. Micah prophesies throughout this chapter, not of certain distinct judgments, but of judgment in general, without any special allusions to the way in which it would be realised; so that the proclamation embraces all the judgments that have fallen upon Judah from the Assyrian invasion down to the Roman catastrophe." This latter conclusion seems to us to be correct. At the date of the prophecy, it is doubtful whether any invasion had taken place, even though Micah may have anticipated the Assyrian attack.

# CHAPTER 3

## A Corrupt Aristocracy

THE social injustices and the indifference of the rich to the plight of the poor, for which Amos scourged Israel, were no less characteristic of Judah in the eighth century B.C. Indeed the intrigues and oppression, avarice and perjury of the period seem to have grown up very largely because of the social and commercial changes of that particular era.

As G. A. Smith (*ibid*, p. 388) remarks, "The enormous increase of money which had been produced by the trade of Uzziah's reign threatened to overwhelm the simple economy under which every family had its croft. As in many another land and period, the social problem was the descent of wealthy men, land-hungry, upon the rural districts. They made the poor their debtors, and bought out the present proprietors. They absorbed into their power numbers of homes, and had at their individual disposal the lives and the happiness of thousands of their fellow-countrymen. . . . Micah pictures the recklessness of those plutocrats—the fatal ease with which their wealth enabled them to dispossess the yeomen of Judah." Many of Britain's present difficulties may probably be traced to the development of similar practices and attitudes in the Victorian and Edwardian eras. History frequently repeats itself.

As Micah makes clear, however, the wrongs of his day went

even farther and included judicial corruption, subornation and perversion of justice. More than once in history, these have appeared as the concomitants of social injustice, and have inevitably met with the same Divine intervention.

*Woe to those who devise iniquity and work evil upon their beds! When the morning dawns, they perform it, because it is in the power of their hand. They covet fields and take them by violence; and houses and take them away. So they oppress a man and his household, even a man and his inheritance (Mic 2:1, 2).*

The wickedness of those with power and authority was patent, for they evidently made no effort to conceal it. The inspired speaker accordingly pronounced a woe upon them for their premeditated and deliberate injustice and oppression. He declared that they planned their rapacious designs and evil schemes upon their beds. Their actions sprang from no mere passionate impulse or mental lapse, but from shameless and criminal intent. "When honest toilers sleep," says one writer, "and good men meditate on God (Psa. 63:6), or at least are still (Psa. 4:4), these avaricious landlords form plans to increase their wealth at the expense of the people and even work out their plans in thought."

According to Micah, they took the earliest opportunity to put their schemes into operation. As soon as day dawned, they took action. They were able to do so because it was within their power: they controlled the judges and there could, therefore, be no appeal by those whom they so meanly defrauded.

The prophet was concerned primarily with the wealthy landowners, who sought to add field to field and house to house. They saw a field and immediately, coveting it, seized it for themselves, gradually enclosing the smaller holdings of the peasants in their large estates. Their schemes of expropriation always succeeded. They oppressed the poor man and his family and robbed them of their inheritance.

In the execution of their nefarious schemes, they ignored the fact that ownership of property was inalienable and that, according to the law, all properties must revert to their original owner in the year of jubilee (Lev. 25:13). The permanent dispossession of a poor proprietor was diametrically opposed to the Divine principles of inheritance, but these capitalists deemed that might was right and cared nothing for the stability of the social order nor for the Divine provisions for the continuity of the people.

"In an agricultural community like Israel", writes Taylor (*The Minor Prophets*, p. 51), "the possession of land was all-important, and for the small peasant it was a matter of life or starvation. Each citizen had his entitlement to a portion of the city-lands and this had been handed down to him and kept in the family for many generations. This . . . inheritance was regarded as a sacred trust, which he sought to pass on to his children intact."

## DIVINE RETRIBUTION

*Therefore thus says Jehovah, Behold, against this family am I devising evil, from which you cannot remove your necks, and you shall not walk haughtily, for it will be an evil time. In that day they shall take up a taunt song against you, and wail with bitter lamentation, and say, We are utterly ruined: he has changed the allotted possession of my people. He has removed it from me! Among the apostates he has divided our fields. Therefore you will have none who shall cast the line by lot in the assembly of Jehovah (Mic. 2:3-5).*

Jehovah now made it evident that nothing escaped His eye. These evildoers had carefully devised their evil schemes. God declared that He also was devising evil for them, He no longer regarded them as His people and He disparagingly referred to them as "this family". Because the wealthy landowners had the power, they did as they pleased and oppressed the peasantry without a qualm. But now One of almighty power was purposing to deal with them. They had defrauded the poor man of justice by corrupting the judges, but the One who now spoke was the origin of absolute and implacable justice. Well might they fear!

The calamity God planned for them was inescapable: they could not remove their necks from it. It was a yoke of disaster which would bear down upon them. They had imposed oppression on others: a well-deserved oppression was to be their penalty. They had walked in arrogance and pride: no longer would they walk haughtily. They had broken the pride of their defenceless victims: now retribution of a similar character was to fall upon them.

"It will be an evil time," Jehovah declared. The prophecy undoubtedly looked beyond the Assyrian invasion to the Babylonian (and possibly to a still future fulfilment), but that it included the people's captivity may be deduced from the implied reference to the yoke for the neck. Nation and land would suffer in that day. It would certainly be an evil time. God took account (and still does) of every action taken and of the motivation and He acted accordingly to rectify by correction what was wrong.

In that day, when His plan of punishment was put into effect, a taunt song would be taken up against Judah and the wailing of the dirge would be bitter lamentation indeed. There would be cause for it. They had forcibly dispossessed their unfortunate victims, but God intended to dispossess them. Bitterly would they cry, "We are utterly ruined". A just penalty was to be exacted. Not only the lands they had stolen, but their own inheritance, properly allotted to them, was to be snatched from them and their ownership permanently alienated. The property was to be transferred to the apostates or rebels of the heathen. The fields were no longer theirs, but the property of the conqueror.

There was no trace of penitence in the cry of Judah. These people were only concerned with what they had lost. Oblivious to their own apostasy, they were completely unable to understand the awarding of their possessions to other nations who were apostates. They utterly failed to see the perfect justice in what was happening.

The common land around every town was annually divided by lot among the citizens. The actual demarcation of these allotments was done by the casting of a measuring line. But the wealthy oppressors of Judah had violated every land custom, and Jehovah declared that they would not be beneficiaries in the annual redistribution of the land.

Inferentially, there would be no restoration to them at Jubilee of lands which had been alienated from them, and no other lands would be allocated to them. They had violated the land principles enunciated by Jehovah and had only regarded their own interests. The retribution was just. Their rights and interests were to be discarded and they themselves would be ignored in the company of God's people.

The prophet's words aroused the antagonism of the upper classes and other interested parties and, not unnaturally, they endeavoured to silence him.

### SILENCING THE PREACHER

*Prophesy not—thus they prophesy—. They should not prophesy of such things. Shame will not overtake us (Mic. 2:6).*

The messages brought by Micah were so disturbing that the rich men bade him to stop speaking in such terms. In their view, it was quite wrong to prophesy in such a manner. ("Stop prattling, said the prattlers," runs one translation.) These constant threats and lamentations were irritating. If only the prophet would keep quiet! His discourses, moreover, were completely irrelevant, they considered. The shame and disgrace of which he spoke could not possibly become their experience. So they clamoured for him to stop his mournful denunciations. They may have referred also to the prophet's contemporaries, whose messages were of the same character. The word of God was disagreeable to them.

The words find their echo today. In the minds of some, it is inconceivable that their actions could be criticised or that God should condemn them and their ways. Consequently, the

35

very word, which should affect their conscience, is rejected as irrelevant and inappropriate. It seems incredible to such that judgment could ever fall upon them and they indignantly refuse to pay heed to any warning. Their only desire is to silence the impertinent messenger.

### THE DIVINE REPLY

*O you who are named the house of Jacob, is the Spirit of Jehovah straitened? Are these his doings? Do not my words do good to him who walks uprightly? (Mic. 2:7).*

The people owned Jacob as their ancestor—a man to whom God had revealed Himself in a remarkable fashion, whom He had renamed and with whom He had entered into a covenant relationship. Jacob may have failed frequently, but his trust in Jehovah was firm and steadfast. Was this corrupt race the house of Jacob? They were so totally unlike their forefather. As Pusey pertinently remarks (*ibid*, p. 33), "God's promise was to Jacob, not to those who were but *named* Jacob, who called themselves after the name of their father, but did not his deeds".

"Is the Spirit of Jehovah straitened?" asked God. Did they imagine that that Spirit had lost His power or that it was shortened? Did they think He was impatient? It was the Holy Spirit who sustained the universe and sustained the life of every living thing. It was scarcely likely that He who was so great would indulge in fretful impatience or that the prophet's words were inspired by His irritation.

Impudently the people threw back the question, "Are these His doings?" If Jehovah is the unchanging One who promised blessing to their forefather, how could the prophet's words be true? What he threatened was not the action of the God with whom they were in covenant relationship. It was completely irreconcilable with His character. In their view, Micah had painted Him as a wrathful tyrant, a vengeful despot, whereas they were convinced that anger was not characteristic of Him and that punishment was out of harmony with His nature and

36

relationship to them. How could Micah's words represent His doings?

They had misjudged the character of the One with whom they had to do. They had argued that His words could not possibly mean that He intended them harm or suffering. They were His people and that was an impossible interpretation of His intentions. What they had failed to appreciate was that the Divine promises were not made with plundering oppressors. His blessings were for those who walked uprightly: to such His words would do good. But if He showed kindness to such, it was perfectly consistent that He should punish the guilty who declined to walk according to His will. The threatened judgments were the indisputable evidence of their failure to do His will.

### EVIL PRACTICES

*Even yesterday my people rose up as an enemy. You pull the robe clean away from the garment from those who pass by trustingly with no thought of war. You drive out the women of my people from their pleasant houses. You have taken away my glory from their children for ever* (Mic. 2: 8, 9).

So blind were Judah to their faults that Jehovah condescended to specify the abuses and injustices of which they were culpable. Their violation of Divine principles and requirements was tantamount to a violent uprising as an enemy against Him. Their outrages against His people were virtually an attack upon Himself. Their crimes were not in the remote past: they had been committed only recently.

Not content with their legal expropriation of properties and possessions, they had indulged in highway robbery. Peaceful travellers or workers, pursuing their course unsuspectingly, had been attacked and robbed. The *salmah*, or outer garment, which was normally well-made and of some value, had been ruthlessly pulled off the victims, who had been left with only their nether garments. The outer cloak was customarily used as a covering for the night, so that the loss was a double one.

Goldman (*ibid*, p. 163) claims, however, that "the prophet is referring, not to robbery, but to the abuse of the rights of creditors in taking and holding articles of clothing as pledges for loans (cf. Exod. 22:25 f.), or in payment of taxes". This is a possible interpretation, but the violence used and the reference to the unexpected nature of the attack and the peace-loving character of the victims, tend to imply an act of highway robbery rather than the implementation of a court order.

Unprotected women and children were being evicted from their homes by the avaricious aristocracy. Since the houses were described as the property of the women, the latter were presumably widows, and the unscrupulous and cold-blooded action was, therefore, all the more reprehensible. God accused them of taking away His glory from the orphaned children for ever. The implication may be that the children were sold into servitude in a heathen land and thereby lost the privileges of membership of Jehovah's own nation, or it may merely refer to the irreparable loss of all their material blessings.

Pusey (*ibid*, p. 34) writes, "Primarily the glory, comeliness, was the fitting apparel which God had given them, and laid upon them, and which these oppressors stripped off from them. But it includes all gifts of God, wherewith God would array them. Instead of the holy home of parental care, the children grew up in want and neglect, away from all the ordinances of God, it may be, in a strange land." Micah was not, of course, speaking parabolically. He was describing what was actually happening in his day and portraying clearly and unmistakably the character of the ruling classes of that period. And these were the people whom God had so signally blessed!

### EXPULSION

*Arise and go, for this is not your rest. Because it is polluted, it will destroy you with a sore destruction (Mic. 2:10).*

The land had been the resting-place of God's people (Deut. 12:9), but it was impossible that it should any longer be such for those who had indulged in such practices. They had thrust others out of their inheritance and had sold some into heathen countries. Therefore the prophet appropriately called upon them to depart. "Arise and go!" The hour of their banishment was approaching. Although it was well over a century before the Babylonian captivity occurred, it had already become inevitable.

They had polluted the land by their abominable actions, and the land could no longer tolerate the defilement. Centuries earlier Moses had declared that, if the land was defiled, it would be unable to tolerate the people who defiled it and would vomit out its inhabitants (Lev. 18:25). This was now to happen. The punishment to come upon them was meet for their iniquity.

### THE FALSE PROPHET

*If a man walking in wind and falsehood lies, saying, I will prophesy to you of wine and strong drink, he will even be the prophet of this people (Mic. 2:11).*

The people had called upon Micah to stop preaching his gloomy prognostications of the future. Now he turned upon them ironically and declared the nature of the popular prophet who would appeal to them.

If a man walked in wind (the word *ruach*, which he used, could refer to either wind or spirit, and is often used with reference to the Holy Spirit, so that the irony was emphasised) and falsehood—or possibly, using a hendiadys, he may have meant "in the spirit of falsehood"—and such a man deceitfully promised blessings of every kind, including wine and strong drink, this degraded nation would accept him. That was the kind of prophet to appeal to them. He would afford them a sense of security, which the depraved people would unquestionably accept.

The words used by Micah were sarcastic. He declared that the false prophet would promise to *drivel* or *sputter* to the people and that it was such a *driveller* or *sputterer* that they would accept. Their powers of judgment had evaporated;

39

their spiritual discernment was so utterly lacking that anyone could deceive them. Even in spiritual matters, their retribution was just.

*I will surely gather all of you, O Jacob. I will gather the remnant of Israel. I will set them together like the sheep of Bozrah, like a flock in the midst of its pasture, a noisy multitude of men. He who breaks through is gone up before them; they have broken through and have passed on to the gate, going out by it. Their king will pass on before them, and Jehovah at their head* (Mic. 2:12, 13).

In the middle of the prophet's denunciation of Judah's rulers and landowners (continued in Mic. 3), there came an abrupt transition and a sudden parenthetical promise. For their sins, the people were certainly going to be driven into exile from the land which they had so grievously defiled. Yet Jehovah had irrevocably and unconditionally promised that land to them. His pledge was clear and He could not renege. Before He completed the story of their impending fate, therefore, He paused to confirm that His promises would one day be fulfilled.

The whole of the nation was to suffer, guilty and innocent alike, but He had respect to the remnant of the faithful. He would yet gather all His people again. Their dispersion was not to be the final chapter of their history. The experiences, through which they were judicially to pass, would prove the means of refining and purifying them. Inferentially, the guilty would perish, but He would bring back the remnant of Israel to their own land (Deut. 30:3, 4).

God declared that He would set them together like the sheep of Bozrah (R.S.V. renders "like sheep in a fold"). The Edomite city of Bozrah was renowned for its large flocks of sheep (2 Kings 3:4; Isa. 34:6) and the implication was that, despite the many who would perish in exile, God would multiply the host. He would set them "like a flock in the midst of its pasture": they would return to a land of plenty to be well cared and provided for. Switching figures, He declared that their sound would be like the noisy hum of a great multitude of men in that day.

Reverting to the imagery of the flock of sheep, the prophet stated that the breaker had gone up before them and that the breach had been made for them. The Messiah, the great *even* Deliverer, was to break open the gate (Isa. 45:2; 48:20) or *today* to make a breach in the walls, and lead His people out of captivity. He envisions the multitude sweeping through the gate into freedom. As their king, the omnipotent liberator would pass on before them, and they would discover that the One at their head, the Messiah-deliverer, was no other than Jehovah Himself—virtually an identification of Christ with God.

The prophecy had its primary fulfilment, of course, in the return from the Babylonian captivity, but the regathering described by Micah almost certainly anticipates a future day, when the whole of the twelve tribes of Israel will be miraculously restored to their land by the power of the Messiah.

*Yes. It is happening today!*

# CHAPTER 4

## The Ruling Classes

JUDAH had originally been very largely a farming community, and the nobles lived among the peasantry, sharing their toil and participating in their problems. But the development of commerce gradually resulted in a widening gap between the classes: this was accentuated by the inevitable concentration of wealth in the hands of a few and by the increasing impoverishment of those without capital, because of the constant rise in prices resulting from exploitation. It is this which underlies the prophetic addresses contained in Micah 3.

Keil (*ibid*, pp. 449-50) comments that "The threatening of punishment contained in this chapter is specially directed against the heads and leaders of Israel, and proclaims, in three strophes of four verses each, (a) to the princes, who turn right into wrong and flay the people (vv. 1-4), and (b) to the false prophets, who lead the people astray, and confirm them in their sin by lying prophecies of peace (vv. 5-8), retribution for their wicked conduct; and (c) to all three classes of the divinely appointed chiefs of the nation—the princes, the priests and the prophets—the destruction of Jerusalem, and the turning of Zion and the temple mountain into a ploughed field and wooded heights on account of their degeneracy (vv. 9-12)." The whole of the administration was denounced and utter destruction forecast.

*And I said, Hear, you heads of Jacob, and you princes of the house of Israel. Is it not for you to know justice? You who hate good and love the evil, who tear the skin from off my people, and their flesh from off their bones; who eat the flesh of my people, and flay their skin from off them; and break their bones, and chop them in pieces like meat for a kettle, and like flesh in a cauldron. Then will they cry to Jehovah, but he will not answer them. He will hide his face from them at that time, because they have behaved themselves evilly in their deeds (Mic. 3:1-4).*

It was the responsibility of the rulers to be acquainted with the law (Exod. 18:25, 26), and the people were entitled to turn to them. The administration of justice devolved upon them and they should have been the ones to ensure that right was done in the land. Those referred to by the prophet were the judges and their obligations were clear. Yet they had failed disgracefully.

They were so completely unprincipled that they had lost the sense of what was right and wrong. In fact, they hated the good and loved the evil. They had no desire to please God or to benefit the community: they were only concerned with their own desires and their disposition was to sacrifice everything to secure their own ends.

They should have been shepherds of the flock, caring for the people over whom they had been placed. Their administration should have tended to the blessing and prosperity of the people and should have maintained a state of righteousness in the land.

Instead of shepherds, they were described by the prophet as cannibals. The language, of course, was figurative, but aptly delineated their true character. Micah declared that they pulled the skin off the people and tore their flesh from their bones to consume it themselves. He reiterated that they flayed them, broke their bones and chopped them in pieces like meat for a pot. They should have protected the flock from

44

the adversary, but they acted in a worse fashion than wild beasts.

The hyperbolic language so scathingly used by the prophet was appropriate to these inhuman wretches. Micah obviously intended to arrest their attention by the very phraseology he employed, but it was apparently quite fruitless. In their heartless cruelty, these rulers not only deprived the common people of all justice, but stripped them of all they could take. He implied, moreover, that it was the godly man who suffered most at their hands, "Their tyrannical rule," says one expositor, "was directed particularly against 'My people', the God-fearing Israelites, whom they hated for their very uprightness." They acted as if there was no God in heaven to whom they must ultimately give account.

Yet they were not irreligious men. They turned to Jehovah in their hour of need. When the day of judgment came, Micah portrayed them as crying fervently to God for help. But their evil exploitation of their fellow-men and their consistent perversion of justice, rendered their petitions completely ineffective. They had shown no mercy to their people and had refused to give ear to their agonising cries for compassion. Now the heavens would be as brass to them. They would cry to Jehovah, but He would give no answer to them.

Because of their evil deeds, no mercy would be shown to them. The God, who loves to show compassion, would hide His face from them. There was nothing but unmitigated wrath to be meted out upon them. God does take account and the behaviour of men upon earth will one day be recompensed by a righteous Judge. Even for the Christian the words have their significance. Mercy will be shown to the one who has shown mercy, but the one who has betrayed the principles of Christianity for his own selfish benefit, will pay the price.

### THE FALSE PROPHETS

*Thus says Jehovah concerning the prophets who lead my people astray, who bite with their teeth and cry, Peace! but they prepare war against him who puts not into their mouths.*

*Therefore, it shall be night to you, that you shall not have vision: and it shall be dark to you, that you shall not divine. The sun shall go down upon the prophets and the day shall be dark over them. The seers shall be put to shame, and the diviners confounded: they shall all cover their lips, for there is no answer from God* (Mic. 3:5-7).

The moral and spiritual condition of a nation or of any community is directly affected by their spiritual leaders. Where such are blind or dumb or are completely unconscious of the will of God, the people will stumble and fall. Here Jehovah condemned the prophets of Judah for leading His people astray. Had they paused to consider, they would have realised that they were thereby bringing themselves under a Divine curse (Deut. 27:18). Those who lead God's people astray or cause them to err bear a heavy responsibility for which they must inevitably give account eventually.

These false prophets were all the more culpable because they were not merely mistaken in their views: they were deliberately corrupt. Their teaching was governed, not by the dictate of God, but by the material benefits they could secure. They pandered to the wealthy and influential and prophesied what these paid them to utter. They "bite with their teeth and cry, Peace", said the prophet. Pusey (*ibid*, p. 41) claims that the word translated "bite" in this verse "is used of no other biting than the biting of serpents. They were doing real, secret evil . . . they bit, as serpents, treacherously, deadly".

It is possible that there was an additional significance in view of what followed. The prophet probably implied that, when their temporal and physical needs were satisfied by their wealthy patrons, these religious guides were prepared to pronounce everything to be quiet and peaceful. They inculcated a false sense of security by their soothing messages when this suited those who paid their alimony. They preached what the people naturally wanted to hear, instead of arousing them to a realisation of their breaches of the law and of the need for repentance and confession. Their words were hollow assurances without authority or justification. It was a time for warning of judgment and of possible invasion, but they talked of peace.

On the other hand, if they were not granted favours and fed on the fat of the land, the tone of their messages completely changed. When they received benefits from their benefactors, they were prepared to prophesy of peace and prosperity and thereby to lead the people astray. But if no material benefit was forthcoming, they would inveigh against those whom they considered guilty of defrauding them of their due. The message of peace then became a declaration of Jehovah's wrath and of the threat of war.

By slander and abuse they attacked those who had given them no bribes. Their prophetic office was a sham and no more than a means of securing a morsel of bread from their wealthy accomplices. Horton (*ibid*, p. 241) is justified in saying, "This disease of sham and interested prophecy ran side by side with the genuine prophecy all through the history of Israel. And it does still."

The day of reckoning was coming for these men. They had darkened the light of Divine truth. Now they would be engulfed in darkness. The image used by Micah was of an eclipse. The light of the sun was suddenly extinguished and the day became night to these wretched time-servers. This may have been accentuated in the mind of the prophet by the mental darkness which already had fallen upon them.

The calamity was such that they would no longer talk of visions of peace: in the Stygian darkness there was nothing they could see. Derisively, Micah declared that they would no longer be able to divine. Goldman (*ibid*, p. 167) points out that "the word *kasam* is always used of magic, soothsaying and necromancy, never of genuine prophetic activity". The night obliterated all their activities.

Four times the inspired word referred to the darkness which would envelop these false prophets. The sun would go down upon them and the day would be dark over them. Their calamity would be unparalleled. "The sun which sets to them is the sun of salvation or prosperity," writes Keil (*ibid*,

47

p. 452), "and the day which becomes black over them is the day of judgment, which is darkness and not light."

Some commentators have seen a reference to the judgment of the day of the Lord in the words which are used. That awful period is to be one of impenetrable darkness and thick clouds, when the evildoer will be judged and the whole nation suffer, and it is not unreasonable to see a hint of that still future period in the picture that is painted. There is certainly a dire warning to blind leaders of the blind in other days and generations.

The false teachers had claimed to be the spokesmen of Jehovah and to be acquainted with His will. The untrue seers had deceived the people by the visions they declared they had seen. The lying diviners had presented arguments from the misleading divinations which they had carried out. Now they were to be abashed and confounded. Their deceit was apparent. Prevarication and falsehood could no longer cover up their true character.

Despite all that they had maintained in the past, it was now evident to everyone that no answer was given to them by God. Their claims were exposed for what they were. In shame and consternation, they covered their mouths as the lepers and the sorrowing did (Lev. 13:45; Ezek. 24:17). Their prophecies were plainly shown to be lying predictions, and their speech now failed them for God would not answer them. Their guilt had been discovered and was visible to all.

### THE TRUE PROPHET

*But as for me, I am filled with power by the Spirit of Jehovah, and of justice and might, to declare to Jacob his transgression, and to Israel his sin (Mic. 3:8).*

After portraying such wretched caricatures of the true, Micah claimed justification for his own position as a prophet. Those, whom he had denounced, had derived their authority and, by implication, their message from the rich landowners who had bribed them to utter soothing words. Micah, by contrast, emphasised that his power and authority were derived from Jehovah. No human energy or false spirit inspired him. He was filled with the power of the Holy Spirit, who enlightened him to understand what was true and right, so that he was equipped with a sense of justice and with the strength to announce the Divine purpose.

No miserable platitudes were in his repertoire. He realised that the primary purpose of the prophet was to declare the transgressions and sins of the people and to bring the nation to an awareness of its need of God. He had been given the moral energy to utter the unpopular word and obviously had no intention of refraining from fulfilling his mission. He boldly asserted the basis of his ministry: it was to bring rebellious Judah to her knees in contrition and repentance. This is still the purpose of God through His servants today and there was never a greater need of men like Micah than there is in our 20th century.

## PERVERTED JUSTICE

*Hear this, you heads of the house of Jacob, and judges of the house of Israel, who abhor justice and pervert all equity, who build Zion with blood and Jerusalem with iniquity (Mic. 3:9, 10).*

Turning from the prophets to the civil rulers, who were responsible for the administration of justice as well as of the general affairs of the state, Micah made it clear that the conditions prevailing were their responsibility. He said nothing of the king, since he was presumably not in a position to control the practices of the rulers.

Although the princes and judges were responsible to ensure that judicial decisions were fair and that right was done, they were so little concerned with justice that it proved, in fact, to be abhorrent to them. Arguments were distorted and a case destroyed by sophistry. Litigants could never be confident about securing their rights unless they were prepared to bribe the magistrate, and cases were already lost if a true verdict would be against the interests of the upper classes. Instead of upholding righteousness, the rulers perverted all equity. It

49

was a scandalous situation: the fountain-head of justice was utterly defiled.

The period was one of extraordinary wealth and prosperity, and the rich indulged in the building of palaces and winter and summer resorts. But the means of doing so were often acquired by oppression, extortion and rapine. The prophet declared that they built Zion with blood (Isa. 1:15; Ezek. 22:2-6)—a synecdoche for the cruelty which resulted in the ruin and possibly even death of others. They built Jerusalem, he added, with iniquity. Their marvellous palaces and fortifications were based on a prosperity derived from the spoliation of the poor and the maltreatment of the less privileged.

### FALSE CONFIDENCE

*Its heads judge for reward, its priests teach for hire, and its prophets divine for money. Yet they lean upon Jehovah and say, Is not Jehovah in the midst of us? No evil shall come upon us. Therefore, for your sake, Zion shall be ploughed as a field, and Jerusalem shall become a heap of ruins, and the mountain of the house like a wooded height (Mic. 3:11, 12).*

Micah traced the source of the corruption to its root—the love of money. The civil authorities were responsible for the execution of the law, but they were subject to bribery. They were venal judges, prepared to sacrifice all principle and to countenance any sordid action provided they were suitably rewarded.

The priests were no better. It was their function to teach the Torah (Mal. 2:7), to explain and interpret it to the ordinary man, or to interpret its ritual and other requirements for the benefit of the judiciary (Deut. 17:8-11). All this was to be done gratuitously and in the fear of God. Yet these priests were charging for their services: they demanded fees for consultation, and only taught for reward.

The prophets, whom he had already scathingly denounced, were again accused for their materialistic concept of their call. They would only divine for money. In place of the delight

they should have found in revealing the will of Jehovah to the
people, they were only concerned with the profit they could
make out of their ministry. The sanctification demanded of
the servant of God was conspicuous by its absence.

Despite their character and conduct, these guilty men
boasted that no evil could possibly come upon them. Jehovah
was in the midst of His people. That was the guarantee of
complete immunity from trouble. Their false confidence was
a sheer impertinence as well as an utter misconception of the
relationship between Israel and Jehovah. They placed their
reliance upon the assurance that God was in their midst and
that consequently no misfortune of any kind could possibly
fall upon them. There was a complete blindness to their sinful
condition: they were utterly oblivious to the fact that a holy
God cannot tolerate sin, even in His people.

Micah announced bluntly that, because of their conduct,
destruction would fall upon the city. Their disgraceful
hypocrisy was intolerable to Jehovah. Because of their evil-
doing, Zion with its royal palace would be ploughed as a
field, the holy city of Jerusalem would be reduced to a heap of
rubble, and the hill of Moriah, where the temple of Jehovah
had stood in its glory, would be covered with a forest (Lam.
5:18). It was the complete annihilation of the city that was
envisaged. The destruction was, of course, postponed because
of the repentance of Hezekiah, but it was subsequently fulfilled by more than one invader—first by Nebuchadnezzar in
621 B.C. (Neh. 2:17), later by Titus in 70 A.D., and further
by later invaders. The malpractices of the guilty were fully
recompensed.

Micah's prediction was the only one to be specifically
quoted in the prophetic literature of the Bible (Jer. 26:18).
He was also, as Goldman (*ibid*, p. 168) points out, "the first
of the prophets to threaten Judah with the annihilation of its
capital and the destruction of its temple. So marked was the

effect of this prophecy that it remained fresh in the minds of Judeans for many a decade, and it is quoted more than a century later by the elders in defence of Jeremiah's right to prophesy in like strain (Jer. 26:18)."

## CHAPTER 5

### The Age of Blessing

With the prediction of the complete destruction of Jerusalem and the judgment of Judah's civil and ecclesiastical authorities, with which the previous section concluded, it might perhaps be deduced that there was no future for the people or the land, that the outrageous sins of the rulers, prophets and priests had excluded the people permanently from all possibility of blessing. Yet this would have negated the reiterated pledges of the Almighty and would have accounted His covenants as ineffective. The promises made to Israel's ancestors, however, were irrevocable and not even the heinous sins of the people could annul the unconditional promises of God. Extraordinary although it may appear, therefore, the prophet proceeded to turn from judgment to paint the blessings of a future day.

#### JEHOVAH'S TEMPLE

*It shall come to pass in the latter days that the mountain of the house of Jehovah shall be established as the highest of the mountains and it shall be raised up above the hills, and peoples shall flow to it. And many nations shall come and say, Come, let us go up to the mountain of Jehovah, to the house of the God of Jacob. He will teach us his ways and we will walk in his paths. For the law shall go forth out of Zion and the word of Jehovah from Jerusalem (Mic. 4:1, 2).*

Micah 3:12 portrayed the temple of Jerusalem as completely destroyed and the site overgrown with trees to such an extent that it looked like a forest. But the prophet now announced that, in the latter days (a term with, of course, an eschatological significance), this would be entirely reversed (cf. Isa. 2:2-4).

Moriah was not the highest mountain in the country. Yet it was now disclosed that it would be "established as the highest of the mountains" and "be raised above the hills". This does not necessarily indicate that the mountain will physically be raised to a higher altitude than at present. The implication is rather that it will be supreme over all others. Aben Ezra, for example, says, "It is well known that the house of the temple is not high. The meaning then is that its fame shall go forth, and there shall return to it from all quarters persons with offerings, so that it shall be as if it were on the top of all the hills, so that all the inhabitants of the earth should see it."

There is, moreover, a clear implication that the temple will be rebuilt; otherwise there would be no point in the nations flocking to it. In the Messianic era, to which the prediction doubtless refers, degradation will be reversed and honour and dignity restored to Jehovah's dwelling-place on earth. No details are given of the temple or of its rebuilding. Details of this must be gleaned from Ezekiel, but the inference is clear.

The temple was not portrayed by Micah as a centre of worship, as might have been expected, but as the centre of Divine revelation. The nations will flock to Jerusalem and to the temple, because God is there (and the verse specifically refers to the temple or "house of the God of Jacob"). Jehovah will then be known in the earth and the nations will seek the knowledge of Him in His temple.

There the seekers will receive instruction (cf. Deut. 17:11) and, as a direct consequence, they will walk in His paths. Disputes and differences will no longer create problems, for His law will be known universally. The *torah* (instruction rather than the Mosaic law) will issue from that centre and the word of Jehovah will go forth from Jerusalem.

*He shall judge between many peoples and shall decide concerning strong nations afar off. And they shall beat their swords into ploughshares, and their spears into pruning-hooks. Nation shall not lift up a sword against nation, neither shall they learn war any more. But they shall sit every man under his vine and under his fig tree; and none shall make them afraid: for the mouth of Jehovah of hosts has spoken it (Mic. 4:3, 4).*

The rulers and judges of Judah had proved their worthlessness. Their judgments were frequently unjust and they personally were subject to corruption. But, in a coming day, righteousness will be enthroned and a just Judge will be established in Jerusalem. He will fulfil the functions of a judge perfectly and no bias will be evident in His decisions. The nations will gladly submit to His arbitration and even remote states will apparently accept His verdicts.

Where such an arbitration court exists, war will naturally be superfluous. Disputes will no longer be decided by conflict but by the Supreme Judge. The prophet accordingly describes the conversion of military weapons into agricultural implements and the complete abolition of war.

Peace and security will be evidenced on every side and every man will sit under his own vine and fig tree—a recognised eastern picture of happiness and peaceful tranquility. In fact, the prophet explicitly added that no one will make others afraid and that this was the declaration of Jehovah of Hosts Himself.

It is extraordinary that, in face of such plain statements, Hailey (*ibid*, p. 206) should say, "The prophet certainly did not envision a time when God would dominate and control the world by force, or an age when men of all political kingdoms would live at peace on this earth. Only in God's spiritual kingdom established by Christ would this blessed experience be realised." But if Micah's words are not intended to be taken literally, they do not make sense. He referred to the literal rule of Jehovah over the earth and to the physical presence of Messiah at Jerusalem to arbitrate in the problems of the nations. The allegorisation of explicit promises destroys the value of the Word.

*For all peoples walk each in the name of his god, but we walk in the name of Jehovah our God for ever and ever (Mic. 4:5).*

When the nations are streaming to Jerusalem to learn the will of Jehovah and to walk in His paths, it seems strange that the conditions described in this verse should be applicable. Micah clearly reverted to current conditions to state the current practice. At his time, the nations were all following their own gods, but in the day to which he had previously referred, they would seek to walk in the ways of Jehovah (verse 2). Judah, by contrast with other nations, would set her eyes upon Jehovah. He was their God and they would for ever walk in His name.

The character of a nation reflects the character of its god. People walk "in the name" of their god, i.e. according to the nature, characteristics and teaching implied in the name. Those who walk in the name of Jehovah observed His character in their ways and conduct.

The verse is patently a separate paragraph. As one writer points out, "It cannot be a continuation of the preceding prophecy, which represents all the nations as acknowledging the God of Zion; nor can it logically be connected with the following verses. It contrasts the present or pre-Messianic age, when each nation serves its own god, with that future age when all men will recognise the one God."

### HOPE FOR THE LAME

*In that day, says Jehovah, I will assemble the lame, and gather those who have been driven out and those whom I have afflicted. And I will make the lame a remnant, and those who were cast far off a strong nation; and Jehovah will reign over them in mount Zion from this time forth and for evermore (Mic. 4:6, 7).*

Continuing his description of the Messianic era ("in that day"), the prophet foretold the regathering of the dispersed of Judah. With a touch of tender compassion, Jehovah said that He would assemble the lame (cf. Zeph. 3:19), using a word employed elsewhere only in Gen. 32:31 and Zeph. 3:19. There was doubtless an allusion to the lameness of their forefather Jacob after his wrestling with God. Jacob's descendants too were regarded as spiritually lame, but Jehovah in His mercy proposed to gather them together and to make of them a remnant, a term normally used to denote those faithful to Him, upon whom His love rested.

Because of their sins, the people were to be driven out of their own country into captivity. Jehovah made it clear that it was His hand which was going to inflict the punishment upon them. The affliction He imposed by dispersing them among the nations was a just retribution for their wrongdoing and waywardness. But His compassions never fail and He now intimated that, in the days of Messiah, those who had been cast out and dispersed would be regathered, not now in weakness, but to become a strong nation.

They would have suffered much in the dispersion. As Scoggin (*Micah*, p. 210) says, "When Jerusalem finally fell to the Babylonian forces, the people were subjected to all kinds of indignities and abuses. The old and indigent were either killed or left to die in misery. The able-bodied were driven like cattle to Babylon as slaves. The pace of the march was set, not by the needs of the captives, but by the standards of a victorious army on its way home from conquest. As a result many exiles died on the way. The less hardy, the women and especially those women with small children, fell by the wayside in large numbers. Those who had the strength finally to arrive in Babylon were bruised, broken, and exhausted, a small percentage of those who began the march . . . this pitiful broken remnant is going to be the nucleus for a completely new and restored strong nation." To anyone reading the prophecy with an unprejudiced mind, it is an inescapable conclusion that God has yet destined a glorious future for the whole nation of Israel.

If these predictions were insufficient, there came a convincing guarantee that they would be fulfilled, for Jehovah declared that He would reign over them in mount Zion from the time of their restoration and for ever. Never again would this people be deported from their land. Never again would the heathen invader grind them under his foot. This was Jehovah's land and Jehovah's people and gloriously He would reign over it and them. This, of course, has not yet been fulfilled and awaits the advent of the Messiah in power and glory.

### THE KINGDOM

*And you, O tower of the flock, the stronghold of the daughters of Zion, to you shall it come, the former dominion, the kingdom shall come to the daughter of Jerusalem (Mic. 4:8).*

Migdal-Edar (Gen. 35:21), a mile from Bethlehem, was a watch-tower erected by the shepherds so that they could keep a watch over their flocks and also a lookout for possible marauders or dangerous beasts. Micah took up the figure metaphorically and stated that it would be the stronghold or shelter for the returning exiles in the coming day.

Then triumphantly he announced that the kingdom would come to Zion, to the daughter of Jerusalem, and made it clear that the reference was not merely the smaller kingdom of Judah but to the united kingdom of the twelve tribes—"the former dominion", Jerusalem was once more to be the capital of Israel and not merely of Judah. Again, the words have not yet been fulfilled, but there can be no dubiety regarding their significance. The prophet referred to a literal kingdom and not to some spiritual fantasy. Israel's future is unquestionable.

58

*Now why do you cry out aloud? Is there no king in you?*
*Has your counsellor perished that pangs have seized you like*
*a woman in travail? Be in pain and labour to bring forth, O*
*daughter of Zion, like a woman in travail. For now you shall*
*go forth out of the city and dwell in the field. You shall go*
*even to Babylon. There you shall be delivered; there Jehovah*
*will redeem you from the hand of your enemies (Mic. 4:9, 10).*

The prophet turned from his picture of the glories of the
Messianic age to glimpse the troubles which would precede it.
He anticipated the horrors of the Babylonian invasion, but
probably looked beyond that, in his description, to the great
tribulation which is still to be experienced. The suggestion
that the allusion was primarily to the campaigns of Sennacherib in 701 B.C. is nullified by the specific mention of
Babylon, although many of the experiences may have been
repeated.

Why were the people crying out aloud? Had they no king?
he enquired. Visualising the awful period which was to come,
he imagined the loud cry of distress like that of a woman in
travail. Was the lamentation due to the loss of the king?
If the king had perished or had been carried away captive, the
land was in a desperate plight. The monarch was the visible
representative of God. His removal meant the loss of Divine
counsel and the clear indication that Divine wrath was to be
poured out upon them. Well might they writhe in agony and
groan in their distress! Their panic was well justified.

Micah bade them to be in pain and to suffer the travail
pains, for a fate far more dreadful than they had even contem-
plated lay before them. Stage by stage he depicted the catas-
trophic happenings. They had lived in comfort and security
in the city. Homeless and unprotected, they would be compelled to leave the city and dwell in the open country, exposed
to every conceivable danger and with nothing to shelter them.

The dominant power of that day was Assyria, but the
prophet revealed that their destination was not Assyria but
Babylon. It was a remarkable prediction, for it was another

century before Babylon (then a vassal of Assyria) became an independent power. Outside the walls of Jerusalem, the unfortunate captives would be herded together for the long march of over 500 miles to distant Babylon (cf. Isa. 39:1-6). The prospect must have seemed appalling.

Yet, at the same time, came the promise of ultimate deliverance from captivity. From Babylon they would be rescued. As a kinsman-redeemer, Jehovah would redeem them from the hand of their enemies. When coupled with the threat of servitude in a far-distant country, the promise of salvation must have seemed almost incredible. But what God promised was actually accomplished (Ezra 1:3).

### THE NATION'S FATE

*Now many nations are gathered against you, saying, Let her be profaned and let our eyes gaze upon Zion. But they do not know the thoughts of Jehovah, nor do they understand his plan. For he has gathered them as sheaves to the threshing-floor. Arise and thresh, O daughter of Zion: for I will make your horn iron, and I will make your hoofs bronze. You shall beat in pieces many peoples, and shall devote their gain to Jehovah, and their wealth to the Lord (Adonai) of the whole earth (Mic. 4:11-13).*

The imminent fate of Jerusalem would attract the attention of her heathen neighbours. The nations would gather around, gloating over her downfall and watching her agony with glee. The holy city would be desecrated by the invading soldiers, defiled by their presence and actions. There was no pity for the doomed nation. Her neighbours merely desired to feast their eyes on the spectacle of her suffering and presumably to participate in humiliating her. The very holiness of former days made her an even more pitiable gazing-stock in the time of trouble, and the nations maliciously rejoiced at her tribulations.

This patently goes much farther than the experiences of the Babylonian invasion and seems to anticipate the trials of

60

the awful period of judgment yet to come. This is confirmed by what follows.

The harassed and desolate nation might well have surrendered all hope of recovery. But the prophet declared that the heathen nations were totally unaware of God's plan. They obviously could not understand what He had purposed. They had gathered together to gloat over the suffering of victims. They did not realise that it was Jehovah who was gathering them together to the threshing-floor, to be flailed and trodden down. In rejoicing over Judah's fate, they had not been conscious that their own doom was sealed. The destruction they had proposed for Judah would recoil upon their own heads.

It was the common practice to use oxen to tread out the corn (Deut. 25:4). God pictured Judah as treading down her enemies and called upon the people to rise and thresh the heathen. The strength of the oxen's hoofs was important in this task, and God declared that He could make Judah's hoofs as strong as military bronze and give them a horn of iron to toss the chaff. They would trample down and break in pieces their foes.

The prophet clearly foresaw the day when Divine power will enable Israel to destroy all her foes. The material possessions of the heathen would be devoted to Jehovah and the wealth of these would-be destroyers would be dedicated to Adonai, the Lord of the whole earth. The defeat and crushing of the nations will naturally result in a tremendous amount of booty. This was not to be appropriated. Deliverance and victory would come by the power of God, and to Him these material things were to be devoted.

The Divine purpose can never be frustrated. Despite all the vicissitudes of the past, Israel is yet to be seen as the chosen people of Jehovah, victorious over every foe. Yet the opening verse of Micah 5, which is regarded as the closing verse of chapter 4 in the Hebrew, showed the people as still suffering.

61

THE SIEGE

*Now gather yourself in troops, O daughter of troops. He has laid siege against us. With a rod they will smite the judge of Israel upon the cheek (Mic. 5:1).*

The Septuagint renders the first sentence of this verse, "Now shall a daughter be hedged in with a hedge", and the R.S.V. adopts a somewhat similar rendering "Now you are walled about with a wall". The N.E.B. takes a somewhat similar line in its translation "Get you behind your walls, you people of a walled city". There is admittedly some question as to the most appropriate wording and the R.S.V. rendering is possibly more consistent with the next clause.

Goldman (*ibid*, p. 174) suggests that the correct rendering may be, "Now you are cutting yourself severely", i.e. in mourning, and he sees "an allusion to the old mourning cult which is forbidden in the Torah (Lev. 19:28; Deut. 14:1). The subject may then be Jerusalem, described as 'daughter of troops', i.e. one suffering from the inroads of invading armies." It may, however, refer "to the heathen nations who will mourn the losses which they will suffer as a punishment for their attack on Jerusalem and insult to its ruler".

Even if the A.V. rendering is adopted as above, there is some doubt as to the correct interpretation. It is argued by some commentators that Jerusalem at this time was filled with violence and that guerillas or marauding bands roamed the city, bent on evil, and that such were now gathered together for destruction. On the other hand, there are those who see in the words a picture of the people of Judah huddled together in bands in fear and distress.

The cause of the consternation was that siege had been laid to the city, presumably by Assyria, although this is not stated. That the siege was victorious is plain from what follows. The ruler of Judah (or Israel, according to Micah) was to be insulted by the invader. The king was described as "the judge of Israel" and the prophet declared that he would be smitten on the cheek with a rod; the word "judge" was apparently employed because of the assonance with the word "rod"

62

(*shophet* and *shebet*). There is no historical record of the shameful ill-treatment of the king in this way. Some have rather fancifully interpreted the description as applying to the treatment of our Lord in the court of Caiaphas (Matt. 26:67), while J. M. P. Smith considers that it may apply to the insults addressed by Rabshakeh to Hezekiah (Isa. 36:4-10), but it is really impracticable to identify the incident.

The term "the judge of Israel"—and not of Judah—was a further indication that the ruler of Judah was regarded by God as the true sovereign of Israel. As in other instances in Micah, the southern kingdom was evidently deemed to be representative of the whole of the ten tribes, with their true capital at Jerusalem and not Samaria.

# CHAPTER 6

## Days of Messiah

TURNING from the ruler of Israel who had been grossly insulted by the besieger, Micah predicted the advent of another ruler in Israel, who was clearly of an entirely different order. It is true that, on the assumption that Mic. 5:1 refers to the maltreatment of the Lord Jesus Christ at His trial, some expositors have related both verse 1 and verse 2 of that chapter to the same Person. While the smiting in verse 1 may obviously be applied to our Lord, it is doubtful whether the primary reference was to Him. The prophecy of verse 2, on the other hand, indubitably related to Him.

### THE COMING RULER

*But you, Bethlehem Ephratah, though you are little among the thousands of Judah, yet out of you shall come forth to me one who is to be ruler in Israel; whose goings forth have been from of old, from the days of eternity (Mic. 5:2).*

The prophet now voiced one of the most remarkable predictions of his ministry, one that was to be fulfilled in Bethlehem Ephratah. The tribe of Zebulun included another city of Bethlehem in their inheritance (Josh. 19:15), but the town of which Micah spoke was the smaller one originally known as Ephrath (Gen. 35:16, 19; 48:7). It was the home of David (1 Sam. 17:12) and certain of his ancestors (Ruth

65

1:1, 2). Its unimportance is clear from its omission from the list of cities initially allocated to Judah (Josh. 15:21-63); it evidently had a population of fewer than a thousand at that time. Indeed, the prophet declared that it was small to be counted among the "thousands" or clans of Judah.

Yet, out of this small town, one was to issue who was destined to be the country's ruler. The identity of that one was made clear centuries later when Herod enquired of the chief priests and scribes where Messiah was to be born. Unhesitatingly they replied, "In Bethlehem of Judea, for so it is written by the prophet, And you, Bethlehem in the land of Judah, are not the least among the princes of Judah: for out of you shall come a governor, who shall rule my people Israel" (Matt. 2:4-6). That this was generally held by the people is clear from John 7:42, for they declared, early in our Lord's ministry, that the Scriptures stated that the Messiah would be a descendant of David and would come from David's village of Bethlehem. Astonishing although it might seem, the Messiah was to come, not from Jerusalem, but from David's home town of Bethlehem, and this was predicted centuries before His birth. And the prophet made it clear that God had purposed that He should be the ruler of His people, Israel.

Micah's statement was even more amazing, for he stated of this One that His "goings forth have been from of old, from the days of eternity". The Septuagint rendered the words, "His goings forth have been from the beginning—from the days of an aeon", but the Peshitta worded it as "whose goings forth have been predicted of old, from eternity". *The Modern Language Bible* translates the clause, "His goings forth are from of old, from days of eternity", but the R.S.V. renders it, "whose origin is from of old, from ancient days", thereby implying that the Messiah had an origin and was not eternal. Goldman (*ibid*, p. 175), writing from a Jewish angle, says, "It is possible that this phrase gave rise to the later Jewish doctrine that Messiah existed in the mind of God from time immemorial, as part of the Creator's plan at the inception of the universe."

While the inspired statement did not specifically declare the eternal generation of the Babe of Bethlehem, it clearly implied His eternal existence, and it is unfortunate that the R.S.V. should leave any doubt on the subject. "Micah does not announce here the eternal proceeding of the Son from the Father, or of the Logos from God, the *generatio filii eterna*", writes Keil (*ibid*, p. 480), but "the words affirm the origin of the Messiah before all worlds". What was described was more than an ancient lineage. Here was One whose existence stretched back into eternity: He was, in fact, one with the Eternal God.

No new personality came into existence at Bethlehem when Jesus was born. The Eternal had become incarnate. God had taken manhood unto Himself and the Child of Mary was—and always will be—the God-man. What He had ever been in the ages of the past, He continued to be in incarnation (see Appendix).

### RETURN OF THE REMNANT

*Therefore he will give them up until the time when she who is in travail has brought forth. Then the remnant of his brethren will return to the children of Israel (Mic. 5:3).*

Micah had already indicated that, because of their infidelity and apostasy, Judah would be delivered up to oppression and suffering inflicted by the heathen. He now reaffirmed it but, at the same time, showed that the nation's humiliation would not be permanent. God would give them up until the one who was in travail had brought forth. He had already declared that the Ruler would come forth from Bethlehem Ephratah. Now he revealed that the birth of the Messiah would bring the nation's servitude to an end.

The prophet patently referred to the prediction by Isaiah of the virgin birth of Christ (Isa. 7:14), as well as to the clear statement regarding the return of the remnant (Isa. 11:12). It has been suggested that the woman who was to give birth to the Messiah was the faithful remnant of Judah, who passed through the Babylonian captivity before the birth of the future ruler of Israel. Certainly, either the nation or the remnant was regarded as giving birth to the coming Ruler.

That event would, in any case, mark the end of the captivity, for then the remnant of Messiah's brethren (i.e. the tribe of Judah) would return to the land of Israel. The coming of the Messiah would be the signal for the happening of these events. The return from exile did, in fact, take place before the First Advent of our Lord and could scarcely be said to have been closely linked to His birth. But a more complete fulfilment awaits a coming day. Israel's tribulations have not yet come to an end and there has not yet been a complete return from the dispersion.

*started already today*

### MESSIAH THE SHEPHERD

*And he shall stand and feed his flock as a shepherd in the strength of Jehovah, in the majesty of the name of Jehovah his God. And they shall abide: for now shall he be great to the ends of the earth. And this shall be peace. When the Assyrian comes into our land, and when he treads in our palaces, then we will raise against him seven shepherds and eight princes of men. And they will waste the land of Assyria with the sword, and the land of Nimrod within its gates. Thus shall he deliver us from the Assyrian when he comes into our land and when he treads within our borders (Mic. 5:4-6).*

The prediction concerning the Messiah went even farther, and the prophet declared that the promised Ruler would stand and feed (or govern) His flock like a shepherd. His care for Israel would be displayed by His government and His provision for their every need. Just as a shepherd watched over his flock of sheep, protecting them from danger, leading them into the best pastures, binding up their wounds, satisfying their thirst, and so on, so would the Shepherd of Israel care for His people.

His rule would be in the strength of Jehovah and in the majesty of God's name. The might and power of the Supreme

Ruler would equip Him and all the regal panoply of heaven would, by implication, be His. Here, quite patently, was no insignificant princeling or chieftain: the prophet was virtually painting the glory and power of the Son of God. To those with the New Testament in their hands, there can be no dubiety about the identity of this great Ruler. Centuries earlier, in the symbol of the Angel of Jehovah, this One had been described as the leader and deliverer of God's people, and Jehovah had stated, "my name is in him" (Ex. 23:21).

Because this Ruler would stand steadfastly as their protector and shepherd, the people would abide securely and permanently, said the prophecy. And He would be great to the ends of the earth. His dominion in the day to come will not be restricted to a small Middle Eastern state. He will rule over the whole earth as King of the kings and Lord of the lords, every knee bowing to Him in homage and every ruler paying obeisance to Him. Peace then will pervade the scene. One rendering of the first clause of Mic. 5:5 is "He is our peace", and it is possible that Eph. 2:14 refers to this verse. Messiah is our peace.

From the glimpses of the greatness of the future Ruler of Israel, Micah turned to the minor needs and problems of his people. Their trials were not yet over and, by divine inspiration, he became conscious of the invasion yet to come. The Assyrians would invade the land and ravage its palaces and strongholds. It seems clear that the prophet's revelation referred, not to the Assyrian of the past but to the Assyrian of the future—the king of the north of Dan. 11:40-45. Babylon, Medo-Persia, Greece and Rome were yet to conquer the country, but his prediction leapt over their domination to portray events of the end-time. The Assyrian empire of his day was symbolic of the future invader.

Against the Assyrian invader, the prophet declared that Israel would raise up seven shepherds and eight princes. These numbers were not, of course, intended to be taken literally. They are on a par with the three and four transgressions of Amos 1:3, etc. The implication was that there would be no

69

lack of leaders to resist the foe. These leaders were described as shepherds because the duty of the prince is to care for his people as a shepherd would for his sheep. In this instance, however, they were to shepherd or feed the enemy's land with the sword instead of a crook (Jer. 6:3). They were to lay Assyria waste and desolate in retaliation for her attack upon Israel.

They were to ravage the land of Nimrod within its gates. Nimrod was, of course, the founder of Babylon (Gen. 10:8 ff.), but the land of Nimrod signified the whole Babylonian–Assyrian empire. The term "gates" was used, not as a synonym for the borders of the country, as claimed by some commentators, but rather as a figure for the cities and fortresses of that country (cf. Isa. 3:26; 13:2). The ultimate deliverer, however, was not any of the leaders raised up in the crisis, but the Great Shepherd of Mic. 5:4. No other would be adequate: the princes were but the executors of His design. In consequence of His power, the Assyrian invader would be completely destroyed. This was remarkably confirmed by Daniel in Dan. 11:45.

### THE REMNANT AMONG THE NATIONS

*Then the remnant of Jacob shall be in the midst of many peoples as dew from Jehovah, as showers upon the grass, which tarries not for man, nor waits for the sons of men, And the remnant of Jacob shall be among the nations, in the midst of many peoples, as a lion among the beasts of the forest, as a young lion among the flocks of sheep, who, if he passes through, treads down and tears in pieces, and none can deliver. Your hand shall be lifted up over your adversaries, and all your enemies shall be cut off* (Mic. 5:7-9).

With the coming of the Messiah, the whole situation for Israel will be fundamentally transformed. Many of the Old Testament prophecies foretell the nation's blessing and exaltation and Micah's predictions were completely *ad idem* with these. He clearly anticipated the establishment of Israel as the supreme nation in the world, all other nations being subordinate to her. He described the nation as "the remnant of Jacob". The term "remnant" is frequently used by the prophets (e.g. Isa. 10:20-22) of those who would eventually turn to God in repentance and be saved. Ibn Ezra explains the phrase of the Israelites who remain in exile after the restoration of Zion, but who subsequently return, but this is rather too restricted an interpretation. In its general use, the term refers to those who remain faithful to God through the vicissitudes of life: throughout the centuries there has always been a remnant for God.

The prophet declared that the remnant would be in the midst of many peoples as dew from Jehovah. It is interesting that, when Jacob received his brother's blessing from his father, the climax was apparently reached in the blessing of "the dew of heaven" (Gen. 27:28), and that a dying Moses again prayed that the heavens of Israel might drop down dew (Deut. 33:28). The "dew" was rather a night mist resulting from the sudden cooling of the westerly rain-bearing winds by the cold nights which succeed the hot eastern days. This mist precipitates its water during the six rainless months and copiously compensates for the lack of rain. Without it the ground would be dried up, plants scorched, and vegetation withered. Through its means, fruits and herbs receive moisture at the critical period and flourish accordingly. It is said that, in Israel, the greatest quantity of such dew falls in the autumn, about the time of the day of atonement (Lev. 16): many students have suggested that there is an indication here that every spiritual blessing is based upon the work of Calvary, to which the sacrifices and ritual of that day pointed.

A remarkable reference to the night mist is found in Jud. 6. As a sign to Gideon, a fleece was one night saturated with dew, while the ground around remained dry, and a second night remained dry while the ground was drenched with dew. It is perhaps not fanciful typology to see a reference to our Lord in the incident of Gideon's fleece. During His life on earth, divine blessing was centred in Him, and spiritual life and power were found in Him alone. Through His atoning death at Calvary, blessing now flows out to all.

The manna, an appropriate type of Christ in incarnation, also fell with the dew. The food of the Christian is in that One who came forth to bring life and refreshment.

A practical aspect of the subject is presented in Psa. 110:3, which declares, "Thy people are freewill offerings in the day of Thy power, in holy beauties (i.e., as priests); from the womb of the morning. Thou hast the dew of Thy youthful ones". In the day of Messiah's reign, Israel is viewed as (1) a consecrated people, (2) priests, and (3) a source of refreshment to others. All this the believer of the present era should be.

The picture painted by Micah was of a restored Israel in the centre of the nations of the earth and functioning as a channel of blessing to the nations. The refreshment (or dew) which they brought to others was derived from Jehovah Himself; and could not, therefore, pall. It fell in rich abundance and independently of the co-operation of men. It came like showers upon the grass: it did not depend upon men because it proceeded from Jehovah. "So," writes Keil (*ibid*, p. 489), "will the spiritual blessing, which will flow over from Israel upon the nations, not depend upon the waiting of the nations, but will flow to them against and beyond their expectation. This does not deny the fact that the heathen wait for the salvation of Jehovah, but simply expresses the thought that the blessings will not be measured by their expectation."

Furthermore, Micah declared that the remnant of Jacob would be among the nations, in the centre of many peoples, like a lion among the beasts of the forests and a young lion among the flocks of sheep. They would trample and tear the heathen and no one could possibly deliver their foes from their hand. If Israel passed through the enemy's land, it would be to tread down and tear in pieces. Their hand would be lifted high over their adversaries and all their enemies would be cut off.

*And in that day it will come to pass, says Jehovah, that I will cut off your horses out of your midst, and I will destroy your chariots. And I will cut off the cities of your land, and throw down all your strongholds; and I will cut off all the sorceries from your land; and you will have no more soothsayers. And I will cut off your graven images and your pillars from among you; and you shall no longer worship the work of your hands. And I will root out your Asherim from your midst, and will destroy your cities. And I will execute vengeance in anger and indignation upon the nations which did not hear (Mic. 5:10-15).*

Still continuing his forecast of the character and happenings of the Messianic period, the prophet described the complete destruction of everything upon which the people had relied. God was their sufficiency, but they had turned to military supplies and armaments with which to defend themselves: they had relied upon horses, chariots and fortifications. They had placed their trust in witchcraft and idolatry in lieu of Jehovah. God now declared that He would destroy all these things.

The victory over all His people's foes will be won by the Messiah. Horses and chariots will consequently become redundant in that day. Such military resources will no longer be required and Jehovah, therefore, announced that He would destroy them. Similarly, the walled towns and impregnable strongholds, which seemed so essential to provide protection from the invader, were superfluous if Jehovah was His people's captain. Accordingly He would destroy the cities and throw down the strongholds.

Instead of seeking counsel and help from Jehovah, the people had resorted to witchcraft and soothsaying, or divination (Isa. 2:6; 8:19). God now declared that He would remove their sorceries or witchcraft from the land, where so much confidence had been placed in them, and that the diviners or soothsayers would no longer find employment with the people. Was not He sufficient for their need?

73

Jeroboam I had introduced the worship of the golden calves in the northern kingdom, and other idols had been adopted by the southern kingdom. This was virtually an insult to Jehovah, and He informed Judah that He would destroy the engraved wooden and metal images which they so foolishly worshipped. Wood or metal pillars, dedicated to the goddess of nature, had also been set up (Ex. 34:13; Deut. 16:21, 22; 27:15), which were intolerable to God and these too would be swept away and the people would no longer worship the works of their hands.

Jehovah reiterated that He would root out the Asherim and destroy the cities. The Asherim (usually translated "groves") were wooden posts erected near the altar of the false deity. They represented the goddess Asherah or Ishtar and the people had been commanded to destroy them when they entered the land of Canaan (Ex. 34:13). Nevertheless, before long they were paying their allegiance to the goddess. If Jehovah was to be acknowledged as their God, these pagan practices must discontinue.

He finally declared that, in His anger and indignation, He would exact retribution from the nations which did not hear. As Cheyne (ibid, p. 49) says, "Jehovah, being the God of the whole world, is de jure 'King of the nations' (Jer. 10:7); and if the natives have enthroned other gods in His place, and have almost forgotten Jehovah's existence, they are still responsible to Him." None can escape their accountability on the plea that the message was not heard or understood.

# CHAPTER 7

## The Divine Controversy

IN HIS *Minor Prophets* (p. 137), F. W. Farrar sees Micah 4 and 5 as the springtide of hope, and chapters 6 and 7 as the paler autumn of disappointment. Certainly there is a marked change of tone in the last two chapters of the book. At the same time, this section of Micah is of the greatest significance, both to the student of prophecy and to the observer of history. The opening utterance has been described as the most important statement in the prophetic literature and it concludes with a definition of religion which is unsurpassed in the whole of the Old Testament.

### JEHOVAH'S COMPLAINT

*Hear what Jehovah says: Arise, plead your case before the mountains, and let the hills hear your voice. Hear, O mountains, Jehovah's controversy, and you enduring foundations of the earth; for Jehovah has a controversy with his people, and he will plead with Israel (Mic. 6:1, 2).*

Taking the mountains and hills as an independent jury, Jehovah arraigned the nation as the defendant and Himself assumed the roles of prosecutor and judge. The mountains had often been called upon to witness events in Israel's history, to rejoice in her blessing, or to listen to the Divine proclamation (Deut. 32:1; Isa. 1:2; 44:23; 49:13; 55:12). Acting as

Jehovah's plenipotentiary, the prophet argued His case against the people in the court of the great mountains and hills and the "enduring foundations of the earth". These works of nature were regarded as immutable spectators of the lawsuit between God and His people.

He bade Israel to plead her case, and to enter into the legal argument. "It is the same Hebrew word," says one commentator, that is "translated 'let us reason together' (Isa. 1:18). The appeal is based, not on God's power and authority, but on reason and truth." He had a lawsuit with them and when they had presented their case, He would argue it with them.

### THE DIVINE FAVOURS

*O my people, what have I done to you? In what have I wearied you? Answer me. For I brought you up from the land of Egypt, and redeemed you from the house of bondage. I sent before you Moses, Aaron and Miriam (Mic. 6:3, 4).*

God might well have condemned His people for their sin and idolatry, and poured scathing denunciations upon them for their unfaithfulness to Him. Instead, He chose most tender expressions, with their implication of deep affection and emotion. In place of detailing their sins, He asked what His faults had been. What had He done to them which might be criticised or questioned? In what respect had He exhausted their patience or wearied them? He had made no harsh, restrictive demands upon them. He had made no rash promises to them which He was unable or unwilling to fulfil. He had not left them to struggle unaided for existence, nor flung them into battle against overwhelming odds. What was their complaint?

His ways with Israel had always been in love and mercy. His dealings with them had not been exigent but compassionate. He reminded them of the outstanding fact of their history. When they had been slaves in Egypt, suffering under the whip of an unreasonable taskmaster, God had delivered them and had redeemed them from the house of bondage. They owed their nationhood to Him.

He had not left them without guides, but had given them Moses, His friend and their mediator and intercessor, Aaron as high priest, and Miriam the prophetess. He had met their every need. Surely He had some claim upon their devotion?

How frequently a similar situation arises with the Christian today! In face of all that Christ has done, we often display the basest ingratitude and neglect. He might justifiably condemn His wayward people, but He pleads in tones of love for a recognition of His affection and reconciliation to Himself. And the compassionate and tender Lover of our souls is no other than the Eternal God, who has the right to command. Yet in our folly we so often ignore His appeals and treat Him in as cavalierly a fashion as we would our fellow-men.

### BALAK AND BALAAM

*O my people, remember what Balak, king of Moab, devised, and what Balaam, the son of Beor, answered him, and what happened from Shittim to Gilgal; that you may know the righteous acts of Jehovah (Mic. 6:5).*

Not only did God provide adequate leadership for Israel from Egypt to Canaan, but He protected them in unforeseen and unrealised dangers as well. In His recital of the case against Israel, He quoted an outstanding illustration of His care for His people. For a second time He used the tender expression, "O my people". There was no harsh rebuke, but rather a gentle persuasive plea, comparable with the parental coaxing of a wayward child.

He called upon them to remember the incident of Balak and Balaam early in their history. After their exodus from Egypt, Israel were attacked by the Amorites, but they completely routed them and moved on into the Moabite plains near Jericho. The Midianites and Moabites consulted together in view of the threatened invasion of their country and decided to solicit the help of a well-known soothsayer named

77

Balaam. The latter did his utmost to earn the reward offered to him by Balak, but every attempt he made to lay a curse upon Israel only resulted in a pronouncement of their blessing (Num. 23, 24). Ultimately the enchanter proposed the seduction of the Israelites by pagan women—an evil scheme which succeeded only too well (Num. 25:1-8; 31:16), although the resultant immorality and idolatry were severely punished (Num. 25:9).

Before Balaam's vicious proposal had been made, the Moabite king contemptuously dismissed him, but it is generally thought that the discussion to which Micah referred took place at that particular time. Jehovah called upon the people, not only to recall the story of Balak and Balaam, but also what had happened between Shittim and Gilgal: thus they might understand the righteous acts of Jehovah. The connection between the story and these two sites is not at first apparent. Shittim was, of course, the last station of Israel before the river Jordan, and Gilgal was the first one in Canaan.

Num. 25:1 states that Israel abode in Shittim and there began to indulge in sexual immorality with the Moabites— presumably the result of Balaam's scheme. But this did not affect the purpose of God. As Laetsch remarks (*ibid*, p. 278), "When Balaam's vicious advice to Balak to seduce Israel to idolatry and immorality (Num. 31:16) proved successful (Num. 25:1-8), the Lord punished them severely (Num. 25:4-9), but did not reject them. From Shittim, the place of their shame and God's forgiving grace, He led them through Jordan (Josh. 3:1-17) to Gilgal, where even during the days of physical weakness of their fighting men (Josh. 5:2-8), the Lord protected them by striking their enemies with panic-like fear (Josh. 2:9-11, 14; 5:2)." If the people had sinned at Shittim, the curse was rolled away at Gilgal, when the rite of circumcision (the symbol of separation to God) was renewed (Josh. 5:3-9). Shittim and Gilgal were, therefore, appropriately associated in the people's minds. As the whole story flooded their memories, they must surely realise the goodness of God and turn in gratitude to Him. Jehovah had really brought to nought the machinations of Balak and Balaam and had shown grace to His people.

*With what shall I come before Jehovah and bow myself before the high God (Elohim)? Shall I come before him with burnt offerings, with yearling calves? Will Jehovah be pleased with thousands of rams, with ten thousands of rivers of oil? Shall I give my first-born for my transgression, the fruit of my body for the sin of my soul? He has shown you, O man, what is good; and what does Jehovah require of you, but to do justice, and to love mercy, and to walk humbly with your God (Elohim)? (Mic. 6:6-8).*

It is usually argued that Mic. 6:6-8 represent the reply of Israel to Jehovah. If it does, then the ignorance shown was deplorable. Acknowledging by implication the grace and mercy of God, they merely enquired how they could discharge their obligations to Him. There was no real consciousness of sin: they were prepared to discuss the number and value of the burnt offerings to be sacrificed to appease Him, as though vast numbers might be more acceptable because of the volume. They were willing to offer hecatombs of rams or yearling calves and vast quantities of oil for their meal offerings. If necessary, they would even sacrifice their first-born son if transgression or sin was alleged against them.

They did not really understand Jehovah, despite their covenant-relationship with Him. As one expositor pertinently remarks, "There is not the slightest realisation of the unalterable holiness of God, which is satisfied with nothing less than perfect holiness in man (Ex. 19:6; Lev. 11:44; 19:2), perfect love toward God and man (Deut. 6:5; Lev. 19:18; cf. Matt. 22:36-39); no recognition of the wickedness and damnableness of every sin (Deut. 27:26; 28:15 ff.; 32:22). Nor is there the least desire for mercy, the faintest plea for grace and forgiveness. As His holiness is an offence, so His mercy is a stumbling-block to them. They will not be poor beggars before God's throne. They are convinced that they can merit

79

God's good-will by their own efforts. They are willing to bargain with God, as if He were a bargainer like themselves. They are ready to buy His favour, as if He were a venal judge who would overlook their failings if only they paid His price." Men never seem to learn that there is nothing good in themselves and that God is the infinitely holy One.

No sacrifices could compensate for the absence of ethical living. The demands made by the Eternal were moral and spiritual and nothing could act as a substitute. Sacrifices naturally had their place, but not in lieu of the spiritual qualities and practical living for which God looked.

The Septuagint, however, considers that the words relate to the discussion between Balak and Balaam. The king was eager to know what means to employ to win over Jehovah and was willing to pay a heavy price for His favour. This seems a more satisfactory interpretation, since the words are out of harmony with Israel's knowledge of God. In particular, it is difficult to imagine the nation proposing the possibility of human sacrifice as a means of currying favour with God, although the valley of Hinnom was used for centuries for the sacrifice of children to Moloch.

If Mic. 6:6-8 refers to what took place between Balak and Balaam, it would appear that the revelation of God's purposes of blessing for Israel—which had aroused the anger of the king—finally struck fear into his heart. Balaam's parables had patently shown the power of Jehovah and, by inference, His superiority to Baal. The king's religion was ineffective and his deity powerless. Here was a greater God, whom, by his efforts to secure a curse upon His people of Israel, he must obviously have offended. How could he avert His displeasure? How could he propitiate Jehovah?

These were the questions which he presumably flung at Balaam. By what means could he pacify Jehovah? What ought he to bring to Him as an offering if he was to come before Him and bow low in the presence of the Most High God? Quite naturally his thoughts ran immediately to the sacrifices of bullocks and rams presented to Him by Balaam already on the altars on the mountain-tops. He was prepared to bring burnt offerings of yearling calves if that would suffice. If that was not enough, perhaps Jehovah would deign to accept the sacrifice of thousands of rams. In the multitude of offerings, he reasoned, he might atone for his guilt. The cost seemed to matter little, provided he could regain his peace of mind.

As though he was bargaining with man, he offered to pour out torrents of oil (cf. Job 29:6), or even, if essential, to make what he regarded as the supreme sacrifice of his first-born son. Balak was prepared to give all he possessed to secure the favour of God. He had offered great rewards to secure his own ends and to bind Israel by enchantment. Now he was equally prepared to yield up his best to achieve what he desired. But, as W. Robertson Smith says, "Man convinced of sin is ready to sacrifice what is dearest to him rather than to give up his own will and give himself to God". He acknowledged his transgression and freely admitted the need to atone for his sin, but he was still totally unaware of God's real requirements.

A pagan ruler might well ask what God required, since the revelation had not been made to him. Israel would never have needed to do so. Those requirements had been clearly enunciated in Deut. 10:12 and were well-known, and Mic. 6:8 virtually reiterated what had already been stated. There is, however, an implication in that verse that Balak had, in fact, been made aware by Balaam of what was required and could not, therefore, plead ignorance. He declared that the king had been shown what was good; God required righteousness, kindness and submission to Him.

There must be the establishment in life and practice of the norm of justice. Secondly, there must be demonstrated mercy or kindness in relation to others, a sincere compassion for one's fellows. Furthermore, there must be a realisation of the greatness of God that will induce a quiet, humble walk before Him, without pride or conceit. There could have been no dubiety in the king's mind. Submission to God might well have saved the lives of himself and his people, and might have preserved his kingdom, But he rejected the revealed will of God and, as subsequent events showed, hardened his heart against Him.

The statement of Jehovah's requirements of man was clear and beyond misunderstanding. J. M. P. Smith says that it "lays hold of the essential elements of religion and, detaching them from all else, sets them in clear relief. It links ethics with piety, duty towards men with duty towards God, and makes them both co-equal factors in religion."

To do justice implied more than the letter of the law, and including setting right whatever was wrong and, in daily life, walking in integrity and faithfully. To love mercy or kindness inferred the translation of mercy into unselfish deeds and the consistent performance of acts of kindness to others. To walk humbly meant primarily to conduct oneself modestly, in personal purity and chastity.

### VOICE IN THE CITY

*The voice of Jehovah cries to the city, and it is wisdom to revere thy name. Heed the rod and who has appointed it (Mic. 6:9).*

Micah turned to expose the corruption of the city of Jerusalem and declared that the voice of Jehovah cried to the city. He was about to denounce the dishonest practices and deceit which characterised the commercial life of the day. The citizens would be wise to listen and to pay respect to His name. A rod had been appointed for their chastisement and it would be well to take heed now. The rod was always a symbol of punishment and the one appointed in this instance was probably the Assyrian. God used what instruments He chose for the castigation of the citizens for their malpractices.

### SOCIAL INJUSTICES

*Are there not still the treasures of wickedness in the house of the wicked and the scant measure that is abominable? Shall I count them innocent with the wicked balances and with a bag of deceitful weights? For your rich men are full of violence, and your inhabitants speak lies, and their tongue is deceitful in their mouths* (Mic. 6:10-12).

The treasures of the traders in Jerusalem had evidently been accumulated by oppression and dishonest practices, and Jehovah termed their possessions "the treasures of wickedness" and said that they were to be found "in the house of the wicked". Commercial dishonesty is as intolerable to a holy and righteous God as many other sins which are commonly regarded as much more serious. Yet these business men were using an ephah, i.e. a corn measure containing six bushels, which held less than the specified weight. Thereby they were defrauding the purchaser and were increasing their profits at the expense of the poor.

Moreover, they were using false scales and weights which were either larger than the true weights when purchasing or smaller when selling. Centuries earlier God had declared that these malpractices were an abomination to Him (Deut. 25:13-16). How could He gloss over the iniquity of such men or regard them as guiltless? His words were a condemnation of the unrighteous customs and manner of life of the deceivers.

He declared that the rich men were full of violence. They had acquired their possessions, not only by dishonest business dealings, but evidently also by pitiless oppression of the poorer classes and possibly by deliberate robbery. He denounced the city's inhabitants as a whole as characterised by falsehood and deceit. The corruption was so widespread that no one spoke the truth and all had a deceitful tongue. It was a sweeping condemnation, but apparently a completely justified one. Yet these were the people who had been so richly blessed and upon whom His favour had rested. It is probable that the words have reference to a future day as well as to those who lived in Micah's day.

Business morality seems to have been eroded in the world generally. Standards, which were scrupulously observed only a few decades ago, have been jettisoned, and the general incentive is to get, without being too concerned about the means used. Obviously this tendency, already universal, will inevitably become more pronounced in the future, and Jehovah's denunciation may, therefore, have a future relevance of which Micah could scarcely have been aware.

*Therefore, I have smitten you grievously, making you desolate because of your sins. You will eat, but not be satisfied; and there will be hunger inside you. You will put away, but will not save; and what you save, I will give to the sword. You will sow, but not reap; you will tread the olives, but not anoint yourselves with the oil; you will tread the grapes, but not drink the wine. For you have kept the statutes of Omri and all the works of the house of Ahab. You have walked in their counsels; that I may make you a desolation and the inhabitants a hissing. So you shall bear the reproach of my people (Mic. 6:13-16).*

Because of the oppression and injustice which characterised Jerusalem and its inhabitants, Divine punishment was inescapable. Already Jehovah had inflicted a wound upon them by smiting them. In withholding His blessing, He had left them desolate on account of their sins. The civic well-being was affected, but the individual also would naturally suffer. Wrongdoing, for which there has been no repentance and which is persisted in, must be recompensed.

He picturesquely declared that the people would eat, but not be satisfied (cf. Hag. 1:6); they would still be empty (Lev. 26:26). The description was virtually that of a besieged and starving city, for which there was no hope. The Peshitta substitutes "dysentery" for "hunger", but it is difficult to see the basis for this.

Evidently the enemy were to descend upon Jerusalem so suddenly and unexpectedly that people were deprived of the opportunity of escaping to a place of safety. Unable to remove their possessions, their efforts to hide them away would prove ineffectual; and what they did manage to save in this way would eventually become the spoils of the invader.

Again the Peshitta adopts a different rendering, viz. "you shall thresh wheat, but shall not keep it, and that which you retain, I will give up to the sword". The meaning, however, seems somewhat broader and to have reference to property of any kind. The citizens were to lose everything.

The judgments specified in the law (Deut. 28:38-40) would be their experience. They would sow, but would never reap the harvest: the enemy would have taken it. They would tread the olives, but would never be able to use the oil. Olive oil was normally produced by beating the olives (Ex. 27:20) and this is the only Biblical mention of the practice of treading or trampling them. The oil was, of course, used, *inter alia*, to anoint the body as a relief from the intense heat. The people would tread the grapes, but they would never drink the wine. The judgment upon them was comprehensive: everything would be lost.

The reason for their experience was clearly stated, so that there could be no ambiguity or misunderstanding. God declared that they had kept the statutes of Omri and all the works of the house of Ahab, and had walked in their counsels. This was the cause of their chastisement.

Omri was the father of Ahab and, according to the Scriptural record, he did evil in the sight of Jehovah to a greater extent than any of his predecessors (1 Kings 16:25). His son was an apt disciple in the ways of wickedness. Omri was the builder of the city of Samaria and the founder of a powerful dynasty in the northern kingdom of Israel. Indeed, the Assyrian inscriptions long afterwards referred to Israel as Bit Khumri, "the place of Omri". Goldman considers that the term, "the statutes of Omri", was an allusion to the oppression and injustice practised in the days of that king. It is more probable though that the reference was to the worship of Baal, introduced by Omri and his son as the official religion of Israel.

Ahab similarly was responsible for the development of Baalism in the country, following his marriage to Jezebel, the daughter of Ethbaal, king of the Sidonians. He built a temple to Baal and erected an altar for the worship of Baal (1 Kings 16:31, 32). The "works of the house of Ahab" were exemplified particularly in one significant incident above all others, viz. the notorious murder of Naboth in order to seize the vineyard of Jezreel (1 Kings 21: 1-16). The acts of violence and injustice of the royal household brought the throne into disrepute. Jehovah accused the inhabitants of Jerusalem of adopting the same course and following in the footsteps of the wicked king.

Because the people had chosen to walk in the "counsels" of Omri and Ahab, they must pay the penalty for their evil ways. It was not merely their idolatry that aroused the anger of Jehovah. It was rather their unprincipled cupidity and inequity that invoked judgment. Jehovah justifiably declared that He would make them a desolation and the inhabitants of Jerusalem a hissing. They would be reduced to such a lowly position, a "desolation", that the amazement of neighbouring nations would be aroused and they would become an object of contempt: their neighbours would "hiss" in scorn at them and their humiliation. This shame would be deliberately imposed upon them by God and would be realised when they were taken captive by the heathen. The hand of God is inescapable. In Divine omniscience He is cognisant of every act taken by His people, and in perfect justice He metes out the due reward for their conduct and sinfulness.

# CHAPTER 8

## Through Shadow to Sunlight

THE desolation inflicted by Jehovah upon His ancient people was completely justified: their decadence and spiritual barrenness were evident. Goldman (*ibid*, p. 184) appropriately remarks that "Micah's grief and pain at the evils of his day are nowhere so poignantly expressed as in this account of the depths of demoralisation into which Judean society had sunk. Every man lived for himself and preyed upon his brother." The state was simply deplorable and judgment was accordingly inevitable.

Corruption spread from the top through the whole body politic. Taylor (*ibid*, p. 58) says, "When a nation lacks good leadership it has no sense of purpose, and without that the people live only for themselves. Politicians use their influence to feather their own nests; lesser officials need monetary persuasion before they will perform their necessary duties on behalf of the public; everyone is somehow on the make. Micah saw a situation like that in the Judah of his day. The nation was like a vineyard after the harvest or as barren as the fig tree which the Lord cursed (Mk. 11:13 f.)." It was a lamentable situation.

The prophet painted the dark picture in all its shades of hopelessness and despair. In his initial description there was not a gleam of light to relieve the darkness: no ray of sun dispelled the shadows.

*Woe is me! For I am as when the summer fruit has been gathered, as when the grapes of the vintage have been gleaned. There is no cluster to eat, no firstripe fig which my soul desired (Mic. 7:1).*

Micah portrayed himself (or possibly the nation) as a man wandering through the fields, seeking something to satisfy his hunger, and finding that the harvest had already been reaped and that no gleanings had been left. The summer fruit had been gathered and there was nothing left to eat. Jerusalem was as desolate and unsatisfying as a reaped field: it was completely bare of all that was desirable. The vineyards had been swept clean of all their grapes. There was not a cluster to eat. Orchard and vineyard were empty.

The firstripe fig, which was sweeter than those which ripened later, should have been available in June, but the final picking had taken place and, despite all his natural longings, there was nothing to satisfy the prophet. "Jerusalem is desolate," writes Horton (*ibid*, p. 264). "The city is crowded and rich; but when the goods have disappeared, or become like the mere wisps and gleanings of the harvest, the population is merely prickly stubble, or a barren fig tree." Whatever was left was worthless. There was nothing to satisfy the heart of God.

Well might the prophet cry, "Woe is me," using an expression otherwise employed only in Job 10:15. The situation was hopeless.

*The godly man has perished from the earth, and there is none upright among men. They all lie in wait for blood: everyone hunts his brother with a net. They do evil earnestly with both hands. The prince and the judge ask for a bribe;*

*and the great man utters his mischievous desire: thus they weave it together* (*Mic.* 7:2, 3).

The prevalent decadence, so vividly indicated in the prophet's pictorial language, naturally had its cause, and he expressed it quite succinctly. The godly man had perished from the land and there was no one who was upright among men. The godly or pious man (*chasid*, related to the *chesed* of ch. 6:8) was one who revered Jehovah and who was consequently merciful and kind to his fellow-men. His unselfish regard for others was anathema in those days of anarchy and, not surprisingly, he disappeared from the country. His ways and character were not acceptable to the majority of the people, and those thus described may well have been deliberately put to death.

The upright man, who lived righteously and whose integrity and honesty were beyond doubt, walked before God without deviation or deception, but the prophet recorded that there were none of this character to be found among the people of Israel. All that was praiseworthy seemed to have been banished from the land.

Micah graphically declared that all lay in wait for blood and hunted each other with a net. Keil (*ibid*, p. 504) writes, "They all lie in wait for blood, i.e. not that they all go about committing murder, but simply that they set their minds upon quarrels, cheating and treachery, that they may rob their neighbour of his means of existence, so that he must perish." Their nets, of course, were schemes to entrap their fellow-men (Psa. 35:7; 57:7). Their hands, instead of doing good, were only eager to do evil and to engage in that with all earnestness and diligence.

The rich and influential were scorchingly denounced. They had it in their power to do what was wrong, and they proceeded to do it with the utmost satisfaction. Micah declared that the rich man, having formulated his scheme, bribed the judge to secure the verdict he desired. The judge unscrupulously perverted the law by granting the verdict for which he had been paid. The great man made known his desires, and he, the judge and the rich man all conspired together and weaved their scheme together as strands are woven into a strong cord. The A.V. vividly translates as "so they wrap it up". It was a *fait accompli* which nothing could alter. The corruption was evidently deliberate and widespread.

## CROOKEDNESS PUNISHED

*The best of them is like a briar: the most upright is sharper than a thorn hedge. The day of your watchmen and of your visitation is coming; now is their confusion (Mic. 7:4).*

Such guilty practices as the prophet had detailed must inevitably be Divinely punished. However long the corruption and perversion of justice had continued, the day of reckoning must ultimately come. Indeed, Micah stated plainly that the day of visitation was coming.

The best of Jerusalem's inhabitants was like a briar and the most upright was sharper than a thorn hedge, said the prophet. The rulers and the judges should have been the protectors of their fellows. Instead, the wickedness made them no better than the briar and thorn, which tore and wounded the passer-by. The use of these particular figures may also have been intended as an indication of their utter worthlessness.

Looking on to the awful period of the day of the Lord, God declared that the day of their watchmen and also of their visitation was coming. The watchmen referred, of course, to the prophets (Isa. 21:6; Jer. 6:17; Hab. 2:1), whose ministry had been directed to convicting these people of the evil of their actions. The requital for the evil deeds of the guilty men was now approaching. Bewilderment and confusion would be their experience when the blow ultimately fell (cf. Isa. 22:5).

## FAMILY TREACHERY

*Trust not in a neighbour; put no confidence in a friend. Guard the doors of your mouth from the one who lies in your bosom. For the son despises the father, the daughter rises up against her mother, the daughter-in-law against her mother-in-law. A man's enemies are the men of his own house* (Mic. 7:5, 6).

So universal had deceit become that it was impossible to trust anyone. No longer could a man confide in his most intimate companion. Because of the prevalent perfidy, Micah enjoined the people not to trust in their neighbours or in their closest friends. He even bade them to guard their words even from their wives. Inferentially, even these could be treacherous. This must have seemed almost incredible at the time. Normally the Jewish wife would never dream of betraying her husband and the conditions were extraordinary where this would occur.

Children usually treated their parents with the greatest respect but, in the days of which Micah spoke, the parents were treated with contempt and opposition. There was not merely dishonesty but active antagonism in the home—the saddest possible condition which could be imagined. The day was, as one writer remarks, "a time of complete social rebellion against constituted authority and natural relations". Is not this a characteristic of the present day? Trust and confidence have been largely destroyed. Domestic relationships, in many instances, have been torn asunder. The love and affection which once characterised family life are rarely in evidence.

A man's enemies, God declared, were the men of his own house, i.e. his own servants. Our Lord quoted this sentence in connection with the great tribulation, which has not yet come. History repeats itself and the conditions so clearly portrayed by Micah will be seen again in a future day. If they are beginning to display themselves already, there is strong presumptive evidence of the imminence of the end times.

### GOD'S SALVATION

*As for me, I will look to Jehovah. I will wait for the God*

91

*(Elohim) of my salvation. My God (Elohim) will hear me (Mic. 7:7).*

Injustice and oppression were prevalent, treachery and disrespect were characteristic of the home, apostasy and unfaithfulness were found on every side. In such circumstances, the faithful ones in the nation turned to God. The prophet became the mouthpiece of the people. They looked to Jehovah and waited in hope upon the God whose salvation could not fail them. It was the critical hour of their history and their hope could only be in God.

Knowing His unchanging character, moreover, they could wait in confidence upon Him, assured that He would hear their cry. With what assurance we may always turn to Him, conscious that, amid all the changing scenes of life, He abides faithful.

### THE ENEMY

*Rejoice not against me, O my enemy. When I fall, I shall rise. When I sit in darkness, Jehovah will be a light to me (Mic. 7:8).*

Well might the nation turn to Jehovah. They were conscious of the constant threat of invasion, perhaps by the Assyrian or by the Edomite or by the Babylonians. Judah was weak and her foes might fittingly rejoice over her sad plight (Psa. 35:19, 24). She had no military strength and could become an easy prey to an invader. Yet in humble trust, the nation bade her enemy not to rejoice over her state. Their malignant joy was premature.

Calamities may have caused Judah's fall, but, in unwavering confidence in Jehovah, she declared that she would yet arise. God's purposes for her would never be frustrated. When the catastrophes of life brought her into the darkness of the afflicted (Isa. 8:22; 9:1), Jehovah would continue to be a light to her. His delivering grace would reach out to her need.

What strength there is in the fact that, no matter what the circumstances of life, we may still trust in God. Through all the vicissitudes and trials of the Christian's path, faith rises to discover its sufficiency in heaven. In every circumstance God will prove Himself to those who trust Him.

## DIVINE JUDGMENT

*I will bear the indignation of Jehovah, because I have sinned against him, until he pleads my cause and executes judgment for me. He will bring me forth to the light; I shall behold his rightousness. Then my enemy will see, and shame will cover her who said to me, Where is Jehovah your God (Elohim)? My eyes will look on her: now she will be trodden down like the mire of the street (Mic. 7:9, 10).*

Because Judah had sinned against Jehovah, it was only fitting that the nation should be punished. He had used heathen nations to inflict His chastisement upon them, but the people did not question His action. They merely expressed their readiness to bear the merited punishment because of their sins (cf. 2 Sam. 16:10). There could be no complaint or rebellion in heart against the Divine ways. The judgment would be borne without murmur until Jehovah interposed on His people's behalf.

God would plead the cause of His people against their enemy. He would vindicate Judah before the nations which had attacked and oppressed the nation and which had rejoiced at the calamities which had befallen the people. It was only righteous that He should protect those who were in covenant relationship to Himself. Therefore, they might confidently declare that Jehovah would bring forth His people into the light and that they would behold His righteous actions and rejoice in His deliverance.

The enemy had scornfully asked where Judah's God, Jehovah, was, as though He was totally incapable of delivering His people. God would vindicate them and bring shame upon those who had raised the question. In addition, Judah would gaze in satisfaction at the discomfiture of her enemies, as they were trodden down in the mire of the streets (Isa. 10:6). The tables would be turned. Those who had rejoiced over the distresses of Judah would be trampled down and Judah would gloat over their ignominy and shame. The last word is always with God.

Although the prediction had a relevance to a period not far ahead at the time, it has also a pertinence to the future. Israel is yet to suffer terribly at the hands of the nations of the world, but eventually God will demonstrate His power to deliver them and to bring down judgment upon their oppressors.

## THE DIVINE PURPOSE

*A day for the building of your walls! In that day the boundary will be far extended. In that day they will come to you from Assyria to Egypt, and from Egypt to the River, from sea to sea and from mountain to mountain. But the earth will be desolate because of its inhabitants, for the fruit of their doings (Mic. 7:11-13).*

The prophet now looked on to the future blessing of Israel and declared that a day would come for the rebuilding of the walls. The word he employed was not that used for the walls of a city; he clearly referred to the boundary walls between fields or around vineyards. The old possessions were to be restored and the ancient walls replaced. The LXX renders rather curiously, "The day for anointing a brick wall—that day will be the unanointing of you, that day will indeed destroy your ritual services." But this seems very wide of the true meaning of verse 11.

Some have interpreted verse 11 as applying to the rebuilding of the walls of Jerusalem under Nehemiah, but the circumstances detailed in verse 12 render this inappropriate. The rebuilding is identified with the time when people from all nations will come to Judah and Jerusalem: that still lies in the future.

The "extension" of the boundaries presumably referred to the construction and replacement of the boundary walls throughout the country. Some expositors have seen a reference in the phrase to the fulfilment of the Abrahamic covenant, when Israel will possess the land from the river of Egypt to

94

the river Euphrates, but it is somewhat doubtful whether this was intended by the words.

From Assyria to Egypt and from Egypt to the Euphrates, from all parts of the world—"from sea to sea and from mountain to mountain", i.e. possibly from the Mediterranean to the Persian Gulf and from Sinai to Lebanon, but more probably from all parts of the world—people will come to the Holy Land, declared the prophet. Goldman (*ibid*, p. 187) insists that this refers to the return of the *diaspora*. He says, "This is a prophecy of world-wide restoration from exile (cf. Isa. 27:12)". If this interpretation is accepted—and there is something to be said for it—the prophecy presumably anticipates the return at Messiah's Advent.

The interpretation of verse 13 is also open to question. Most commentators tend to relate it to the heathen world in general, suffering desolation because of the sins of the nations and receiving the just fruit, or deserts, for their actions. On the other hand, it is suggested that the reference is to the land of Israel and to the devastation to be expected before the day of blessing dawns—a clear indication that the coming of the day of verse 12 was not to be anticipated in the immediate future. *Maybe wars since 1914 - 2024?*

## SHEPHERD AND FLOCK

*Shepherd thy people with thy rod, the flock of thy inheritance, who live alone in the forest in the midst of a fruitful land. Let them feed in Bashan and Gilead as in the days of old. As in the days when you came out of the land of Egypt, I will show him marvellous things* (Mic. 7:14, 15).

In the light of the unveiling of the future, Micah breathed a prayer to the Shepherd of Israel for His people and, by implication, the restoration of their territory. Viewing the nation as a flock, he prayed that Jehovah would shepherd the flock of His inheritance with His rod. The shepherd customarily used his rod to lead the sheep out of the fold to the pasture-land or to the brook to drink, to protect them from attack by wild animals, to rescue them from danger, or to urge

*12 June 2023*

them to move more quickly. It was the symbol of all his care and compassion for the sheep, of his control and direction, and of his protection of them.

The prophet referred to the people as living alone in the forest in the midst of a fruitful land ("Carmel", according to the A.V., but the literal meaning is probably what was intended). The Scriptures often portray the people of God's pasture as living alone (e.g. Num. 23:9). They were separate from the nations of the earth and were His own personal possession.

"Let them feed in Bashan and Gilead as in the days of old," pleaded the prophet. These two provinces were overrun by Tiglath-Pileser III in 734 B.C., and it may perhaps be deduced from Micah's words that this eastern area was not in his time in Israel's possession and had not been so for a considerable time. He, therefore, besought that these rich territories might be restored to Israel once more for the enjoyment of their flocks and herds. *12 June 2023*

The Divine answer to the brief petition recalled the deliverance of Israel from Egypt. Jehovah had done great things for His people then. His power had not changed and His purpose for His people had not altered. He would show him (or them) marvellous things. Once again His saving power would be demonstrated. What He had pledged Himself to do, He would perform. There was no place for fear or doubt.

### THE NATIONS

*The nations shall see and be ashamed of all their might. They shall put their hand on their mouth: their ears shall be deaf. They shall lick the dust like a serpent. They will come out of their strongholds like crawling things of the earth. They will be afraid of Jehovah our God (Elohim) and will fear because of thee (Mic. 7:16, 17).*

The nations had naturally relied upon their military strength: their confidence was in their own power. But when the salvation of God was seen in Israel's experience and His

以色列 独立战争后

mighty arm reached out again on their behalf, the watching nations were alarmed and ashamed that their own strength was so completely ineffective to thwart the deliverance of Israel. No longer did they control their own might and ability; here was something far greater. 当代的经历和历史

The prophet declared that they put their hand on their mouth—a gesture of reverence and astonishment (Job 21:5; Isa. 52:15). Not only were they speechless in the presence of the Divine power, but they were deaf to all else. They listened no longer to the proud boastings and effusions of shortly before: they were overawed by the infinite majesty and might which confronted them.

So complete was their abasement that Micah said that they would lick the dust like a serpent—an expression frequently used of the humiliating unconditional surrender of defeated enemies (Psa. 72:9; Isa. 49:23). Goldman (ibid, p. 188) says, "In the day of God's vindication of Israel, the nations, ashamed of their oppressive treatment of that people, and realising that, not because of their strength, but as instruments of God's wrath, had they so far triumphed, will abase themselves before Him in anxiety, trembling for their own safety."

Micah pictured them as creeping out of the strongholds (Psa. 18: 45) to which they had fled in their terror of Jehovah. They were no better than worms coming out of their holes in the ground. And all this because of their terror before God and their fear of Him. Well might they be in dread as they realised the retribution which might be exacted from them for their treatment of Israel. Employed as God's instruments for the punishment of His wayward people, they had gone far beyond their commission in oppressing and crushing them. The consciousness of the righteousness of God had at last been borne in upon them and the inevitable result was guilty fear.

### DIVINE MERCY *3rd July 2023*

*Who is a God (El) like Thee, pardoning iniquity and pass-*

*ing over transgression for the remnant of His inheritance? He does not retain His anger for ever, because He delights in loving-kindness. He will turn. He will again have compassion on us. He will trample upon our iniquities; and Thou wilt cast all our sins into the depths of the sea. Thou wilt show faithfulness to Jacob, and loving-kindness to Abraham, as Thou hast sworn to our fathers from the days of old (Mic. 7:18-20).*

The closing verses of Micah's Book are read each year by Jewish worshippers in the afternoon service of the Day of Atonement (Lev. 16), and are singularly appropriate for that occasion. That day is the one on which there is the annual reminder of the nation's sins and on which there is the symbolic removal of those sins.

As he viewed the wonder of God's operations, His grace and His judgment, Micah burst into a sublime hymn of praise to the Mighty One. He was the incomparable One. Who could conceive of any other like the Eternal God? He pardoned iniquity, a Hebrew term which, according to one writer, "is one of the strongest terms for sin, denoting perverseness, crookedness, which makes a man guilty, a debtor before God, with no possibility of ever ridding himself of that guilt." What stirred the prophet's heart was that such sin was pardoned by the God with whom he was concerned. The burden of guilt was lifted and the conscience freed. How could he but worship such an One?

But He also passed over transgression, the continuous wrongdoing which is the natural practice of a depraved heart. All this He did for those who formed "the remnant of His inheritance". Micah, of course, was unaware in his day that the sins of his people were pretermitted because of the work of Christ at Calvary, which was yet to happen. The sins of the believer today are remitted because of a work that has been accomplished.

God did not retain His anger for ever, the prophet declared, because He delighted in loving-kindness. His love and mercy never failed. He punished the guilty, but was ever ready to forgive the penitent. His grace was overwhelming. He was always ready to turn to His people and to display His compassion towards them. Because of the work of His Son, this is still true, and the Christian rejoices in the infinite mercy and unfailing compassion of God.

Micah painted the nation's iniquities as the enemies of God, actively antagonistic to Him because they hindered the outworking of His love and the fulfilment of His purposes. Consequently He trampled them underfoot, rendering them nugatory and powerless.

He went even farther and declared poetically that God would cast all the sins of His people into the sea, a concept which patently indicated the finality of the undertaking. They were banished beyond recall. Never again would their sins be remembered. This phrase is the origin of the "Tashlich" ceremony on the Jewish New Year. The implication of the words still thrill the hearts of God's people today. Their sins have gone—they are buried in the depths of the sea.

Despite the character of Jacob, despite all his duplicity and trickery, Jehovah entered into covenant relationship with him (Gen. 28:14), as with his father and grandfather. Fulfilment of the Divine purpose was not dependent upon the merit of the beneficiary: the intended blessings sprang from the predetermined plan of God and nothing could amend that plan or alter His purposes. He would show His faithfulness to Jacob, affirmed the prophet.

In His own sovereign will He had pledged Himself to Abraham that his seed should be as numerous as the grains of sand upon the sea-shore and as countless as the stars in the heavens above (Gen. 12:2, 3; 15:5; 22:16-18) and had promised that the land of Canaan should be his permanent possession. His promises had been confirmed by oath (Heb. 6:13-18) and were, therefore, immutable. The loving kindness which inspired them would still reach out to Abraham and his descendants. What Jehovah had sworn to Israel's ancestors centuries earlier remained the unchanging purpose of God. Amen, praise be to God the

Eternal King of the earth.

APPENDIX

## The God-Man

THE statement in Mic. 5:2 of the coming of a future ruler for Israel, "whose goings forth have been from of old, from the days of eternity", poses problems which are explicable only in the light of the New Testament revelation that the One predicted was both God and man.

"Jesus Christ," writes Karl Barth in *The Doctrine of the Word of God*, "is also the Rabbi of Nazareth, historically so difficult to get information about, and when it is obtained, one who is so apt to impress us as a little commonplace alongside more than one other founder of a religion and even alongside many later representatives of His own religion." It is not true, however, that—even from a historical point of view alone— the Lord Jesus Christ was entirely unremarkable and devoid of special distinctiveness. "God was in Christ," declared the apostle Paul (II Cor. 5:19), and the profound mystery of the *Theanthropos*, or God-man, can scarcely be dismissed as a commonplace. Indeed, the explanation of the mystery has taxed the minds of theologians for centuries.

Support is still found in some quarters for the Apollinarian explanation of the Incarnation, viz., that Deity and manhood were not united in Christ but that the Logos was enshrined in the physical body, taking the place in Christ's body which is normally taken by the human spirit and soul. Some colour

101

may seem to be lent to this by John's statement that "the Word became flesh and tabernacled among us" (John, 1:14), but the apostle's words cannot really be taken as signifying that, for three decades, God merely inhabited a physical body which was human, the spirit being divine. As Prof. D. M. Bailie admirably puts it in *God Was in Christ*, that "would mean that Jesus was not truly and perfectly human, but that it was a case of God having a partly human experience, or even taking a temporary human disguise . . . It would mean that in the experience of Jesus we could draw a line between the divine and the human element, a boundary where the human ceased and the divine began, so that each was limited by the other. But Christianity teaches that there was no such boundary or limit to either one or other. Each covered the whole field on different planes. Jesus is God and man, without boundary."

The physical union of the divine and the human natures in Christ does not, however, imply any intermingling of them in such a way as to affect the qualities or attributes of either. The divine effected no change in the human nor the latter in the former. It has been suggested by some theologians that, since there could be only one personality in Christ, His actions must have sprung from one whole and not from two independent natures. In other words, each of the two natures communicated its properties to the other by a process of interpenetration. Carried to its logical conclusion, this theory of the *communicatio idiomatum* implies the deification of the human nature, since any impartation of qualities would patently be primarily from the divine side to the human. This clearly cannot be accepted.

Dormer and others propounded a theory that our Lord's two natures were gradually united into one conscious personality—either at His baptism or after His resurrection. But this is obviously fallacious; our Lord was clearly not without a personality from His earliest days on earth. The alternative that each nature was personal infers a kind of schizophrenic being—a concept for which there is no foundation in the historic records.

The theory of Adoptionism, viz., that Christ commenced His earthly life merely as a man but developed into divinity, is equally devoid of Scriptural support. It might reasonably be asked at what point such a transformation took place and by what means it occurred. There is no evidence for this somewhat illogical view and it seems rather a reflection of pagan mythology.

Another explanation, which is also out of harmony with the Biblical account, is that the Incarnation largely followed the pattern of the Old Testament theophanies since it was a manifestation of God in human form. According to this theory, Christ was perfectly human, and the Deity was wholly contained in the humanity. Mackintosh, for example, says, "There is realised on earth the human life of God, and it is a life whose chiefest glory consists in a voluntary descent from depth to depth of our experience. It is the personal presence of God in One who is neither omniscient nor ubiquitous nor almighty—as God *per se* must be—but is perfect love and holiness and freedom in terms of perfect humanity." This is little more than a metamorphosis of the Deity into a human being, with the surrender of the Divine attributes following as a matter of course. But the New Testament portrays One who is both divine and human and who, while on earth, still retained all the attributes which belonged to Him in eternity.

It is commonly taught that Divine action upon the human soul takes place in the subliminal consciousness, and Sanday has suggested that the Deity found a seat in the subliminal consciousness of the human Christ. But as Griffith Thomas points out, this theory that the Deity underlay the humanity in the incarnate Christ "really makes Christ to possess one nature . . . and reduces our Lord to a purely human Christ, in whom God dwelt in fuller measure than He dwells in all men." Our Lord was not merely indwelt by God: He was equal with God (e.g. John 5:18).

In his *Gospel of St. John*, Godet maintains that there were not "two natures or two opposite modes of being co-existing in the same subject; but a single subject passing from one mode of being to another, in order to recover the first by perfectly realising the second." He adds, referring to John 1:14, that "the word *become* shows indeed that this change reached even the foundation of the existence of the Logos. This natural sense of the word *become* is not invalidated by the expression *is come in the flesh* (I John 4:2), in which Reuss finds the affirmation of the preserving of His original nature with all its attributes, but which really involves only the continuity of His personality. The personal subject in the Logos remained the same when He passed from the divine state to the human state, but with the complete surrender of all the divine attributes, the possession of which would have been incompatible with the reality of the human mode of existence. If He ever recovers the divine state, it will not be by renouncing His human personality, but by exalting it even to the point where it can become the organ of the divine state." Whilst there seems a measure of truth in this view, Godet overlooks the fact that our Lord never renounced His divine nature. He could never divest Himself of what was inherently His, nor relinquish attributes which, *in rerum natura*, were virtually part and parcel of His being. The suggestion that the incarnation involved a change which "reached even the foundation of the existence of the Logos" and that the retention of the divine personality was accompanied by the surrender of divine attributes is a contradiction of the plain evidence of the New Testament.

This view is more fully developed in what is commonly termed the doctrine of the kenosis. The theory of Christ's incarnation or kenosis (so called from the verb *keno* to empty), used in Phil. 2:7 is that, during His earthly life, the Son divested Himself completely of all Divine functions, attributes and consciousness, and restricted Himself to the normal limitations of humanity. If this was so, many problems pose themselves. Although he expresses himself rather crudely, Archbishop Temple's comment in *Christus Veritas* is pertinent: "What was happening to the rest of the universe during the period of our Lord's earthly life? To say that the Infant Jesus was from His cradle exercising providential care over it all is certainly monstrous; but to deny this, and yet to say that the Creative Word was so self-emptied as to have no being except in the Infant Jesus, is to assert that for a certain period the history of the world was let loose from the control of the Creative Word." The absurdity is obvious.

The kenotic theory is based on the words used in the description of our Lord's self-abnegation in Phil. 2: "Christ Jesus, who, subsisting in the form of God, did not count equality with God a thing to be grasped, but emptied Himself, taking the form of a slave, being born in the likeness of men" (Phil. 2:5-7). It is clear from this statement that:

(1) Christ subsisted—and must have subsisted eternally—in the form of God, i.e. in the essential nature and character of God. This would have been utterly impossible, of course, if He had not Himself been God.

(2) He did not regard equality with God as a treasure to be grasped. It was His inalienable possession.

(3) He emptied Himself. (This is the real crux of the passage.)

(4) He assumed the form of a slave.

(5) He was born in the likeness of men.

There is probably a parallel between Phil. 2:7-8: ("emptied Himself . . . unto death") and Isa. 53:12 ("poured out His soul unto death").

The kenotic theory is that Christ "emptied" Himself of His Godhead and consequently His divine attributes (and not merely of the use of them) when He became incarnate. The Philippian passage, as James Orr says, is "taken to mean that, during His earthly life, the Son ceased to exist in the form of God even as respects His heavenly existence. The place of the Son in the life of the Godhead was for the time suspended." As Orr pertinently remarks, "The difficulties in the way of this conception of the temporary obliteration of consciousness and activity on the part of one of the members

12 June 2023

of the Holy Trinity appear insuperable." He could not have divested Himself of the inner reality of Deity, even if He surrendered its outward manifestation. Moreover, Vincent maintains that the word "emptied" in Phil. 2:7 cannot possibly indicate "surrender of Deity or paralysis of Deity, nor a change of personality, nor a break in continuity of self-consciousness."

Of what then did the Son empty Himself, since renunciation of His Deity would have been a denial of His own nature? He laid aside the glory He shared with the Father in a past eternity (John 17:5). He divested Himself of the external insignia of His dignity and majesty. While never ceasing to be what He ever was, He veiled the blazing light of eternity to reveal Himself in flesh. The attributes, which are the essential possession of Deity, could never be surrendered but, during His earthly life, He chose to use or to leave them in abeyance at will. As Orr so admirably remarks, "While the Son submits to the conditions of humanity, it is still the Son of God who so submits, and behind all human conditionings are still present the undiminished resources of the Godhead. Omniscience, omnipotence, all other divine attributes, are there, though not drawn upon, save as the Father willed them to be." A statement issued by 16 signatories several years ago said, "Christ was essentially God and possessed of all the Divine attributes throughout eternity, including the period of His earthly career, not by derivation from the Father but in His essential deity. The attributes that were His by sovereign right were still His during the period when He took upon Himself the form of a servant. He never divested Himself of them and there is nothing inconsistent with this view and His dependence upon the Father, for He was very God and very man."

Our Lord then had (and will forever have) two natures, the divine and the human, and these were inseparably united by a hypostatic or personal union. Christ is not a dual being, possessing two personalities, nor some intermediate being, partly divine and partly human. The Son's personality obviously existed prior to His incarnation and belongs to His

106

divine nature and not to the human. Personality cannot be ascribed to His human nature and it could have no subsistence apart from its union with the Divine Person. When He became man, the impersonal human nature (see Luke 1:35) was taken up into the personality of the Logos, and the Divine Person assumed a second nature (i.e. a human) in addition to that (the divine) which He already possessed. Liddon pertinently remarks, "The Son of Mary is not a distinct human person mysteriously linked with the Divine nature of the Eternal Word. The Person of the Son of Mary is divine and eternal; it is none other than the Person of the Word . . . Christ's Manhood is not of itself an individual being; it is not a seat and centre of personality. . . . In saying that Christ took our nature upon Him, we imply that His Person existed before, and that the Manhood which He assumed was of itself impersonal." Schaff clearly defined the difference between nature and personality when he wrote, "Nature (essence, Greek *ousia*) denotes the totality of powers and qualities which constitute a being; while person (Greek *hypostasis, prosopon*) is the ego, the self-conscious, self-asserting and acting subject."

The two natures were (and are) not confused, absorbed or converted. Although there was one common life, each nature (as is evident from the Gospel narratives) retained its own attributes and qualities and none were transferred from one to the other. Our Lord possessed a human intelligence, a human will, a human sensibility, etc. His knowledge increased; He hungered, thirsted, wept, sorrowed and died; He knew the practical implications of penury and dependence; He was susceptible to all the experiences of humanity, except those which arose from sin or the promptings of a sinful nature. On the other hand, the characteristics of His Divine nature were also in evidence: He possessed a divine intelligence and will. He could discern the coin in the mouth of the unseen fish; He could stay the storm on the troubled lake; He could read the inmost depths of human hearts.

Notwithstanding this, He remained one Person. His words

and works were those of one Person and were never attributed to one nature or the other, and one cannot, therefore, speak of Him as acting at one time as God and at another as man. He was—and for ever will be—God and man, with two distinct natures but one personality. If this seems incomprehensible to a finite mind, it is because the mystery of God is, in fact, beyond the limits of human understanding.

# BIBLIOGRAPHY

| | |
|---|---|
| C. J. ALLEN: | *Hosea–Malachi* (Broadman Bible Commentary, Vol. 7), Marshall, Morgan & Scott Ltd., London, 1973. |
| G. R. BLISS: | *The Book of Micah* (in Lange's Commentary—see below). |
| J. CALVIN: | *Commentaries on the Twelve Minor Prophets*, Wm. B. Eerdmans Publishing Co., Grand Rapids, n.d. |
| T. K. CHEYNE: | *Micah*, Cambridge University Press, Cambridge, 1909. |
| A. COHEN: | *The Twelve Prophets*, Soncino Press, London, 1970. |
| S. R. DRIVER: | *The Minor Prophets*, Edinburgh, 1906. |
| G. H. A. EWALD: | *Commentary on the Prophets of the Old Testament.* |
| C. L. FEINBERG: | *Jonah, Micah and Nahum*, American Board of Missions to the Jews, New York, 1951. |
| S. GOLDMAN: | *Micah* (in *The Twelve Prophets*, by A. Cohen—see above). |
| H. HAILEY: | *A Commentary on the Minor Prophets*, Baker Book House, Grand Rapids, 1972. |
| E. HENDERSON: | *The Book of the Twelve Minor Prophets*, London, 1845. |
| R. F. HORTON: | *The Minor Prophets*, T. C. & E. C. Jack, Edinburgh, n.d. |
| C. F. KEIL: | *The Twelve Minor Prophets, Vol. I*, Wm. B. Eerdmans Publishing Co., Grand Rapids, 1961. |
| W. KELLY: | *Lectures Introductory to the Study of the Minor Prophets*, W. H. Broom & Rouse, London, 1897. |
| H. W. P. KLEINERT: | *Micah* (in Lange's Commentary—see below). |

109

| T. LAETSCH: | *The Minor Prophets*, Concordia Publishing House, St. Louis, 1956. |
| J. P. LANGE: | *The Minor Prophets*, Zondervan Publishing House, Grand Rapids, n.d. |
| H. MCKEATING: | *Amos, Hosea, Micah*, Cambridge University Press, Cambridge, 1971. |
| J. MARSH: | *Amos and Micah*, S.C.M. Press, London, 1959. |
| E. B. PUSEY: | *The Minor Prophets, Vol. II*, Baker Book House, Grand Rapids, 1970. |
| B. E. SCOGGIN: | *Micah* (in Broadman Bible Commentary—see above). |
| G. A. SMITH: | *The Book of the Twelve Prophets, Vol. I*, Hodder & Stoughton Ltd., London, 1905. |
| J. M. P. SMITH: | *Micah, Zephaniah, Nahum, Habakkuk, Obadiah, Joel*, T. & T. Clark, Edinburgh, 1911. |
| N. H. SNAITH: | *Amos, Hosea and Micah*, Epworth Press, London, 1956. |
| A. J. TAIT: | *The Prophecy of Micah*, 1917. |
| F. A. TATFORD: | *Prophet from the Euphrates*, P.W.M.I., Eastbourne, 1973. |
| J. B. TAYLOR: | *The Minor Prophets*, Scripture Union, London, 1970. |
| G. W. WADE: | *Micah, Obadiah, Joel and Jonah*, Methuen, London, 1925. |

# PROPHET OF ROYAL BLOOD

# PROPHET OF
# ROYAL BLOOD

*An exposition of the Prophecy
of Zephaniah*

by

Fredk. A. Tatford

# CONTENTS

Contents

FOR the student of Biblical prophecy, one of the most important features of eschatology is the Day of the Lord —a subject referred to in the Old and New Testaments nearly a hundred times. The descriptions given of that period portray it as one of clouds and thick darkness; of cosmic and celestial disturbances, of unparalleled tribulation for man, and of the outpouring of the unmitigated judgments of God.

The prophet Zephaniah, however, takes a somewhat different viewpoint from that of his predecessors. "To the earlier prophets," writes Sir George Adam Smith (*The Book of the Twelve Prophets*, vol. II, pp. 49-50), "the Day of the Lord, the crisis of the world, is a definite point in history: full of terrible, divine events, yet 'natural' ones—battle, siege, famine, massacre and captivity. After it, history is still to flow on, common days come back and Israel pursue their way as a nation. But to Zephaniah, the Day of the Lord begins to assume what we call the 'supernatural'. The grim colours are still woven of war and siege, but mixed with vague and solemn terrors from another sphere, by which history appears to be swallowed up, and it is only with an effort that the prophet thinks of a rally of Israel beyond. In short, with Zephaniah the Day of the Lord tends to become the Last Day. His book is the first tinging of prophecy with apocalypse. . . . Nevertheless, though the first of the apocalyptic writers, Zephaniah does not allow himself the licence of apocalypse. As he refuses to imagine great glory for the righteous, so he does not dwell on the terrors of the wicked. He is sober and restrained, a matter-of-fact man, yet with power of imagination, who, amidst the vague horrors he summons, delights in giving a sharp, realistic impression. 'The Day of the Lord,' he says, 'what is it?'. 'A strong man—there!—crying bitterly' (Zeph. 1: 14 b)".

He lived in a day of reformation, but the elements seemed to be loose, and the prophet was more concerned with the impending visitation of Divine wrath upon a guilty people than with the effects of the royal reforms.

Yet he closed his prophecy with the remarkable picture of the Eternal resting silent in His love.

All the Minor Prophets seem to have their message for the present day, but even a casual reading of Zephaniah will probably lead to the conclusion that his book is of more than average pertinence to our own day. *12 Jan 2023*

FREDK. A. TATFORD.

CHAPTER 1

## The Fruitless Reformation

O<sup>F</sup> all the Old Testament prophetical books, that of
Zephaniah is probably the widest in outlook and the
most comprehensive in content. In his commentary of 1528,
Bucer, for example, said, "If anyone wishes all the secret
oracles of the prophets to be given in a brief compendium,
let him read through this brief Zephaniah", and Keil declared
(*The Twelve Minor Prophets*, vol. II, pp. 123, 124) that Zephaniah reproduced "in a compendious form the fundamental
thoughts of judgment and salvation which are common to all
the prophets." Whilst his matter was original, the prophet
did not ignore the writings of his predecessors, but freely
borrowed words and expressions from Isaiah, Joel and Habakkuk, at the same time using many similar terms in relation
to some subjects as those used by his contemporary, Jeremiah.

The primary subject of his book was the universal judgment of the day of Jehovah (in fact he quoted the term more
frequently than any other Old Testament writer), although
he apparently saw the Divine judgment, not only as a future
eschatological event, but also as an immediate visitation upon
a sinful people.

He lived in an atmosphere of unbelief: paganism and
idolatry were prevalent, and the prophet's scathing denunciations and his threats of punishment were pertinent and justified
by the conditions. A popular syncretism approved the
association of the worship of Jehovah with that of false

11

deities, and a tolerant eclecticism produced a grave unconcern for justice and a strong inclination to materialism. Resolute condemnation of the people's attitude and an urgent call to repentance were demanded by the circumstances of the day.

The book is not quoted or alluded to in the New Testament, although its message and contents virtually find their full confirmation in the Apocalypse.

The prophet described himself as Zephaniah—a name used of others in 1 Chron, 6: 36; Jer. 21: 1; 29: 25, 29; Zech. 6: 10, 14, and meaning "he whom Jehovah hides". It has been claimed by some writers that he was a member of the tribe of Simeon and came from the mountainous area of Sarabatha, but there is no evidence to substantiate this. D. L. Williams identifies him with a priest of the same name, who was slain by the King of Babylon at Riblab (2 Kings 25: 18-21; Jer. 21: 1; 29: 25, 29; 37: 3; 52: 24-27), but this theory is equally without factual support, although this priest was obviously contemporaneous with the prophet.

Zephaniah specifically claimed to be a descendant of Hezekiah. The only pre-exilic individual named Hezekiah of whom there is any record is King Hezekiah (2 Kings 20), and most commentators have accepted the conclusion of Aben Ezra that this king was the prophet's ancestor and that he was consequently of royal blood. Although there were only two generations (Manasseh and Amon) between Hezekiah and Josiah (during whose reign Zephaniah prophesied), Manasseh reigned for 55 years (2 Kings 21: 1) and there was, therefore, time for the four generations mentioned in Zeph. 1: 1.

On the basis of Zeph. 1: 4, 10, 11, it is usually considered that Zephaniah was resident at Jerusalem (as might perhaps be expected of a member—however remote—of the royal family), but there is no definite confirmation of this.

No serious question has been raised regarding the canonicity of the book, although some critics have argued that more than one hand took a part in its compilation.

It is explicitly stated in the opening verse of the book that Zephaniah prophesied during the reign of Josiah, i.e. during the period 641 to 609 B.C., and he was consequently—as already indicated—a contemporary of Jeremiah (see Jer. 1: 2). There is, however, no conclusive indication of the precise dates of the prophet's ministry.

Josiah had been preceded by two evil kings, Manasseh and Amon, whose idolatry, witchcraft and spiritism undid most of the good done earlier by Hezekiah (2 Chron. 32,33). The worship of the Baalim, the host of heaven (the sun, moon and stars) and Molech had corrupted the land. In the eighth year of his reign, however, the heart of young king Josiah turned to Jehovah and he began to remove the altars of the false gods and the images of those deities, and to restore the worship of Jehovah (2 Chron. 34: 3-7). Ten years later a copy of the book of Deuteronomy was found in the temple and, at the king's instigation, a reformation commenced in Judah. Kleinert (*Zephaniah*, p. 4) points out that the principal royal reforms were all crowded into Josiah's eighteenth year, *viz.* "the appointment of the temple repairs (2 Chron. 34: 8 ff) and the events which followed the discovery of the law on this occasion (2 Chron. 34: 15 ff; c.f. 2 Kings 22: 8 ff); the consultation of the prophetess Huldah (2 Chron. 34: 20 ff), the convocation of the people (29 ff), and the feast of the passover (2 Chron. 35 : 1 ff)".

It is argued by some expositors that Zephaniah's messages must have been uttered prior to the king's reformation, because he did not allude to these events and because he specifically referred to the false cults which were current in the days of Manasseh and Amon.

*Per contra*, there is the reference in Zeph. 1: 4 to "the remnant of Baal", implying that, however large the remnant, the majority of Baal-worshippers had been destroyed and that the worship of Baal had very largely been checked. Moreover, the prophet frequently quoted the book of Deuteronomy, inferring thereby that the book had, by this time, been discovered in the temple and that its contents were known to the people through the public reading mentioned in 2 Kings 23: 1 ff. Furthermore, the prophet's description of current conditions is parallel to the description given by Jeremiah, who began to prophesy in the thirteenth year of Josiah, so that Zephaniah presumably prophesied at approximately the same time.

It is evident from Zeph 2: 13 that the fall of Assyria and the destruction of Nineveh, which occurred in 612 B.C., had not yet taken peace. Zephaniah's prophecy must, therefore, have antedated them. The most common view is that his messages were uttered after the period of reformation (630-624 B.C.), but before 612 B.C.

It has been suggested that the prophecy was originally inspired by predatory attacks made upon Judah by the Moabites and Ammonites in 597 B.C. (Jer. 49: 1-6; Ezek. 25: 1-11), but these apparently occurred some time after Zephaniah. Eakin (*Boardman Bible Commentary,* vol. 7, p. 270) maintains that the prophecy sprang from an attack by the Scythians on Palestine. Whilst it is probable that an invasion of some kind did precipitate the outburst of Zephaniah, he gave no information regarding it which would enable us to identify the invader or to determine the date of the prophecy thereby.

Taking all the relevant factors into consideration, it seems reasonably certain that the prophecy should be dated within the period 624 to 609 B.C.

### BACKGROUND

The reformation carried out by Josiah and his advisers was neither complete nor fully successful when the prophet commenced his ministry. Despite the attempts to put a stop to the worship of Baal, a remnant of Baal-worshippers (probably of appreciable numbers) was still firmly entrenched in the land. The astral deities, whose shrines had been removed from the temple of Jehovah, were still openly worshipped: in the evenings men blatantly bowed down to them and to the queen of heaven on their flat housetops. Children were still being sacrificed to the god Molech. Priests of the false gods served the idols unashamedly and without concealment. Idolatry continued to be woven into the warp and woof of life: indeed, commerce was partly dependent upon the acknowledgment of the gods of the nations. The disregard for the claims of Jehovah may not have been as widespread as in the days of Manasseh, but it was still characteristic of the upper classes. Even if the king was not personally involved, his closest relations were.

The nobility had adopted foreign fashions as well as foreign gods. Materialism had displaced spirituality and, in their pursuit of riches, the wealthy indulged in cruelty and oppression. Justice was prevented and corruption prevailed. The sceptics cynically concluded that God was so little interested in this conduct that He would do neither good nor evil. The tide continued to flow against the king's efforts to effect a spiritual reformation in the nation.

At the same time, the storm clouds were once more gathering in the north, "black and pregnant with destruction." The threat this time was not from Assyria, but from another frightening power. "From the hidden world beyond" Assyria, writes Smith (*ibid.* p. 15), "from the regions over Caucasus, vast nameless hordes of men arose and, sweeping past her unchecked, poured upon Palestine. This was the great Scythian invasion recorded by Herodotus. . . . Living in the saddle, and with no infantry nor chariot to delay them, these centaurs swept on with a speed of invasion hitherto unknown. In 630 they had crossed the Caucasus, by 626 they were on the borders of Egypt. Psamtik I succeeded in purchasing their retreat, and they swept back again as swiftly as they came. . . . But they shook the whole of Palestine into consternation. Though Judah among her hills escaped them, as she escaped the earlier campaigns of Assyria, they showed her the penal resources of her offended God. Once again the dark, sacred north was seen to be full of the possibilities of gloom". There are not wanting those, however, who see in

15

the threatened judgment, not the Scythian invasion, but the Babylonian, and there is something to be said for this view.

These were the circumstances in which Zephaniah lifted up his voice to his people.

APOCRYPHAL ADDITIONS

Clement of Alexandria (*Strom.* v. 11, § 77) quotes an apocryphal prophecy attributed to Zephaniah. It runs: "And the spirit took me and carried me up into the fifth heaven, and I saw angels called lords, and their diadem placed upon them by the Holy Spirit, and the throne of each of them was seven times brighter than the light of the rising sun, dwelling in temples of salvation, and hymning the unspeakable God Most High." There are also other fragments, for which his authorship has been claimed, which have been preserved in a Coptic version.

# CHAPTER 2

## The Warning to Judah

DESPITE the superficial revival under Josiah, the moral and spiritual condition of the nation of Judah rendered judgment inevitable. Opinion differs regarding the instrument used by God to inflict the judgment, but C. I. Scofield and others consider that the Babylonian invasion was in view and that the Babylonian captivity was the impending punishment to which Zephaniah referred. His message may have received greater emphasis because of the character and status of the messenger.

### THE SUPERSCRIPTION
*The word of Jehovah, which came to Zephaniah, the son of Cushi, the son of Gedaliah, the son of Amariah, the son of Hezekiah, in the days of Josiah, the son of Amon, king of Judah* (*Zeph.* 1: 1).

The introductory formula to the book is identical with that found in other prophetical books (e.g. Hos. 1: 1; Joel 1: 1; Mic. 1: 1) and is a claim that the words which follow are of Divine authority and inspiration.

Zephaniah is unique in tracing his genealogy to the fourth generation. Pusey (*The Minor Prophets*, vol 2, p. 235) provides an i n t e r p r e t a t i o n of the names mentioned: "Zephaniah, 'whom the Lord hid'; Gedaliah, 'whom the Lord made great'; Amariah, 'whom the Lord promised'; Hezekiah, 'whom the Lord strengthened'." It is certainly interesting to note that there is a reference to Jehovah in each of the names. If the Hezekiah referred to was the king of that name, Zephaniah was evidently his great-grandson.

The messages of the book were uttered, according to this opening verse, in the days of Josiah, king of Judah. Wm. Kelly (*Lectures Introductory to the Study of the Minor Prophets*, p. 348) says, "there was but a short space indeed that separated Josiah's bright burst of pious effort for God's glory from the awful evils which succeeded and brought an insupportable judgment from God on the guilty people. Zephaniah was one of those who spoke in Jehovah's name during those promising times." But the period was probably not quite so bright as Kelly implies: the first flush of enthusiastic repentance seems to have vanished.

Having announced himself, his authority and his status, the prophet proceeded immediately to a declaration of the Divine message to the guilty nation.

## UNIVERSAL JUDGMENT

*I will sweep away everything from the face of the earth, says Jehovah. I will sweep away man and beast; I will sweep away the fowls of the heaven and the fish of the sea and the ruins with the wicked. I will cut off mankind from the face of the earth, says Jehovah* (Zeph. 1: 2, 3).

When the message came, it must have shattered the complacency and self-sufficiency of Josiah's subjects, for Jehovah announced a universal judgment. Every living thing was to be affected. Although, as one writer remarks, "the cosmological upheaval usually associated with apocalyptic is not present," the intention was evident. The ultimate day of Jehovah will be cataclysmic, but what was now predicted was such a complete destruction as to be an apt symbol of what still lies in the future.

God declared that the earth was to be swept clean of every living thing; man and beast would be destroyed ("I will cut off man", *adam*, "from the fact of the earth", *adamah*— the land man had defiled). The heavens would be denuded of bird life and the sea of aquatic life. The destruction would be more effective and more extensive than even the Noahic deluge. The opportunity to repent, which had been afforded by the royal reformation, had been despised: the opportunity had only increased the responsibility of the people, and punishment for the hardened impenitent and sceptic was inevitable.

The term "stumbling blocks", used in the A.V., is better rendered "ruins" (c.f. Isa. 3: 6). The reference is possibly to "the objects and rites of their idolatrous worship" (c.f. Ezek. 14: 3, 4, 7). The Septuagint renders the last two clauses of verse 3, "As for the wicked, they shall be without strength; and I will remove transgressions from the face of the land". Man had rebelled against the rule of God and against his ordinances; in consequence, every moral, social and political institution ultimately fell into ruins. The ruins would be swept away with the sinners who were virtually the cause of the desolation.

There is no doubt that what is envisioned is the final collapse at the end of time, as described, for example, in Rev. 15 et seq. The immediate judgment was intended as a warning of what was yet to come—the dread day of Jehovah, which still lies in the future. If the impending troubles were terrifying, they were but a pale reflection of that ultimate judgment day. The adumbration was, however, certainly one to cause fear and to awaken men to the need to turn to God in repentance.

Judgment always commences with the house of God, and the prophet turned from the general picture to portray the hand of discipline falling upon the degenerate theocracy of Judah.

### THE CHASTISEMENT OF JUDAH

*I will also stretch out my hand against Judah and against all the inhabitants of Jerusalem. And I will cut off from this place the remnant of Baal, and the name of the Chemarims with the priests, and those who, on the roofs, bow down to the host of the heavens, and those who bow down and swear by Jehovah and yet swear by Malcham; and those who have turned back from Jehovah, and those who have not sought Jehovah, nor enquired of him* (Zeph. 1 : 4-6).

The storm clouds of Divine wrath were gathering and the whole earth was threatened, but the lightning struck first on the nation of Judah and the capital city of Jerusalem. If the hostility of the Gentile nations demanded judicial action in retribution, how much more richly deserved was the punishment of God's own people. Blessed above all other nations, their base ingratitude to and despite of the One who had covenanted with them were all the more reprehensible. They boasted arrogantly of their relationship with Jehovah and yet turned their backs upon Him, but now He would stretch out His hand against them. He had seen their disloyalty to Him and their association of other deities with His worship, and the day of reckoning had now come.

His stretching out of His hand against them symbolised His preparation for punitive action. He saw the towers of the city of Jerusalem, He discerned the idolatrous practices of the citizens, and announced His intention of dealing with them all. Each class of offender was to feel the weight of His hand.

"I will cut off from this place the remnant of Baal." It seems almost incredible that in the metropolis itself in spite of all the efforts of the king to put an end to idolatry and to restore the true worship of God there were still some who paid their homage to Baal. Originally a personification of the sun, Baal was also a fertility god. Literally the word means "lord" or owner, and he was regarded as supreme in the Canaanite pantheon. The name was often attached to deities of varying characteristics, and even sometimes to Jehovah Himself (e.g. in 1 Chron. 12 : 5 the name Bealiah means "Jehovah is Baal", i.e. lord). Tablets discovered at Ugarit in northern Syria show that Baal was regarded, not only as the god of fertility, but as the lord of clouds, rain and storm. He was frequently confused with other gods, and the Old Testament often refers to a Baal of a certain district as well as to the plural Baalim (i.e. lords or gods of various locales).

Baal's consort was his own sister Anat, a warrior-goddess, who was not infrequently confused with Astarte (or the plural Ashtaroth). Their cult involved the utmost licentiousness, usually carried out on the summits of hills and mountains or in the woods ("under every green tree").

Baalism was apparently first introduced into Israel by Jezebel, the wife of Ahab (1 Kings 16: 31, 32) although it was in evidence in much earlier days (Jud. 2: 13). It was anathematised by true followers of Jehovah, who usually replaced the name of Baal by *Bosheth* (shame). The worship of Baal certainly continued up to the time of the exile and it was obviously in existence in Judah in Josiah's day. The king's reformation had not completely ousted this false religion, with all its attendant dangers to morality, and Jehovah now declared that he would cut off the remaining worshippers of Baal.

The name of the Chemarim and the priests was also to be wiped out. The Chemarim were idolatrous priests, who officiated in the heathen cults, offering sacrifices on the high places or mountain-tops. Feinberg says that the Hebrew root means "black" and that they were so termed because of the black garments they wore, or that it also has the significance of "zealous", referring to their fanatical enthusiasm in their idolatrous services. The implication of the Divine judgment upon these deceivers was that their posterity would be blotted out.

Judgment was also to fall upon the men and women who were to be seen at the point of sunset on their flat roofs, paying homage to "the host of heaven". From early days of human history, the sun, moon and stars have been worshipped. In Egyptian, Sumerian and Akkadian religion, the sun has been regarded as a deity, and there were certainly sun worshippers in Babylonia and Assyria. Sabaism (the worship of the stars) was also practised widely among the Semitic peoples. Manasseh not only introduced astral worship into Jerusalem, but set up altars to the astral deities in the temple of Jehovah, which Josiah subsequently destroyed (2 Kings

21: 3-5; 23: 4, 5). Jeremiah implies that this worship was almost universal in Jerusalem (Jer. 19: 13).

The worship of Baal and of the host of heaven was one of the sins leading to the collapse of the northern kingdom of Israel (2 Kings 17: 16). Yet the people of Judah were foolishly following the same course, despite the action taken by the king. The time had come for judgment to fall upon them.

There were others who bowed down to Jehovah and simultaneously to Malcham. The latter was a reference to Milcom or Molech (or Moloch). The word has sometimes been interpreted as "their king", but it is reasonably clear that it was the god Molech wtho was intended. There are repeated references to Molech or Milcom in the Old Testament, from Lev. 18: 21 onwards, and his worship was common in Israel. He was the principal god of the Ammonites, and his service demanded human sacrifice (e.g. 2 Kings 16: 3). This was an abomination to God, but children of His people were often sacrificed to Molech by their parents.

The condemnation of Zephaniah is that this evil system was being combined with the worship of Jehovah—a syncretism even more objectionable than some of the other practices condemned. Any attempt to associate others with God is intolerable to Him: He claims sole and absolute loyalty.

Finally there were two other classes: first, those who had known the truth but had apostasised from God. Whether or not they followed false religions is not stated but it is not really relevant. They had turned their backs upon Jehovah after tasting His grace and favour. The second class were those who did not seek Jehovah or enquire of Him. They were not openly opposed to Him, nor did they adopt the policy of the syncretist: they had not turned to idolatry, but they were completely indifferent to Jehovah. They had dispensed with Him and lived their lives independently of Him. Upon those also the hand of judgment was to fall .

22

Zephaniah lived and prophesied in a day over 25 centuries ago, but the picture he painted still retains its relevance today. The world of the twentieth century seeks other lords and is prepared to be tolerant of all beliefs and principles. Sincerity is all that matters. It is often said that a study of comparative religion indicates the common origin of all religion and that every attempt should, therefore, be made to draw the various faiths together again.

If we do not worship the pagan deities of the nations, we bow at the feet of power or mammon. Those who have deliberately turned their backs upon the true to follow their own inclinations are not restricted to the occupants of the pew, but often tragically include deniers of the faith in the pulpit. And who shall say that the majority do not completely ignore the claims of God and view religion with apathetic indifference? The prophet's picture is a mirror reflecting not only conditions of a past age but the attitudes of our own day.

The warning, however, is clear. The God, who has shown amazing grace and mercy and who has withheld the merited punishment for so long, will not always delay and the indications today are that judgment cannot much longer be postponed. The clarion note of warning should be sounded loud and clear.

## CHAPTER 3

### Terror Strikes

IT was patent that nothing had escaped the eye of Jehovah. The idolatrous practices of His people and their complete disregard of His claims upon their allegiance and loyalty had reached a stage where punishment was inevitable. His purpose had been announced but, before the blow fell, He called for a pause to give the nation the opportunity of realising what was about to happen.

JEHOVAH'S SACRIFICE

*Be silent at the presence of Adonai Jehovah: for the day of Jehovah is at hand. For Jehovah has prepared a sacrifice: he has hallowed his guests. And it shall come to pass on the day of Jehovah's sacrifice that I will punish the chiefs and the king's sons and all who clothe themselves with foreign apparel. On that day also, I will punish everyone who leaps over the threshold and those who fill their masters' houses with violence and fraud (Zeph. 1: 7-9).*

The announcement of the impending judgment had been made by the prophet. Now, in the guise of the herald who enjoins silence on the approach of his ruler, he commands the people to be silent before the coming of the Sovereign Lord, Adonai Jehovah. There is ample reason for quietness: the day of Jehovah was at hand. The awfulness of that day seems to have seized the prophet himself. He was aware of the description given by other prophets of that day. Now the dreaded moment approached.

25

Like many another Biblical prophecy there has been more than one fulfilment of the predicted day of trouble and the ultimate and complete fulfilment is still delayed. But the experiences confronting Judah were so dire that they were aptly deemed a reflection of the final day of judgment. Under Divine inspiration, Zephaniah was adopting the same pattern as his predecessors.

The day of Jehovah will be the culmination of all judgment and is consistently depicted as a period of unparalleled trouble, starting suddenly and unexpectedly, coming "as a thief in the night" (1 Thess. 5: 1, 2). The character of that period is indicated in Isaiah's words, where he enjoined the people to "Enter into the rock and hide in the dust, for fear of Jehovah and for the glory of his majesty . . . and they shall go into the holes of the rocks and into the caves of the earth, for fear of Jehovah and for the glory of his majesty, when he arises to shake terribly the earth" (Isa. 2: 10-19; Joel 1: 15; 2: 1, 2, 31; 3: 16; Amos 5: 18; Isa. 34: 1-8; 2 Pet 3: 10, etc.).

In 2 Thess. 2: 2-4 the apostle Paul stated that the day of the Lord will not come until the appearance of the man of sin. Our Lord's words in Mark 13: 14-19, coupled with Daniel's in Dan. 9: 27, revealed that that would occur half-way through the seven years referred to in the latter verse. It will apparently conclude with the dissolution of the earth and the heavens (2 Pet. 3: 10). During that long period Divine wrath will be poured out upon earth, but the dark clouds of trouble will be dispersed for a thousand years during the reign of Christ upon earth, only to regather at the end of the millennium and to break in a final outburst at the end of time.

If that awful period was near, a silence might well fall upon the people. Zephaniah declared that Divine preparations had been made for the outpouring of wrath upon the guilty. But he described judgment, not as a slaughter, but as a sacrifice. In the words of one writer, what was to happen assumed the character of a holy sacrificial act. The symbolism was, of course, taken from the Levitical offerings and the term employed had its application primarily to the peace offering. The animal to be sacrificed as a peace offering was brought to the priest, and the offerer identified himself with the animal by laying his hands upon its head. If the animal was accepted, he was accepted in it; if it was rejected, he was rejected also. Part of the sacrifice was consumed upon the altar as the food of Jehovah, part became the portion of the officiating priest, and the remainder was eaten by the offerer and his family (Lev. 3: 1-17; 7: 11-21). The sacrificed animal had to be consumed within two days, any part left after that period being destroyed (Lev. 7: 15-18).

Jehovah used this type of sacrifice as a symbol of the destruction He was about to inflict upon the guilty (Isa. 34: 6; Jer. 46: 10; Ezek. 39: 17-21). He regarded Judah as no better than her Gentile neighbours, and she would accordingly be destroyed at the same time.

The worshipper under the Levitical economy invited guests to share the meal with him. So God declared that He had bidden, or hallowed, or consecrated guests to feast upon His sacrifice (c.f. Isa. 13: 3). Kleinert (*ibid.* p. 14) maintains that the guests will be the heathen nations whom Israel was about to destroy, but most commentators take the view that Israel (or Judah) and the nations are themselves the sacrifice and that the identity of the guests is deliberately left vague— that the feature is introduced merely to complete the picture.

Jehovah specifically stated that, on the day of His sacrifice, He would punish five classes of people in Judah. The first were the civil leaders, the "princes" or "chiefs", who were officers of the royal court and advisers of the king. They were the magistrates and dispensers of justice, but they had, in fact, become the principal oppressors of the poor (1 Kings 4: 2; 9: 23; 20: 14; Jer. 24: 1; 36: 12). The Divine sentence upon them was executed in due course (2 Kings 24: 12-14).

King Josiah was not himself named. His heart beat true to God and the Divine hand did not fall upon him (2 Kings 22: 19, 20). But "the king's sons" were to suffer, since they

27

had evidently declined to walk in the ways of their pious father. Some difficulty arises over the interpretation of this class. In the 18th year of Josiah, his son, Jehoiakim was only 12, Jehoahaz was 10, and Zedekiah had not yet been born. At that early age they could scarcely have exhibited the impious character that merited destruction. The prophecy may have anticipated a later period when they also would be punished for their sins, or it may have referred to other members of the royal household who are not named. Whoever they were, it is made clear that Jehovah was perfectly well aware of their manner of life and of their sinfulness in His sight.

The third class to come under sentence were those who arrayed themselves in foreign apparel. Certain regulations had been laid down for the people's costume (Num. 15: 38; Deut. 22: 11, 12), but full details of God's requirements were never given. Some of the people, who had adopted the idols of the heathen, also adopted the dress of their neighbours. Assyrian fashions, in particular, were being aped. These people were making themselves like the world around them, whereas it had always been God's purpose that they should be separate from the nations of the earth.

"The strange apparel shows the estranged heart," writes Kleinert (*ibid.*, p. 15). "The infringement of the popular manners and the contempt of the natural costume evince the decay of the nation's spirit." It is possible that the change of dress was partly due to the desirability of getting on with neighbours, and that a spirit of compromise gradually developed. As clothes are to the body, so are habits to the real man, and the judgment of these people probably has a significance for this day as well as for Zephaniah's.

The fourth class singled out for particular mention were described as those who leap over the threshold.. Eakin (*ibid.*, p. 279) writes, "The threshold was judged in antiquity to be the abode of a demon (or demons), thus a place of particular danger. In Roman times this belief found expression in the protective carrying of a bride across the threshold". One version renders the clause, "who ascends the pedestal", i.e. the pedestal upon which stood a pagan altar. This would merely be a further description of idolatry. The ward translated "threshold", however, is used also in 1 Sam. 5: 4, 5; Ezek. 9: 3; 10: 4; 46: 2; 47: 1; and in every instance (as well as in non-Biblical literature) has reference to the threshold of a temple or a sacred building; it was never used of the threshold of a private house or of any other building.

The significance must, therefore, be related to the incident described in 1 Sam. 5. The Philistines had captured the ark of God and had placed it in the temple of Dagon at Ashdod. The following morning the image of Dagon had fallen down before the ark. The next day they found the image across the threshold of the temple, decapitated and minus its hands. From that time, no one entering the temple stepped on the threshold (v. 5), and it became a cultic practice to leap over the threshold. In time, the reason for the practice was doubtless forgotten, but the practice continued. Jehovah condemned those who adopted this heathen rite in their religious observances. He had judged Dagon by destroying his image on the threshold of his temple. Those who followed the pagan mode of access by jumping over the threshold were virtually aligning themselves with paganism against the true God.

Some expositors link the fifth class with the fourth and conclude that the servants of the wealthy, in their zeal to despoil others of their goods, would leap over the threshold of their master's house, to rush out to the scene of robbery and violence. This is untenable for the reason already stated. Others have suggested that the servants were those of the temple and that their purpose was to enrich the house of their master, the false god, and, in leaving the temple, they would follow their normal custom of leaping over the threshold. But the word used for "master" is the common one, *adonim*, and not the word *baalim*, which would be used of the gods.

Those described were evidently dishonourable servants of unscrupulous masters, who used violence and cruelty to extort treasures from the poor and unprotected. By their

29

oppression and fraud, they filled their masters' houses with ill-gotten gains. But their actions did not escape the eye of omniscience and Jehovah announced His intention of calling them to account.

The day of Jehovah would be a day of reckoning for all who had offended Him, and as the hour of that day burst upon the consciousness of the people, lamentations would arise from every quarter.

### WIDESPREAD GRIEF

*And it shall come to pass on that day, says Jehovah, that there will be the noise of crying from the fish gate, and a wailing from the second quarter, and a great crashing from the hills. Howl, inhabitants of Mortar, for all the traders are cut down; all who weigh out silver are destroyed* (*Zeph.* 1: 10, 11).

The realisation of what was involved in the punitive justice of the day of Jehovah will produce universal consternation, according to the picture painted by Zephaniah. The victorious shouts of the invaders in their ruthless onslaught of plunder and rapine, will scarcely be heard because of the shrieking and howling of the besieged. The wailing and lamentation will resound through the streets of the city, echoing from the fish gate through the lower part of Jerusalem to re-echo in the hills as the crashing of falling houses and palaces reverberates through the valleys.

The fish gate was the nearest of the city gates to the road to Jaffa and the coast (Neh. 3: 3; 12: 39; 2 Chron. 33: 14), although one writer insists that it obtained its name from its proximity to the fish market where fish, caught in the lake of Tiberias or in the River Jordan, were brought for sale. Although some place this gate in the western wall and others in the north, Keil confidently asserts that it was in the eastern wall. Unfortunately, he provides no evidence to support his theory. It has also been identified with the present Damascus Gate, but the evidence for this is slight.

The "second quarter", or the lower city, was located to

30

the north and west of the temple area. It was here that the wealthy lived in their luxurious dwellings. It was here also that the prophetess Huldah lived (2 Kings 22: 14; 2 Chron. 34: 22).

When attacked, the people usually fled to the hills, but the sound of crashing was to echo from the hills. Destruction was to sweep through the city. Feinberg (*ibid.*, p. 48) says that verse 10 "indicates the progress of the enemy until they occupy the prominent positions in the city". This would certainly be appropriate if the thesis is accepted that the prophet is referring throughout to the impending Babylonian invasion, as a type of the ultimate day of Jehovah.

The wailing extended to the inhabitants of Maktesh, or Mortar, the lower, basin-like section of the city. This name was applied to the Tyropoeon Valley. It was in this area that the Phoenician and Jewish merchants engaged in their occupations, whom the prophet termed "Canaanites", i.e. traffickers, a term expressive of contempt. "Hammackhtesh, the mortar (Prov. 27: 22), which is the name given in Jud. 15: 19 to a hollow place in a rock, is used here to describe a locality in Jerusalem", writes Keil (*ibid.*, p. 133), and perhaps as an indication of the unscrupulous trading and usury of these merchants. Both the traders and the money changers (as there was no standard coinage, silver was used for transactions and it was weighed out by the money-changer or the banker) were to be destroyed. There was no need for them in the day of Jehovah.

#### JUDGMENT OF THE IRRELIGIOUS

*And it shall come to pass at that time, that I will search Jerusalem with lamps, and punish the men who are settled on their lees, who say in their heart, Jehovah will not do good, neither will he do evil. Therefore, their goods shall be plundered, and their houses laid waste. They will build houses, but shall not inhabit them. They will plant vineyards, but they shall not drink wine from them (Zeph. 1: 12, 13).*

There were others who also merited judgment and who

could not be allowed to escape, and Jehovah declared that He would search Jerusalem with lamps to discover them, i.e. the most diligent and minute search (c.f. Luke 15: 8). His penetrative glance would discover the guilty, wherever they might take refuge. To quote Laetsch (*The Minor Prophets,* p. 361), "There is no possibility of hiding from Him; not even the huge natural and artificial caves and tunnels, which honeycombed the hill on which Zion was built, will safeguard them from His avenging wrath (c.f. Psa. 139: 7 ff; Amos 9: 1 ff)". Jerome says that "princes and priests and mighty men were dragged even out of sewers and caves and pits and tombs, in which they had hidden themselves for fear of death".

The prophet picturesquely described these as men who had settled on their lees. The figure was, of course, drawn from that of new, fermenting wine, which was left on the "lees", the solid matter and the impurities which had settled at the bottom, only long enough for it to acquire sufficient strength, colour and flavour. It was then strained off, being poured from one vessel to another to free it from sediment and any further impurities (Isa. 25: 6; Jer. 48: 11). If allowed to remain longer, the liquid became thick and syrupy and soon became unpalatable. The expression used by Zephaniah was a stronger term than "settled" and meant "thickened" or "hardened"—possibly a reference to the hard crust which forms on the surface of fermented wine if it is left undisturbed for a long time.

"The characters stigmatised by Zephaniah are obvious," writes Smith (*ibid.,* pp. 52, 53). "They were a precipitate from the ferment of fifteen years back. Through the cruel days of Manasseh and Amon, hope had been stirred and strained, emptied from vessel to vessel, and so had sprung sparkling and keen into the new days of Josiah. But no miracle came, only ten years of waiting for the king's majority and five more of small, tentative reforms. . . . Of course, disappointment ensued—disappointment and listlessness. The new security of life became a temptation; persecution ceased, and religious men lived again at ease. So numbers of eager and sparkling souls, who had been in the front of the movement fell away into a selfish and idle obscurity."

Left undisturbed, these people had become "thickened" or callous and unresponsive to the claims of God. They had become hardened in iniquity and religious indifference. So flagrantly did they dishonour Jehovah that they concluded that He was of no different character from the idols of the pagans, with neither the interest nor the ability to intervene in the affairs of men. They denied Divine providence in the universe and declared that Jehovah produced neither blessing nor calamity.

There could be only one reply to such impious impertinence. Hence Jehovah announced that He would search them out to bring them to account. But is the attitude of God's people very different today? The apathetic indifference to His claims, the unresponsiveness to the challenge of spiritual need, the general inertia on the part of Christians, all suggest another period in which people have "settled on their lees". Another writer refers to the "pubescence of respectability" and says that "respectability may be the precipitate of unbelief". Certainly we are more concerned with our respectability than the claims of Christ. Zephaniah's thunderous tones warned that the day of Jehovah was at hand, but with equal fervour and force the Holy Spirit today warns that "the coming of the Lord draws nigh". When the Lord Jesus Christ returns for His church, the Christian will be manifested at His *bema*, to give account of life and deeds on earth. That moment is imminent. It is time for the complacent and slothful, who are settled on their lees, to awake and realise the seriousness of their attitude. The eye of the Eternal still searches the heart.

The morons of Zephaniah's day foolishly ruled out the possibility of Divine interest in human affairs. Everything in life, they argued, happened in accordance with natural laws. There was virtually no place for the supernatural. It was a tacit denial of the authority and immanence of God. Yet there are Christian leaders today who adopt a similar doctrine, and declare that the One, who redeems a soul, leaves the individual to guide his own life and choose his own course and never intervenes to encourage or to check. This is not the character of the God of the Bible.

Condign punishment was to fall swiftly and unexpectedly upon these irreligious characters of Judah. Their possessions would be plundered by the invader and their wealth would become the spoil of their enemies. Their houses would be laid low. There would be ample evidence now that there was a God in the heavens who had not surrendered His rule to any other. The punishments specified for those who despised His name would be meted out (Lev. 26, 32, 33; Deut. 28, 30, 39; Amos 5: 11; Mic. 6: 15). Life would be completely disrupted. They might build houses, but they would never be allowed to inhabit them. They might plant vineyards, but they would never drink of the wine therefrom. Those who despised Jehovah would pay the penalty for their insensate folly.

## CHAPTER 4

### The Character of the Day

L EST there should be any dubiety about the nature of the forthcoming judgment, Zephaniah vividly described some of the features of the day of Jehovah. All sense of security must have dissolved at his words. There was no place now for complacency. But it was too late to avert the storm: the rumblings of thunder could already be heard in the distance. The armies of the enemy were on the march.

*The great day of Jehovah is near. It is near and hastening fast. The sound of the day of Jehovah is bitter: the mighty man cries bitterly there (Zeph. 1: 14).*

Possibly still with the intention of arousing the slothful and lethargic, of disturbing the self-complacent, and of shaking the irreligious out of their condition, the prophet warned that the day of trouble was near and was speeding fast to fulfilment. Nothing could now stop its course. The sounds could be heard with ever-increasing distinctness. Zephaniah continued to describe the approaching judgment as the day of Jehovah, although it was but a prefiguring of that calamitous period. It was, however, so terrible that even its sound would strike fear into the heart. Even the experienced warrior, who had passed through battle and strife, would be so awed by its character that he would shriek out in abject terror at the sight. This will certainly be true when the actual period commences and the unprecedented sufferings of the great tribulation are experienced by earth. Indeed, our Lord Himself declared that, so dreadful would that period be that, unless it was shortened, no one would be saved (Matt. 24: 21, 22).

The Septuagint renders the last clause of verse 14 as "dreadful things are ordained", but it is difficult to see the origin of this.

Zephaniah's note needs to be struck again in our twentieth century. The coming of Christ is near and it is now speeding on to the day of fulfilment. The opportunities of the present will soon be gone and the potentialities of life will be for ever behind our backs. With all the urgency of which we are capable, we should proclaim the fact that that day is coming. "It is near and hastening fast."

### THE NATURE OF THE DAY

*That day is a day of wrath, a day of tribulation and distress, a day of ruin and devastation, a day of darkness and gloom, a day of clouds and gross darkness, a day of trumpet blast and battle cry against the fortified cities and against the high battlements (Zeph. 1: 15, 16).*

The day of Jehovah is pre-eminently one of wrath and Zephaniah made this clear at the outset. The hymn on judgment, written by Thomas of Celano in 1250, entitled *Dies irae, dies illa* ("That day is a day of wrath") was based on verse 15.

The advent of that period of judgment would mean the complete devastation of everything for man: he would be utterly helpless, suffocated by the overwhelming flood which submerged him. The universal distress would be increased by the darkness and gloom, the clouds and thick darkness (Joel 2: 31; Matt. 24: 29). These are the features described by all the prophets who refer to that day. The light and glory of Divine favour will be hidden in the outpouring of His judgments upon a guilty world.

The prophet went on to use the metaphor of an attacking army. The sound of the trumpet was to be heard on every side. The war cry of the enemy was to ring out as the fortified

36

cities were besieged. The hordes of foes sweeping into the land threatened every inhabited town. The corners and battlements of the fortified walls would re-echo the trumpet blast, as the signal for the destruction which was about to commence. The immediate instruments of the Divine wrath may have been the ruthless, terrifying Scythians, or the prophet may have anticipated the later Chaldean invasion. God was not limited for instruments (see Note at end of chapter).

(see Note at end of chapter)

### DISTRESS FOR ALL

*And I will bring distress upon mankind, that they shall walk like blind men, because they have sinned against Jehovah; and their blood shall be poured out like dust and their flesh like dung. Neither their silver nor their gold shall be able to deliver them in the day of Jehovah's wrath. But the whole earth shall be consumed by the fire of his jealous wrath; for he shall make a full, even a sudden end of all the inhabitants of the earth (Zeph.* 1: 17, 18).

The Divine visitation in that day will be universal. All mankind is to suffer and the affliction will obviously be sore. Because of their sin, men would walk as those deprived of sight, declared the prophet. This was precisely what was foretold in the law as part of the punishment of the disobedient—they would be smitten with blindness (Deut. 28: 28, 29). Just retribution was, therefore, predicted. There would be no escape: they would stagger about hopelessly like blind men, exactly in accord with the provisions of the law. All attempts to seek a way out of their trouble and distress would be unavailing; all sense of direction would be lost.

Man's life is in the blood (Lev. 17: 11), but so worthless would be the blood of those men that it would be poured out like dust (c.f. 2 Kings 23: 7; Isa. 49: 23), and their bodies would be regarded as of no more value than offal. They had discounted Divine providence and had insulted God by declaring, not only that He had no interest in mankind, but that He was virtually unable to affect the course of life. Now

37

the full penalty would be exacted by One who estimated them as worthless.

In the past they had purchased immunity from punishment by heavy payments of silver and gold to venal judges. They had even possibly bought off potential invaders of their country. They would soon be faced by invaders who could not be bought off and, in the ultimate, they would face the Eternal, whose dread judgments could not be warded off by effort or by payment (c.f. Ezek. 7: 19). There will be no salvation in the day of Jehovah's wrath.

The whole earth will be consumed by the fire of God's wrath. In perfect justice that fire will sweep over a guilty world and all mankind will be speedily destroyed. Zephaniah looked far beyond the immediate to the ultimate, and his words related, not merely to the terrible period of the great tribulation but, in all probability to the final outpouring of the wrath of God, when the fire of heaven will destroy the rebels of earth and the world itself be dissolved (Rev. 20: 9, 11; 2 Pet. 3: 10-12).

### CALL TO REPENTANCE

*Gather together, yes, gather together, O shameless nation, before the decree is implemented, before the day sweeps you away like drifting chaff, before the fierce anger of Jehovah come upon you, before the day of Jehovah's anger come upon you. Seek Jehovah, all you humble of the land, who do His commands: seek righteousness, seek humility. It may be that you will be hidden in the day of Jehovah's anger (Zeph. 2: 1-3).*

The judgment of the whole earth had been predicted, and Judah, in particular, had been warned of the imminence of the impending tribulation. But, almost unexpectedly, there came a call to the nation to repent. They were called to gather together. Feinberg (*ibid.*, p. 53) says, "The word translated 'gather together' ordinarily means to gather together stubble as fuel for burning. . . . The nation is addressed in a derogatory manner because of their sin."

38

These people were summoned to assemble like slaves bending down to gather the stubble for the fire, in recognition of their worthlessness and sinfulness.

Judah was even called upon as a *nation*—a Hebrew word used for a Gentile nation whom God did not recognise as related to Him. So low had Judah sunk that she was regarded as no better than her pagan neighbours. If there was to be any reconciliation to Jehovah, there must be penitence and an acknowledgment of guilt and shame. The Authorised Version describes her as a "nation not desired", but the real significance is a "nation without shame". Sin had so hardened their sensibilities that they were dead to shame.

Yet the opportunity was given to them to repent. Let them seek Jehovah before His decree, or sentence of punishment, was put into execution—before it was too late. If they failed to do so, the storm of Divine wrath would sweep them away like chaff, and the fury of Jehovah's anger would be meted out upon them. In the immediate context, there was, of course, no repentance. Nor will there be when the great tribulation breaks upon God's ancient people. The pleas of the age will continue to fall upon deaf ears.

If the people had striven to carry out the commandments of God and to fulfil His ordinances, if they had made it their earnest desire to seek righteousness and humility, there would have been a complete transformation in their prospects. They would have been sheltered from the storm in the day of trouble. In a still future day, the same facts are appropriate. Repentance and contrition for sin, a determination to walk aright and humbly in the fear of God, would still protect them from the outpoured wrath of the great tribulation. But there is no sign of penitence or of humbling before Him, and the judgment must inevitably fall.

The conclusion is a tragic one. Unrepentant to the end, unaffected by the warnings of the prophet or his predecessors, blind to the claims of the Eternal, the people faced the inevitable and inescapable chastening of God—and still do!

## Note.

It is usually contended that the events of the day of Jehovah, described by Zephaniah, were practically fulfilled in the Babylonian invasions and the subsequent captivity of the people of Judah. On the other hand, there are many who consider that the fulfilment was through the medium of the Scythians. This is doubtful because the Scythians did not overrun Judah and they left Jerusalem untouched at their invasion of Palestine.

The Scythians were a very ancient race, who claimed descent from Targetaus, the son of Zeus. They were a nomadic race, extremely backward in civilisation, and seem to have originated in the highlands of Asia. As Scoloti, they settled in the area to the north of the Black Sea and the Caspian Sea.

They invaded Persia but were checked by Sargon II. They attacked the Medes and Cimmerians, and later swept through Palestine to invade Egypt about the time when Zephaniah was prophesying. Psammetichus, king of Egypt, a contemporary of Josiah of Judah, bought them off and saved his country from the cruelties and sufferings which these fierce and ruthless barbarians would have inflicted.

Some later settled at Bethshean (which acquired the name of Scythopolis), but they played little part in Judah. The New Testament refers to them in Col. 3 : 11.

## CHAPTER 5

## The Gentiles Under Review

THE judgment predicted by Zephaniah was not a local one, restricted to the relatively small country of Judah. It was a universal one, covering all the Gentile nations. All, however, were not specifically detailed by name. Four countries which bordered on Judah were selected as illustrative of the whole.

PHILISTINE CAPITALS

*For Gaza shall be deserted, and Ashkelon shall become a waste. They shall drive out Ashdod at noonday, and Ekron shall be rooted up (Zeph.* 2: 4).

Four of the five cities which constituted the Philistine league (Josh. 13: 3) were named for judgment. The fifth, Gath, had ceased to exist at this time. These old foes of Judah were to be dealt with by Jehovah. Pusey pertinently points out (*ibid.*, p. 254) that the names of these cities "expressed boastfulness and so, in the Divine judgment, carried their own sentence with them, and this sentence is pronounced by a slight change in the word. Thus *Azzah* (Gaza), *strong,* shall be *Azoobah, desolated; Ekron, deeprooting,* shall be *Teaker, uprooted;* the *Cherethites, cutters off,* shall become *Cheroth,* diggings; *Chebel,* the *land* of the sea-coast, shall be in another sense *Chebel, an inheritance,* divided by line to the remnant of Judah; and *Ashdod, the waster,* shall be taken in their might, not by craft, nor in the

41

way of robbers, but *driven forth* violently and openly in the *noonday*."

Gaza was one of the most ancient cities of the world and it existed before the times of Abraham. It marked the southern limit of Canaan (Gen. 10: 19). Originally inhabited by the Avims, it was conquered by the Philistine tribe, the Caphtorims (Josh 13 : 2; 3). It stood on the main road from Egypt to Mesopotamia and an important trade route. It was captured by Judah, but changed hands many times, Philistines, Assyrians, Egyptians and Greeks capturing it. It was captured and held for some time by the Maccabees and later fell into the hands of the Romans. It was, of course, the scene of Samson's greatest exploit (Jud. 16: 21-31). Under the hand of Jehovah, Gaza was to be deserted. The proud city, with its centuries of history, was to become an abandoned site. The present city is, in fact, on a new site.

Ashkelon, 12 miles north of Gaza, was occupied from Neolithic times. It was captured by Judah (Jud. 1:18), but was later taken by the Philistines and subsequently by the Assyrians, Babylonians, Persians, Greeks and Maccabees and ultimately by the Romans. It was set on fire by the Jews in Roman times. It was the birthplace of Herod the Great. Philo said in 40 A.D., "The Ascalonites have an implacable and irreconcilable enmity to the Jews, their neighbours." Their recompense had come. The city's doom was pronounced by Jeremiah about the same time as Zephaniah (Jer. 47: 5-7). The latter declared that it would become a waste, a prediction fulfilled centuries ago.

Ashdod, 18 miles north-east of Gaza, was one of the principal ports of Philistia. It contained the chief temple of Dagon (1 Sam. 5: 1-6). Like other Philistine cities, it passed through the hands of most of the great powers. Originally a city of considerable importance, it evidently wasted away (Jer. 25: 20). Zephaniah declared that the Ashdodites would be driven out at noon—the hottest time of the day and the most unlikely time for any military action.

Ekron was captured first by Dan at the conquest of

Canaan, and then by Judah, but was retaken by the Philistines, falling later into the hands of greater powers. It was the centre of worship of Baal-Zebub. The prophet declared that Ekron would be rooted up. So completely has this been fulfilled that today there is not a trace of the city.

The hatred of these Philistine cities for the Jews continued in terrible atrocities committed later against Christians. The judgment which fell upon them was well-merited.

### THE COAST LANDS

*Woe to the inhabitants of the sea coast, the nation of the Cherethites! The word of Jehovah is against you, O Canaan, the land of the Philistines; I will even destroy you till no inhabitant is left. And the sea coast shall become pasture land, caves for shepherds and folds for flocks. And the sea coast shall become the possession of the remnant of the house of Judah. They shall feed therefrom. In the houses of Ashkelon they shall lie down in the evening. For Jehovah their God will be mindful of them and turn away their captivity (Zeph. 2: 5-7).*

As long ago as the time of Abraham, Philistines had settled along the Mediterranean coast (Gen. 21 : 32, etc). A Hamitic nation, they had apparently originated in Caphtor (Amos 9: 7) or Crete. Zephaniah referred to them as the nation of the Cherethites (see also 1 Sam 30: 14; Ezek. 25: 16), a name which is assumed to have been derived from Cretans: indeed, the Septuagint uses the latter word. They were associated with the Pelethites as David's guard (2 Sam. 8: 18; 20: 23) and T. C. Mitchell maintains that the Cherethites were Cretans and that the Pelethites were Philistines, but there is no evidence to confirm this. The Cherethites evidently settled in southern Palestine along the sea-coast.

A woe was pronounced upon these people and the prophet stated that the word of Jehovah was against them. The storm which was to sweep the rest of the country was to

43

affect them also. The land itself was described as "Canaan, the land of the Philistines". Pusey (*ibid.*, p. 259) says, "in that name lay the original source of their destruction. They inherited the sins of Canaan and with them his curse." They were to be completely blotted out. The curse laid by Noah upon his grandson was to be fulfilled in his descendants (Gen. 9: 25). Not a single inhabitant of the region was to be left.

The depopulated coastlands would then become pasture lands, in which the nomadic shepherds would provide themselves shelters, either in caves or in huts dug out of the ground as a refuge from the sun, and where folds would be constructed for their flocks. The area which had once teemed with life and bustling activity was to revert to the quiet of pastoral life—a prediction which has been completely fulfilled. The hordes of Scythians wiped out the inhabitants and left the land bare.

According to Zephaniah, the coastlands were to become a possession of the remnant of the house of Judah. Philistia, for her sins, had forfeited all entitlement to it, but the mass of Judah were in no better spiritual state. The land was, therefore, to become the possession, not of the nation as a whole, but of the restored remnant. An area, once covered with cities and the scene of trade and commerce, was to provide food for Judah from its fertile soil.

If Ashkelon had become a desolation, the remnant was to find shelter for the night in the empty houses of the city. There they would be able to lie down in quiet security, fearing no ferocious beast or evil intruder. For the prophet's vision rises above the storm-clouds of the present to the Divine mercy of the future. Jehovah would once more be mindful of His people and He would restore them again. The immediate and the distant future seem inextricably entangled, but the prophet unquestionably saw not merely the return of Judah from the Babylonian captivity (which had not then commenced), but doubtless the ultimate restoration to the land and the peace and blessing of the millennial age.

44

*I have heard the taunting of Moab and the revilings of the Ammonites, wherewith they have taunted my people and have boasted against their territory. Therefore, as I live, says Jehovah of hosts, the God of Israel, surely Moab shall be like Sodom, and the Ammonites like Gomorrah, a possession of nettles and salt-pits, and a permanent desolation. The remnant of my people shall pillage them, and the remnant of my nation shall possess them. This shall they have for their arrogance, because they have reviled and vaunted themselves against the people of Jehovah of hosts (Zeph. 2: 8-10).*

The Philistines were located to the west of Israel and Judah, but the Moabites and Ammonites were on the east. These two nations had, of course, descended from the sons born of an incestuous relationship of Lot with his daughters (Gen. 19: 36-38). They were consistently opposed to God's people and were frequently denounced by the prophets as the inveterate foes of Israel and Judah (Jer. 48: 1—49: 6; Ezek. 25: 1-11, etc.). They were notorious for their pride and haughtiness (Isa. 16: 6), their idolatry (1 Kings 11: 7) and their inhumanity (2 Kings 3: 27).

The Moabites claimed that their land had been bestowed upon them by their principal god, Chemosh (see Appendix), and described themselves as the people of Chemosh (Num. 21: 29). The Ammonites similarly claimed that their land was the gift of their god, Molech (1 Kings 11: 7). The two deities have often been identified with each other, but there seems no doubt that they were separate. Both demanded human sacrifice (Jer. 7: 31) and were, therefore, abhorred by Israel and Judah.

Not only were they bitterly opposed to God's people, but they rejoiced at every calamity suffered by them. They displayed their enmity on every possible occasion and reviled and reproached the nation of Judah. The day of reckoning was to come, however. Those who attack God's people are virtually opponents of Him. He declared that He had heard their taunts and had observed their boastful arrogance and

45

the way in which they had vaunted themselves against His people.

Moab and Ammon had come into existence in consequence of Lot's escape from the judgment which had fallen on Sodom and Gomorrah. But now Jehovah would make them like Sodom and Gomorrah. Their insults would boomerang. Their punishment would be permanent and irrevocable, being confirmed by the Almighty's solemn oath—"as I live, says Jehovah of hosts, the God of Israel." Sodom and Gomorrah had once flourished in wealth and glory, only to be destroyed. Now Ammon and Moab were to share their fate. The two countries were located in the vicinity of the Dead Sea and it seemed appropriate that the fate of the ancient cities of that area should become theirs also.

Their fertile land was to become a mournful waste. The nettles (Job 30: 7), which grew lavishly and in abundance in waste places, would overrun the land of Moab and Ammon. The southern shore of the Dead Sea provides an almost inexhaustible supply of rock salt. The land would be covered with salt pits, declared the prophet: the symbol was one of utter ruin and sterility. Pusey (*ibid.*, p. 271) says, "The soil continues, as of old, of exuberant fertility; yet in part, from the utter neglect and insecurity of agriculture, it is abandoned to a rank and encumbering vegetation; elsewhere, from the neglect of the former artificial system of irrigation, it is wholly barren. At the present day it seems irretrievably lost, but this is precisely what Zephaniah foretold: the land was to become a permanent desolation with no hope of recovery."

They had despised Judah, but God declared that the remnant of His people would plunder the Ammonites and Moabites and possess them personally (by implication, as slaves). So complete would be the ruin and humiliation of these arrogant nations. There is a God in the heavens with whom men have to do and although, as Longfellow wrote, "the mills of God grind slowly, yet they grind exceeding small; though with patience He stands waiting, with exactness grinds He all". (*Retribution*). It is a lesson which men still

46

need to learn. We cannot please ourselves how we live and what we do. Nor can we escape the consequences of our actions to others.

The fate of the two nations was well-deserved. They had scoffed at and condemned Jehovah's nation. Their pride was now to be recompensed. What He had threatened would be their lot in return for their arrogance and haughtiness and their vaunting of themselves against His people. The higher the boaster exalts himself, the greater is his fall.

### THE FALSE GODS

*Jehovah will be terrible against them: for he will make all the gods of the earth waste away. And men shall bow down to him, each in his place, even all the lands of the nations (Zeph. 2: 11).*

The nations of the earth have their gods, whom the Bible regards as nonentities. In His wrath against the nations, Jehovah would also deal with the idols they worshipped. In the language of the prophet, He would famish them or make them lean; He would so deprive them of strength and sustenance that they would waste away. Without the worship and support of their adherents the idols would exercise no influence or power. It was the Divine intention to destroy them and leave men and nations again with the choice of submission or not to Himself.

Deprived of their false deities, men from every land will, in the day envisioned by the prophet, bow down to Jehovah, each in his own place. Submission to the true God may not be universal, but from every tribe and nation praises will ascend to Him. In a glimpse into the golden age of the millennium, Zephaniah saw the widespread recognition of the Eternal of which other prophets speak. Elliott (*ibid.*, p. 28) says that one of the "objects of these judgments upon the nations is that Israel may come thereby to the knowledge of the glory and power of his God, and learn to stand in fear of His severity and bow to His goodness." But the prophecy reaches beyond Israel to the Gentile nations of earth and to

47

the destruction of their false objects of worship that the only true God may be exalted.

The A.V. uses the term "the isles of the heathen" or nations, an expression taken from the islands and coastlands to symbolise the whole of the world (Isa. 41: 1).

### ETHIOPIA'S SUFFERING

*You Ethiopians also, you shall be slain by my sword (Zeph. 2: 12).*

The prophet's glance swung away from the west and east to focus on the south, where the Cushites had made their home in the south and southwest of Egypt.

The Ethiopians, or Cushites, were descendants of Cush, the son of Ham (Gen. 10: 6). They ruled Egypt from 720 to 654 B.C. and some commentators consider that it is Egypt that Zephaniah has in view in this verse. The invasions of Esarhaddon and Ashurbanipal reduced Ethiopia and Egypt to mere tributary states. They had little connection with Israel, although they did attack Asa and were soundly defeated (2 Chron. 14: 9-13). Their judgment at God's hands was not, therefore, as in other cases, related to their attitude to the chosen people.

No reason for their trials is given. They may have been included as an indication of the universality of the judgment. Their sentence, however, was to be executed by the sword. In other words, their country would be ravaged by war and the people would perish at the hands of whatever invaders Jehovah employed as His instrument.

### ASSYRIA CALLED TO ACCOUNT

*And he shall stretch out his hand against the north and destroy Assyria; and will make Nineveh a desolation and a dry waste like the desert. Herds shall lie down in the midst of her, all the beasts of the nations. Both the pelican and the hedgehog shall lodge in her capitals; a voice shall sing in the windows; rubbish shall be on the thresholds; he shall lay bare the cedar work. This is the exulting city which dwelt in security, which said to herself, I am and there is none beside me. What a desolation she has become, a place for wild beasts to lie down in. Everyone who passes by her shall hiss and wag his hand* (*Zeph.* 2: 13-15).

From the south the prophet now swept to the north, the direction from which trouble so often emanated for Israel. Assyria was actually situated to the northeast of Israel, but her armies always invaded Israel from the north and the prophetical books always refer to her as the power in the north.

The great Assyrian empire dominated the ancient world from the 9th to the 7th centuries B.C. By the time of Zephaniah's prophecy the great colossus had begun to totter but it had not yet fallen. The prophet now declared that Jehovah was about to stretch out His hand to destroy Assyria. This could not have been foreseen at the time, but very shortly afterwards the joint armies of Media and Babylonia attacked the empire and completely broke her power. As instruments in God's hands, they were employed to bring about a speedy fulfilment of the prophecy. "The ruins with which for nigh three centuries she had strewn Western Asia," says another, "to these were to be reduced her own impregnable and ancient glory. It was the end of an epoch."

The proud capital of the empire had a long and glorious history. It was built by Asshur in the earliest days of human history (Gen. 10: 11) and became the centre of government and the residence of the emperor. A centre of learning and with a very large library, it was yet renowned for its cruelty. Indeed, Nahum describes her as "the bloody city" (Nah. 3: 1).

This great city, according to Zephaniah, was to become a complete desolation and a dry barren waste, inhabited only by desert animals. When the Medes, Babylonians and Scythians besieged the city, a sudden rise of the River Tigris swept away a great part of the city's wall of sun-dried bricks and rendered her defenceless. Her devastation was complete.

The description given of the forsaken city was a lamentable one. Every detail spoke of its ruin.

Herds of beasts of every conceivable kind would lie down in the middle of the city. Pusey pertinently remarks (*ibid.*, p. 275), "No desolation is like that of decayed luxury. It preaches the nothingness of man, the fruitlessness of his toils, the fleetingness of his hopes and enjoyments, and their baffling when at their height. Grass in a court or on a once beaten road, much more, in a town, speaks of the passing away of what has been. . . . It leaves the feeling of void and forsakenness. But in Nineveh not a few tufts of grass here and there shall betoken desolation, it shall be one wild rank pasture, where flocks shall not only feed, but *lie down*, as in their fold and continual resting-place, not in the outskirts only or suburbs, but in the very centre of her life and throng and busy activity."

The pelican, an unclean bird (Lev. 11 : 18) which inhabits isolated places, is pictured as finding a home in the deserted city. The R.S.V. translates as "vulture" and the Septuagint as "chameleon", but the "pelican" is probably what was intended. The A.V. "cormorant" can hardly be accepted. The Asiatic hedgehog (rather than "bittern") usually dwells in waste lands. But the pelican and the hedgehog were described as lodging in the carved capitals of the massive pillars, which had evidently crashed to the ground.

The moaning of the wind through the open windows of the city must have sounded like a funeral dirge, so that the prophet declared that a voice would sing through the windows. The R.S.V., without much justification, translates this as "the owl shall hoot through the window", and the Septuagint as "wild beasts shall utter their cries in its vaults", but the explanation suggested above seems more appropriate.

In the destruction of the city it would be logical to expect rubbish on the thresholds of palaces, temples and mansions, precisely as the prophet indicates. Both the R.S.V. and the LXX consider that the reference is to the croaking of the raven on the thresholds or in the gates, but this interpretation is doubtful.

The whole picture is one of tragic destruction, such as actually occurred in 612 B.C.—probably soon after the prophecy. The description of a dry barren waste, in place of the prosperous, bustling city, is remarkably apt in view of its complete disappearance from history. It is only in the last few decades that much has been discovered of it.

The destruction of the palaces and temples left exposed the elaborately carved cedar wood of the ceilings and the panelling of the walls: this valuable work was left to decay in the vicissitudes of weather and circumstances. Nineveh had reached her end.

The glory and majesty of the Assyrian empire were universally acknowledged. Her power had been felt worldwide and Judah and Israel had suffered with others. The imperial victories and triumphs had been boisterously celebrated in Nineveh. In her self-sufficiency, the city deemed herself completely invincible. In her pride she proclaimed that she had no equal and there was none to disturb her serenity. In 401 B.C., however, Xenophon could find few traces of the great city and concluded that it had been destroyed because Zeus had deprived the people of their wits— a conclusion for which there was some justification.

Zephaniah declared that the exulting city would become a desolation, a place where wild beasts might make their lairs. Because of her attitude in the past, she would become an object of scorn and derision. The passer-by would maliciously hiss at her and shake his fist. For centuries the very site of the city was forgotten. The words of God proved true. A well-merited fate was meted out to her.

# CHAPTER 6

## The Condition of Jerusalem

ZEPHANIAH turned once more to his own people and to the capital city of Jerusalem in what was tacitly a final appeal to repentance and a warning of the dangers attendant upon a refusal to repent. Yet the very condition of the city would have dispelled any hope and he pronounced a woe on her.

### THE IMPENITENT CITY

*Woe to her that is rebellious and unclean, the city of oppression. She hearkened not to the voice; she accepted not correction. She trusted not in Jehovah: she drew not near to her God* (*Zeph.* 3: 1, 2).

Jerusalem was no better than her pagan neighbours whose doom had been announced. So low had she sunk in the spiritual scale that the prophet ignored her proper name, which meant "city of peace", and described her instead as the "city of oppression". She had been far more highly privileged than the Gentile nations; the revelation of God had been made to her; she had received the oracles of God; a Divinely appointed ritual and form of worship had been prescribed for her; messengers had been sent repeatedly with the message of Jehovah. Yet she had rejected every means of grace and had obstinately turned her back upon her God.

Not only was she refractory but also unclean—an active rebel against the Divine will and defiled by the sin in which she delighted. Above all others, she might have been expected to render loyal obedience to Jehovah and to conduct herself

in conformity with His revealed will. Her superficial ortho-
doxy and her external observance of the Levitical ceremonial
could not compensate for her heart rejection of God and her
long continuance in wrongdoing. Hence the only message the
prophet could bring was one of denunciation.

Faithfulness would have induced a consideration for the
poor, a practical sympathy for the widow and orphan, a protection of the rights of the under-privileged. Instead,
Jerusalem was a city of oppression: the rights of others
were completely ignored, the help for others which should
have been in evidence was conspicuous by its absence, and
the compassion to be expected from a city so favoured was
displaced by a vindictive cruelty.

Sin must meet with correction, but Jehovah had dealt
leniently with His erring people: admonition and rebuke and
even specific punishment had been employed to win them
back to His ways. Yet this city refused to listen to the witness
of the law or to the warnings of the prophets; she declined to
accept discipline, and the lessons intended to be learned,
through the chastisements inflicted, were ignored. Her faith
should have been reposed in God, but she turned her back
upon Him to serve the idols of the pagans. She should have
drawn near to Jehovah, in penitence and contrition, to re-
dedicate herself to Him, but she showed no inclination for
communion with Him. He was deemed unworthy of her trust
and confidence.

It is a deplorable picture, but of how many believers
today the same expressions would be applicable. Every
spiritual blessing has been bestowed upon the Christian, but
the love and devotion to Christ, which ought to be in evidence,
are often gravely lacking; the duty to friends and neighbours
is grievously ignored; the ways of the world are reflected in
the church; the power of the Holy Spirit is completely
missing; and the radiant glory of the Christ is not to be seen.
Woe to the city, declaimed the prophet. Woe to such a
believer too!

*Her officials within her are roaring lions. Her judges are evening wolves which leave nothing for the morning. Her prophets are vainglorious and faithless persons. Her priests have profaned the sanctuary; they have done violence to the law (Zeph. 3: 3, 4).*

Zephaniah proceeded to denounce the leaders in every sphere, and his words patently referred to the country as a whole and not merely to the metropolis. A nation takes its character, at least partially, from its rulers. A church reflects, to some extent, the nature of its leaders and ministers. Every community is inevitably affected in attitude and outlook by those who stand in the forefront: this is inescapable. Hence the appropriateness of the prophet's words. If a cancer affected the whole body, its roots were to be found in the head. He dealt with all four categories of leaders.

The princes or civil officials were described as roaring lions. Instead of respect, they inculcated fear. They should have been guides and monitors to the people: instead they sought to devour. They fed upon power and were not conconcerned for those for whose condition and safety they were responsible. They were like roaring lions, constantly seeking a prey instead of caring for the flock.

The magistrates were the ministers of justice. In the administration of the law, their work was to protect the innocent and to punish the guilty. But Zephaniah implied that they utterly ignored their responsibilities and were concerned only with their own well-being. He painted them as the evening wolves from the Arabian desert who, in insatiable greed, issued forth ravenously at sunset, to seize the prey. Like the wolves they gluttonously devoured what they caught and even gnawed the bones lest something should be left till the morning. In their rapacious greed they devoured all. "Under the pretence of law and justice", says one writer, "they mercilessly fleece their victims and are never satisfied, always hungry for more gain (Amos 2 : 6-8; Matt. 23 :

14, 25)". Our Lord used similar expressions in respect of the teachers of the law of His day.

The prophets were even more seriously reprehensible perhaps. Called of God to warn the people of evil practices and to reveal to them the mind and will of the Eternal, they practised the very sins which they should have condemned. They were wanton or vainglorious, utterly frivolous and irresponsible, empty boasters claiming to be the messengers of God. They were treacherous or faithless, deceiving those whom they should have enlightened. It was a serious indictment.

The priests were virtually the mediators between the nation and Jehovah. The whole sacrificial system was, in effect, dependent upon them. It was through them that communion with God was established and maintained. Yet the prophet declared that they had profaned the temple. They had made the sacred common. Jeremiah, at roughly the same time, exposed their shameful wickedness (Jer. 7: 9-11). The prescribed ritual mattered little to them; the spiritual needs of the worshippers were discounted; they did violence to the law which had been entrusted to them to implement. Laetsch (*ibid.*, p. 375) says scathingly, "They manipulated the law of God chiefly for the purpose of filling their purses and paunches". The whole religious system was being distorted.

When the leaders were so culpable, it is little wonder that the nation was corrupt. "Like master, like man", wrote George Farquhar nearly three centuries ago, and he was quite right. The character of the leaders is inevitably reflected in those who are led.

### A RIGHTEOUS GOD

*Jehovah, in the midst of her, is righteous: He does no wrong. Morning by morning He brings His justice to light without fail. Yet the unjust knows no shame (Zeph. 3: 5).*

Despite the perversity of His people, Jehovah remained in their midst. In view of their shameless conduct, His grace was amazing. Yet He made it clear that He was the righteous

One with Whom there was no iniquity. By inference, the very presence of the One, who was infinitely holy and perfectly just, was a condemnation of the guilty city and nation.

In the east, the early morning is the most suitable time for conducting business and it was formerly the hour for the administering of justice. Appropriately, therefore, Zephaniah declared that Jehovah unfailingly brought His justice to light each morning. "God's justice," says Kleinert (*ibid.*, p. 27) "is neither His teaching nor His righteous administration, but the announcement of the judgment which it was right for Him and obligatory upon Him to bring those mad practices." By whatever method He might speak (and it could conceivably be in the circumstances of life), the significance ought to have been born home to the sinner.

"Yet the unjust knows no shame," said Zephaniah. Lifting up his voice at approximately the same time, Jeremiah said, "Were they ashamed when they had committed abomination? Nay, they were not at all ashamed, neither could they blush" (Jer. 6: 15). Not only was there no sign of contrition: there was not the slightest indication of shame. The people were oblivious to the holiness of God and the shamefulness of their iniquity. They could not even blush. When there is a consciousness of guilt and a sense of shame that evil practices had been tolerated or engaged in, there is some hope. But when all sense of shame at doing wrong has disappeared, the probability of a change of attitude is negligible.

### JUDGMENT EXEMPLIFIED

*I have cut off the nations: their battlements are in ruins. I made their streets waste, that no one walks in them. Their cities are desolate, so that there is no man, there is no inhabitant. I said, Surely she will fear me, she will receive correction, so that their dwellings should not be cut off. However I punished them, but they rose early and corrupted all their doings (Zeph. 3: 6, 7).*

God condescended to provide examples to His people of

the character of His judgments by reference to His dealings with other nations, who were not identified. It was only necessary for Judah to recall the facts of recent history, or to gaze upon the ruined fortifications on the hill-tops surrounding them, to realise that the hand of God had been laid upon the nations which had perished. The empty streets of the devastated cities were a silent reminder of the Divine visitation upon the guilty nations. The decimated populations of their neighbours was a fact which could not be ignored. Yet they were insensitive to the message and unheeding of the Divine voice.

With these examples before them, surely Judah and Jerusalem would heed the lesson and, if only to avert the judgment which must otherwise fall upon their own dwellings, would listen to admonition and turn in filial fear to the One through whom these judgments came. The warning was clear. The enemy was almost within the gate, but grace still lingered to provide the opportunity for repentance. After God's strenuous efforts to make clear their danger, surely they would flee to Him for shelter from the oncoming wrath.

They did not. In blind and insolent obstinacy, they pursued their evil occupations with unabated—if not increased —vigour. Pusey (*ibid., p.* 282) writes, "There are as many aggravations of their sin as there are words. The four Hebrew words bespeak eagerness, wilfulness, completeness, enormity, in sin. *They rose early,* themselves deliberately *corrupted,* of their own mind made offensive *all* their *doings,* not slight acts, but *deeds,* great works done with a high hand." There was not a sign of repentance: they were eager to do wrong, to engage in what was offensive to God. How could longsuffering continue?

The conditions are not entirely dissimilar to those of the present day. The grace of God has been revealed in an incomparable way at Calvary. His judicial acts have been seen in the fall and suffering of the nations. His message has rung out clearly in the happenings of life. But men refuse to listen to the warning. They are eager to pursue what they

58

know to be evil. The sense of shame has gone. No more can they blush. But a holy God will not permanently delay His judgment. His longsuffering has postponed the hour for long, but the lightning seems now about to strike.

## CHAPTER 7

### The Golden Age

BEFORE the blessings of the future burst upon his vision, Zephaniah brought a final message regarding the judgment of the nations and the outpouring of the Divine wrath, leading on quite naturally from the preceding section.

*Therefore, wait for me, says Jehovah, for the day when I rise up to the prey. For my fixed purpose is to gather together nations, to assemble kingdoms, to pour out upon them my indignation, the full fury of my anger; for in the fire of my jealousy shall all the earth be consumed* (Zeph. 3: 8).

This verse is the only one in the Old Testament in which all the letters of the Hebrew alphabet are included.

The evidence of the justice of Jehovah was now to be demonstrated. He had, in longsuffering, permitted men to follow their own course, and even His own people had deliberately indulged in wrongdoing in defiance of Him. Now He called upon the nation to wait for the day when He would rise up to the prey or, according to Sir George Adam Smith, the R.S.V. and other versions, when He would rise up as a witness or to testify. It matters little which translation is taken; the intention is clear. God was about to arise as His own witness, to testify of His perfect justice, and to demonstrate it as, like a hunter, He seized the prey.

Nations and kingdoms would be gathered together in

order that His indignation might be poured out upon them, His intolerance of sin would be evidenced by the unmitigated punishment resulting from His wrath. The whole earth would be consumed by the fire of His zeal. There would be no doubt as to His attitude to sin and to the unrepentant sinner. The day of mercy would be past: Divine vengeance would exact the full penalty from the inhabitants of the earth.

The language employed clearly anticipates the final judgment of earth, although earlier partial fulfilments (even including the outpouring of wrath preparatory to the introduction of the millennium) are plainly visualised. God's ways in judgment are made clear in the pages of history and will continue to be until the final day of reckoning comes. The thinking man must recognise that a Supreme Ruler sits upon the throne and that His authority has been delegated to no other. Consequently, sin against Him must meet with His condemnation, and His sentence must inescapably be executed.

### A NEW SPEECH

*At that time, I will change the language of the people to a pure language, that they may all call on the name of Jehovah, and serve him with one accord (Zeph. 3: 9).*

*Prima facie,* the first promise in connection with the restoration of Israel was a reversal of the judgment at Babel when language was confused (Gen. 11: 7-9). The word used, however, means "lip" rather than "language". The lip was regarded as the organ of speech. The lips express the inward thoughts, and the character of the thoughts of the heart was figuratively imputed to the lips. Those who invoked the names of idols were deemed to have unclean lips, defiled by the names of the false gods (Hos. 2: 19; Psa. 16: 4). Those, whose hearts had been purified, called upon Jehovah with clean lips because their thoughts were clean (c.f. Jer. 32: 39). Implicitly, Jehovah promised a cleansed heart and thereby a cleansed lip, which would enable the individual of whatever nation to call upon Jehovah.

Such would serve Him "with one shoulder", i.e. in perfect accord and unanimity. The metaphor was derived from the practice of two men bearing a burden between them, possibly suspended from a yoke on their shoulders. The regenerated people of all nations in the future millennial age will be one in the worship and service of Jehovah.

## ISRAEL'S RESTORATION

*From beyond the rivers of Ethiopia, will they bring my worshippers, the daughter of my dispersed ones, as my offering. On that day you shall not be put to shame because of your doings whereby you have transgressed against me. For then will I take away from the midst of you those who exult in your pride, and you shall no longer be haughty on my holy mountain. I will leave in the midst of you a humble and poor people, and they shall trust in the name of Jehovah. The remnant of Israel shall not work unrighteousness, nor speak falsehood, nor shall a deceitful tongue be found in their mouth. For they shall feed and lie down, and none shall make them afraid (Zeph. 3: 10-13).*

Zephaniah once more looked far beyond the immediate future to the ultimate restoration of Israel to her own land. The prophetical books repeatedly predicted that day when God would gather out of all countries those whom, centuries ago, He dispersed as a penalty for their wrongdoing. In this particular instance, the regathering was to be from beyond the rivers of Cush or Ethiopia (c.f. Isa. 18: 1). The rivers of Ethiopia were the Blue Nile, White Nile, Atbara and Astasobas, and it was from the hinterland that the exiles were to be gathered. The Falashas of western Abyssinia, for example, claim Jewish descent and have a knowledge of Judaism and may consequently be among those to be gathered one day.

From these areas the nations were to bring to Jehovah, as an offering, worshippers who were no other than the descendants of His dispersed people. The word used for "offering" was *minchah*, "meal offering" (see Lev. 2). This particular offering is usually considered to be an apt figure of the perfect life of our Lord Jesus Christ. It was composed of fine flour, symbolising the purity and perfect evenness of His character; olive oil, signifying the sanctifying influence of the Holy Spirit in His life; frankincense, indicative of the fragrance of His moral and personal glories; salt, the type of the preserving potency of the Word of God which sustained Him. If Israel is to be such an offering to God, there is a clear implication of a regeneration of such a character and extent that the life will be a reflection of that of the Perfect Man.

The comprehensive cleansing of God's people is confirmed in verse 11. The shame of the past is to be removed: the remorse for the sins and transgressions of earlier days will give place to a quiet satisfaction in Jehovah. Pride and self-exaltation were once characteristic of Israel—and still are to some extent—but that will all disappear in the Messianic era of which the prophet spoke. There will be no room for personal or national arrogance or haughtiness in the temple mount (Isa. 11 : 9).

Those who return to the land in that future day of blessing will be a humble and lowly people, exhibiting none of the characteristics of the past. The stamp of true piety will be seen in their attitude: they will seek refuge in the name of Jehovah; their trust and confidence will be solely in Him.

The picture presented by Zephaniah is stark and austere. Other prophets tell of the glory and blessing of the millennial age, but he is concerned with practical living. To quote Smith (*ibid.*, pp. 70, 71), "A thorough purgation, the removal of the wicked, the sparing of the honest and the meek; insistence only upon the rudiments of morality and religion; faith in its simplest form of trust in a righteous God, and character in its basal elements of meekness and truth—these and these alone survive the judgment".

The restored remnant of Israel, the prophet declared, would not commit iniquity or practise deceit or falsehood. Like sheep they would feed in the lush pastures and lie down in peace, with no fear of being disturbed. The reference is quite clearly, not to the returned exiles from Babylon but to those gathered back by the Messiah at His Second Advent. The words will never be true until then.

*Sing, O daughter of Zion; shout aloud, O Israel; rejoice and be jubilant with all the heart, O daughter of Jerusalem. Jehovah has taken away the judgments against you. He has cast out your enemy. The king of Israel, even Jehovah, is in your midst. You shall not see evil any more (Zeph.* 3: 14, 15).

In the light of the glorious age to come, the people were bidden to give expression to their jubilation in song and shout. Nothing was to hinder their joy. With a full heart they were to exult in the presence of Jehovah.

"Sing, it is the inarticulate yet louder swell of joy, a trumpet-blast; and then too, deep within, *be glad,* the calm even joy of the inward soul; *exult,* the triumph of the soul which cannot contain itself for joy; and this, *with the whole heart,* no corner of it not pervaded with joy. The ground of this is the complete removal of every evil, and the full presence of God" (Pusey, *ibid.,* p. 288).

The causes for praise and jubilation were many. In the first place, Jehovah had removed the judgments against His people. Not only had the judicial charges and sentence been cancelled, but the chastisements, which had been inflicted upon them to teach them the discipline of God, had been lifted. Every burden had gone. Their transgressions had been forgiven. Never would they experience trouble again, for the King of Israel, Jehovah Himself, was in their midst.

The King of Israel was in the midst. "Although it is incorrect to see eschatological ideas monolithically," writes Eakin (*ibid.,* p. 288), "at least one idea associated with the *eschaton* was that the absolute rule of Yahweh would be re-established. This was the event to which Zephaniah points." The kingship of God is a constantly recurring theme in the Old Testament. Jehovah's throne is said to be established in

65

the heavens and His kingdom to be eternal and universal (Exod. 15: 18; Psa. 103: 19). With the election of Israel, the kingdom of God was closely identified with that nation. "With the decline and fall of the Davidic dynasty," says Prof. F. F. Bruce, "the expectation of a future and more permanent manifestation of the kingship of God emerged with increasing clarity and can be traced from the Old Testament prophets right on into our Lord's lifetime."

When our Lord was born into this world, there was no doubt regarding His status as king. Even prior to His birth, in the annunciation to Mary, Gabriel declared, "He shall be great and shall be called the Son of the Most High: and the Lord God shall give unto Him the throne of His father David: and He shall rule over the house of Jacob for ever; and of His kingdom there shall be no end" (Luke 1: 32, 33). When the wise men came to see Him, they were aware of the royal status of the One they sought, for they asked, "Where is he who is born King of the Jews?" (Matt. 2: 2).

It is sometimes argued that the purpose of the incarnation was no more than the atonement and the outcalling of the church, and that it had no reference to the Old Testament prophecies of a literal earthly kingdom and that the Lord Jesus Christ never offered such a kingdom to Israel during His earthly life. This is patently fallacious. "Repent," enjoined John the Baptist, "for the kingdom of heaven is at hand" (Matt. 3: 2). As every Jew who listened must have concluded, his reference was to the promised theocratic kingdom described in Dan. 2: 44; 7: 14, etc. Our Lord, after the temptation, used the same words (Matt. 4: 17) and, in all the synagogues of Galilee, He preached the gospel of the kingdom (Matt. 4: 23). There could, of course, be no kingdom without the king: but the King was now present and the kingdom was available in Him. Acceptance of Him was essential if the kingdom was to be introduced.

After Peter's confession at Caesarea Philippi, the Master charged "His disciples that they should tell no man that He was Jesus the Messiah" (i.e. the One by whom the kingdom would be introduced), and *"from that time"* told them of His impending crucifixion (Matt. 16: 20, 21). When He rode into Jerusalem on Palm Sunday, He specifically stated that it was done to fulfil the prophecy of Zech. 9: 9, "Behold your king comes to you" (Matt. 21: 5). The crowds who gathered cried, "Blessed be the King who comes in the name of the Lord" (Luke 19: 38). Our Lord did not rebuke them for any misconception (v. 40). They were familiar with their own prophets and fully realised the implication of Christ's words: He had come as King and the kingdom was at hand. His claims were clear, e.g. "if I with the finger of God cast out demons, no doubt the kingdom of God is come upon you" (Luke 11: 20). "The law and the prophets were until John: since that time the kingdom of God is preached" (Luke 16: 16). He told the Pharisees, "the kingdom of God is among you" (Luke 17: 21), and the people later concluded, in view of His preaching, "that the kingdom of God should immediately appear" (Luke 19: 11).

The nation had the opportunity of accepting Him and the long-promised kingdom and, referring to His rejection, He said, "The kingdom of God shall be taken from you and given to a nation bringing forth the fruits thereof" (Matt. 21: 43). When Pilate challenged Him, "Art thou the King of the Jews?" He replied in affirmation, "Thou sayest" (Luke 23: 3). Even the dying thief cried, "Lord, remember me when Thou comest into Thy kingdom" (Luke 23: 42).

His disciples plainly anticipated the establishment of the kingdom during His lifetime and, even after His resurrection, they asked Him, "Wilt Thou at this time restore again the kingdom to Israel?" (Acts 1: 6). Words have no meaning if our Lord did not come as King and did not imply that the kingdom was available to Israel by acceptance of the King. We have spent some time on this point in view of the contrary teaching prevalent in some quarters. God has not given up His people and one day Israel will be seen plainly as a kingdom with a king. The abundance of Old Testament predictions will reach their fulfilment. Jehovah is King in the midst of His earthly people. Consequently trials and troubles will then dissolve. The people will "not see evil any more".

*On that day it shall be said to Jerusalem, Fear not: and to Zion, Let not your hands grow weak. Jehovah your God in your midst is mighty. He will save. He will rejoice over you with gladness. He will be silent in His love. He will exult over you with loud singing (Zeph. 3: 16, 17).*

There will be no need for paralysing fear for God's people. The despondency, which would weaken them and cause their hands to fall listlessly to their sides, has no place now, for Jehovah their God, like a mighty warrior will be in their midst to deliver. There should be no abatement in their service for Him: their hands should be strong.

Jehovah Himself would rejoice in His people. The Eternal expressed His pleasure and gladness in this restored nation of the future—a nation which had done despite to Him and had deserted His ways. In a daring anthropomorphism, the prophet declared that He would be silent in His love, "an expression used to denote love deeply felt, which is absorbed in its object with thoughtfulness and admiration" (Keil, *ibid.*, p. 161). He will quietly rest in His love. Eakin (*ibid.*, p. 289) says that the word used is not *chesed* (covenant love) but *ahabah.* According to Snaith, "'*Ahabah* is the cause of the covenant; *chesed* is the means of its continuance. Thus '*ahabah* is God's election-love, whilst *chesed* is His covenant-love".

At the same time Zephaniah declared that God would exult over His people with loud singing. His superabundant joy in His own redeemed and restored nation would be evident in the songs of the celestial heights.

If this is to be true of Israel in a future day, is it not true in the experience of the church today? Of our Lord Jesus Christ, it was specifically said that He loved His own to the end (John 13: 1) and He prayed that His loved ones might be with Him to behold His glory (John 17: 24). His joy is in them (John 15 : 11). In a coming day, He will sing praise to God in the midst of the church (Heb. 2 : 12).

## THE FINAL REGATHERING

*I will gather those who are sorrowing for the set feast, those of you to whom the shame of it was a burden. Behold, at that time, I will deal with all who maltreat you. And I will save the lame and gather her who was driven out. And I will make them a praise and a name in every land where they were put to shame. At that time I will bring you again, at the time when I gather you. For I will make you renowned and praised among all the peoples of the earth, when I turn again your captivity before your eyes, says Jehovah (Zeph. 8: 18-20).*

During their exile, Israel had been unable to make the annual pilgrimages to Jerusalem for the set feasts (i.e. all of them and not merely the feast of tabernacles), and sorrow had filled their hearts. Their mourning over their banishment and consequent separation from these religious observances and the shame they felt were a burden to be borne. Zephaniah now promised that Jehovah would gather them back to their own land and dismiss their shame. Moreover, He would then deal with their oppressors: those who had maltreated them would suffer for their actions.

The lame and the dispersed would be regathered. The prophet echoes the promises made through his predecessors. God fully intends to restore Israel to her own land and will bring them back from the four corners of the earth. When that has been accomplished, Jehovah "will make them a praise and a name in every land where they" suffered shame at the hands of their oppressors. Kleinert (*ibid.*, p. 34) says that "praise and name" is a "hendiadys for a celebrated name, which is praised, so that the original promise (Gen. 12) is fulfilled, and all nations long to be invested with the citizenship of the new community (Psa. 87; c.f. also Zech. 8: 23; Isa. 4: 1)."

The promise of regathering and of the gift of a celebrated

69

name was repeated in the closing verse of the prophecy and Jehovah declared that their restoration would be undertaken before their own eyes. This restoration was promised by law and prophet long before (Deut. 30: 3-5; Isa. 11: 11, 12; Jer. 23: 3-8; Ezek. 37: 21-25). His words implied the exaltation of Israel above the nations of the earth. The promises to the fathers must inevitably be fulfilled. Sir George Adam Smith (*ibid.*, p. 49) does less than justice to Zephaniah when he says that, in the book, "there is no prospect of a redeemed and faithful land, but only of a group of battered and hardly saved characters; a few meek and righteous are hidden from the fire and creep forth when it is over. Israel is left a poor and humble folk. No prophet is more true to the doctrine of the remnant, or more resolutely refuses to modify it." Zephaniah's prophecy, however, concludes with Jehovah's re-gathering of His people and His exaltation of them above all others, their name renowned and other nations prepared to acknowledge them. All this is to be fulfilled in a coming day, even now !

# APPENDIX

## The Moabite Stone

A BLOCK of black basalt, 3′ 10″ high and 2′ wide, and allegedly dating back to the 9th or 10th century B.C., was found in Moab in 1868 by a German missionary named F. Klein. Both the Germans and the French endeavoured to purchase it but, on the intervention of Turkish officials, the Arab owners broke it in pieces in the hope of securing a higher price. The pieces were eventually acquired in 1873 for the Louvre. It is the only writing of any length surviving from Moab. Some of the wording of the stele is not entirely complete, but it is clear that it was made by Mesha, king of Moab, and supplements the account of 1 Kings 16: 23-28 and 2 Kings 3: 4-27. It is also clear that Chemosh was the national god of the Moabites.

The account runs as follows:

"I Mesha, son of Chemosh-Melech, king of Moab, the Dibonite. My father reigned over Moab thirty years, and I reigned after my father; and I made this monument to Chemosh in Khorkah, a monument of deliverance, because he saved me from all invaders and because he let me look upon all who hate me. Omri was king of Israel; and he afflicted Moab many days, for Chemosh was angry with his land. And his son succeeded him, and he also said, I will afflict Moab. In my days Chemosh said I will see my desire upon him and upon his house, and Israel perished with an everlasting destruction. And Omri took possession of the land of Medeba and Israel dwelt in it, in his days and in the days of his son, altogether forty years. But Chemosh dwelt in it in my days. And I built Baal-Meon and I made ditches in it and I built Kiriathaim. And the men of God dwelt in the land of Ataroth from time immemorial, and the king of Israel built for him Ataroth. And I warred against the city; and I took it and I slew all the mighty men of the city, for the well-pleasing of Chemosh and Moab; I captured there the Arel of Doda and dragged him before Chemosh in Kerioth; and I made to dwell in it the men of Siran, and the men of Macharath. And Chemosh said to me, Go, take Nebo from Israel. And I went by night and I fought against it from the break of dawn till noon, and I took it, and I slew all, seven thousand men, boys, women, girls and maid-servants; for I had devoted them to destruction for Ashtar Chemosh. And I took from thence the vessels of Jehovah and I dragged them before Chemosh. And the king of Israel built Jahaz and dwelt in it, while he warred with me. And Chemosh drove him out before me and I took from Moab 200 men, all chiefs, and I took them against Jahaz and took it to add to Dibon. I built Khorkah, the wall of the forests and the wall of the citadel; I built the gates thereof, and I built the king's house, and I made prisons for the guilty in the midst of the city. And there was no cistern within the city, in Khorkah, and I said to all the people, Make for yourselves every man a cistern in his house. And I dug the canals for Khorkah by means of the prisoners of Israel. I built Arnon and I made the high road in the province of the Arnon. I built Beth-Barmoth, for it was destroyed. I built Bergen, for it was in ruins. And all the chiefs of Dibon were fifty; for all Dibon was subject, and I placed a hundred chiefs in the towns which I added to the land. And I built Beth-Medeba and Beth-Diblelathain and Beth-Bad-Meon, and I transported thereto the shepherds and the pastors of the flocks of the land. And at Horonain there dwelt . . . . And Chemosh said to me, Go, fight against Honorain and I went and fought against it. And Chemosh dwelt in it during my days. I went up from thence . . . . And I . . . ."

# BIBLIOGRAPHY

A. B. DAVIDSON: *The Books of Nahum, Habakkuk and Zephaniah,* Cambridge University Press, Cambridge, 1920.

S. R. DRIVER: *The Minor Prophets,* Vol. II, T. C. & E. C. Jack, Edinburgh, 1906.

F. E. EAKIN: *Zephaniah* in *The Broadman Bible Commentary, Vol. 7,* Marshall, Morgan & Scott Ltd., London, 1973.

J. H. EATON: *Obadiah, Nahum, Habakkuk and Zephaniah,* S.C.M. Press Ltd., London, 1961.

C. ELLIOTT: *Zephaniah* in *The Minor Prophets* in Lange's *Commentary on the Holy Scriptures* (see below).

C. L. FEINBERG: *Habakkuk, Zephaniah, Haggai and Malachi,* American Board of Missions to the Jews, New York, 1951.

J. H. GAILEY: *The Book of Zephaniah,* John Knox Press, Richmond, U.S.A., 1962.

R. F. HORTON: *The Minor Prophets,* T. C. and E. C. Jack, Edinburgh, 1906.

W. S. HOTTEL: *Hosea-Malachi,* Union Gospel Press, Cleveland.

H. A. IRONSIDE: *The Minor Prophets,* Loizeaux Bros., Neptune, n.d.

C. F. KEIL: *The Twelve Minor Prophets,* Wm. E. Eerdmans Publishing Co., Grand Rapids, 1961.

W. KELLY: *Lectures Introductory to the Study of the Minor Prophets*, W. H. Broom & Rouse, London, 1897.

P. KLEINERT: *Zephaniah* in *Lange's Commentary on the Holy Scriptures* (see below).

T. LAETSCH: *The Minor Prophets*, Concordia Publishing Co., St. Louis, 1956.

J. P. LANGE: *The Minor Prophets*, Zondervan Publishing House, Grand Rapids, n.d.

E. B. PUSEY: *The Minor Prophets*, Baker Book House, Grand Rapids, 1970.

G. A. SMITH: *The Book of the Twelve Prophets*, Hodder & Stoughton Ltd., London, 1905.

G. E. V. STONEHOUSE and G. W. WADE: *The Books of the Prophets Zephaniah and Nahum*, Meuthen & Co. Ltd., London, 1929.

C. L. TAYLOR: *The Book of Zephaniah*, Abingdon Press, Nashville, 1956.

J. B. TAYLOR: *The Minor Prophets*, Scripture Union, London, 1970.